Sunset
Southern California
TRAVEL GUIDE

By the Editors of Sunset Books
and Sunset Magazine

Lane Publishing Co. • Menlo Park, California

Hours, admission fees, prices, telephone numbers, and highway designations in this book are accurate as of the time this edition went to press.

Maps have been provided in each chapter for the special purpose of highlighting significant regions, routes, or attractions in the area. Check automobile clubs, insurance agencies, and chambers of commerce or visitors bureaus in major cities for detailed maps of Southern California.

Edited by Barbara J. Braasch

Design: Cynthia Hanson

Cartography: Ted Martine

Illustrations: Susan Jaekel

Cover: Excursion boat passes venerable Balboa Pavilion in Newport Beach. Photographed by Gerald R. Fredrick.

Thanks...

to the many people and organizations who assisted in the preparation of this travel guide. Special appreciation goes to the Greater Los Angeles Visitors and Convention Bureau, and to other city and county visitors bureaus and chambers of commerce throughout the area.

Photographers

William Aplin: 118 top. **Craig Aurness:** 50 bottom right. **Barbara Braasch:** 67 bottom. **Glenn Christiansen:** 19 top left and right, 70, 78, 91 top, 99, 102 all. **Ed Cooper:** 91 bottom, 94, 115. **Disneyland:** 50 top right. **James H. Flanagan:** 83. **Gerald R. Fredrick:** 6 top right and bottom, 19 bottom, 22 bottom, 39 top, 47, 63. **Leland Y. Lee:** 42 bottom. **Martin Litton:** 118 bottom. **Long Beach Area Convention and Visitors Council:** 39 bottom. **Marie Mainz:** 14 top. **Steve W. Marley:** 107 bottom, 110. **MGM/Six Flags Movieland:** 50 left. **Josef Muench:** 86. **Norman A. Plate:** 126 all. **Bill Reid:** 3. **Sea World:** 75 top. **Jeffrey Stanton:** 11, 30, 55 top, 58, 75 bottom, 107 top. **Ted Streshinsky:** 34 all, 42 top. **Bill Tara:** 22 top. **Tom Tracy:** 6 top left, 14 bottom, 55 bottom. **Mark Uhler:** 67 top. **Universal Studios:** 27 bottom right. **Robert Wenkam:** 27 top, 123.

Editor, Sunset Books: David E. Clark

Mission San Diego de Alcala

Contents

Special Features

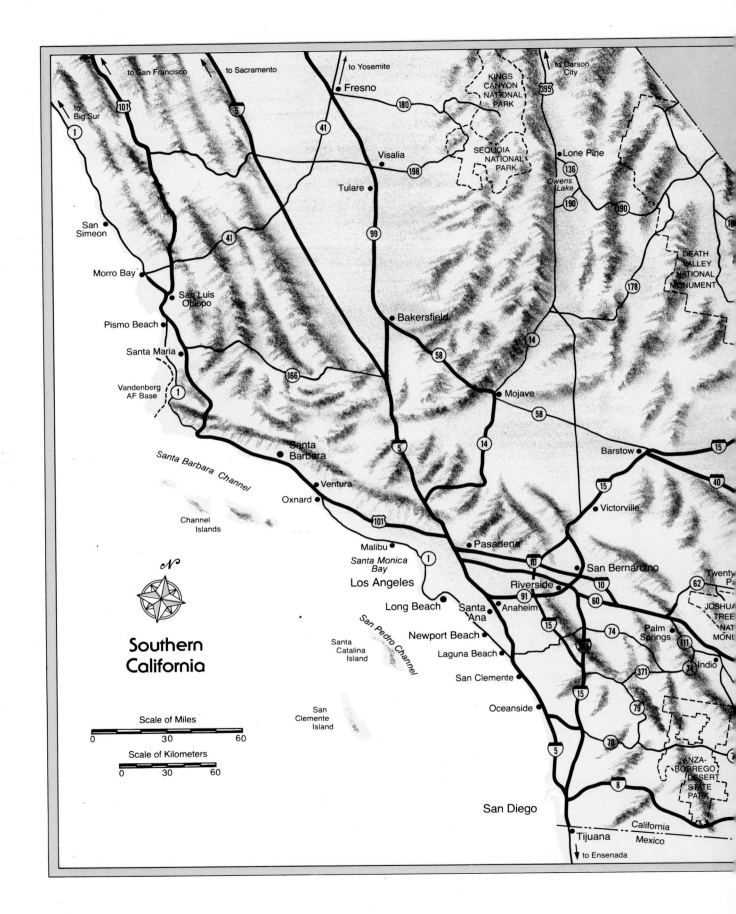

Southern California

Scale of Miles
0   30   60

Scale of Kilometers
0   30   60

Areas of Interest

Hearst Castle—William Randolph Hearst's castlelike "ranch" above San Simeon, now a State Historic Monument; tours give a look at mansion's interior

San Joaquin Valley—southern half of California's Central Valley (state's major producer of cotton, grapes, rice, other hot-weather crops); Bakersfield, one of largest cities, is Basque center

Sequoia & Kings Canyon National Parks—end-to-end parks along Sierra Nevada ridge contain massive giant sequoias and Mt. Whitney, highest peak in the contiguous United States

Death Valley National Monument—legendary desert valley contains land of extremes, contrasts, and surprises: lowest point in Western Hemisphere, dramatic overlooks, rainbow-hued canyons, ghost towns, Scotty's Castle

Santa Barbara—red-tiled roofs and Spanish architecture add to beautiful city setting; drives from here take you up or down the coast on El Camino Real, or into back-country communities of condors (Ojai Valley) and Danes (Solvang)

Los Angeles—West Coast's largest city; county encompasses some of the Southland's most fascinating inland cities (Hollywood, Beverly Hills, Westwood, Pasadena), the San Fernando Valley, plus back door mountains, front door beaches

Orange County—manmade amusement center for Southern California (Disneyland, Knott's Berry Farm, Movieland, Lion Country Safari, others); great beach communities to intrigue surfers, snorkelers, sunbathers, shoppers, and fishermen

Catalina Island—Mediterranean-style isle just a helicopter, boat, or plane ride from the California coast; scenic drives and tours from town of Avalon; glass-bottom and flying-fish boat trips; snorkeler's and diver's paradise

Palm Springs—desert resort capital offers sunshine, sports, and easy access up mountain face by tram or into palm-filled canyons on foot or horseback; nearby are the Salton Sea, Joshua Tree National Monument, Anza-Borrego Desert State Park, date-studded Coachella Valley, and the Colorado River recreation area

Joshua Tree National Monument—high and low desert terrain protected in desert sanctuary; park headquarters at Twentynine Palms; dramatic wildflower show in springtime

San Diego—California's oldest city retains much of her Spanish heritage (Old Town, Cabrillo Monument, Presidio Hill, mission) in a lovely seaside setting; water sports and shows attract visitors, as do historic Balboa Park and the famous zoo; jumping-off spot for coastal and back-country trips plus jaunts across the Mexican border

Anza-Borrego Desert State Park—untamed desert marks one of California's last frontiers; Borrego Springs resort area provides base for exploring; unlimited camping

VARIETY MARKS SOUTHLAND attractions. Skid down snow (above) on plastic wrap, stand in star's steps at Hollywood's Chinese Theatre (right), or take your board (below) into surf at Huntington Beach.

Why visit Southern California? One reason might be that no other single area offers the environmental diversity, natural and manmade attractions, or social and cultural achievements that characterize this region. You could vacation here for a year without running out of exciting things to see and do.

Land of Variety

Nearly a century ago a massive advertising campaign by the Southern Pacific and Santa Fe railroads attracted thousands of settlers here with visions of swimming in the blue Pacific, picking oranges from acres of fruit-filled groves, and playing in the snow of nearby mountains—all in one day. It's still possible.

Variety in the Southland does not stop there. Large cities (each different in character) add overlays to the landscape between ocean and mountains, and desert meets the mountains at their north and east faces. In Death Valley, Badwater is 282 feet below sea level, the lowest point in the Western Hemisphere. Across the valley in the Sierra Nevada, Mount Whitney (14,495 feet) is the nation's highest point outside of Alaska.

Land of Sunshine

Southern California's biggest asset is its dry, subtropical climate—the only one in the United States. Very little rain, low humidity, little variation in temperature, and lots of sun make it possible to enjoy casual outdoor living the year around. Sunbathing around a back yard pool is in the best Southern California tradition.

Known around the country as the queen of desert resorts, Palm Springs offers most of the Southland's year-round outdoor recreational possibilities—golfing, tennis, swimming, horseback riding, biking, and hiking. At nearby Salton Sea you'll find boating and fishing.

On Southern California's beaches, bronzed beauties dot the sand, while surfers "hang ten," trying to avoid a wipeout. Each beach has its own character—Malibu has long been known as a playground for movie stars; Santa Monica is a show place for "muscle men"; Long Beach is home port for the ocean liner *Queen Mary* and the world's largest wooden airplane, the "Spruce Goose"; Newport hosts wildly colored sailboats and offers intriguing shoreside shopping; Laguna Beach inspires artists; San Diego's primary attraction is its beautiful harbor and manmade bay.

Land of Casual Culture

Mellowed by the fine weather, Southern Californians have adopted a new life style, becoming trend-setters in food, fashion, architecture, and gardening. In this capital of casual living, it's possible to enter a fine restaurant without a tie, and a dinner invitation usually means an outdoor barbecue on a garden patio.

(Continued on page 8)

In this chapter we present a sampling of Southern California's myriad attractions and define the boundaries of the Southland. (Also see map on pages 4 and 5.) Any time is the time to visit, and there is always something to see and do. Even residents may find a few "back yard" discoveries.

Introduction

. . . Continued from page 7

However, this region is a center of culture. You can discover some of the world's finest art museums, theaters, and music centers here. Outdoor pageants and "under-the-stars" performances are popular. In summertime, the Universal Amphitheatre provides a showcase for the biggest names in contemporary music. At Hollywood Bowl, the famed Los Angeles Philharmonic performs, while across the Hollywood Hills top-name entertainers draw crowds for evening concerts at the Greek Theatre. In San Diego you'll find performances in Balboa Park; at Hemet you can see the Ramona Pageant in a natural outdoor amphitheater; Santa Barbara offers song and dance spectacles at the Mission Bowl.

Land of Entertainment

Southern California sets the pace for other regions in family fun and entertainment. You'll find more man-made amusement parks and attractions here than anywhere else in the world—all within a few miles of downtown Los Angeles. With a magical wand, that great creative genius, Walt Disney, created the first and foremost of theme parks: Disneyland. Today, Disneyland stands amid a fantasyland of whimsical adventures and great amusement parks.

Whether your idea of adventure is a high-speed ride on Space Mountain, a stomach-jerking stop at the top of Montezooma's Revenge, a log-jamming water-flume run, dancing horses, jumping whales, or an eye-to-eye confrontation with a lion—you'll find it in Southern California.

Celebrity-hunting is a big game in Southern California. Many people come to the area hoping to rub elbows with movie and television stars. One of our special features—*Hunting for Celebrities*, page 28—gives some hints on the best places to "star-gaze."

Another special feature—*World of Entertainment*, page 29—tells you how to get tickets to television shows and which studios you can tour; in short, it's an introduction to the land of illusion.

Boundaries of a Land

Where is Southern California? Though actual boundaries do not exist, the area known as Southern California is nevertheless a real place—one defined as much by personality as by geography.

Our travel guide to Southern California covers a generous scope, stretching north to the San Joaquin Valley and Sequoia and Kings Canyon National Parks, and extending south across the Mexican border. In the east we draw the boundary a bit above Death Valley, taking in both Inyo and Mono counties, major recreation targets for Southland residents. Along the coast we inch north above San Luis Obispo (halfway between Los Angeles and San Francisco) to Morro Bay and San Simeon. The area north of this east-west line is described in the *Sunset* book *Travel Guide to Northern California*.

Beginning with the sprawling Los Angeles region, this book includes the ocean world and coastal resort towns, valleys fronting upon major mountain ranges, peaceful rolling hills with quiet villages and mission memories, desert resorts and wilderness, the winding Colorado River that divides Southern California and Arizona, and the grand southern section of the Sierra Nevada.

In addition to the general map of Southern California, other maps scattered throughout the chapters focus on local points of interest. Detailed street maps of downtown Los Angeles and Santa Barbara, with a general map of sprawling San Diego, aid in planning walking or driving tours. Freeways in the L.A. area are clearly marked to help motorists find their way around.

With each map in the book, a "Points of Interest" box keys some of the interesting attractions to their locations in that region. Many are famous, others not so well known. Intended only as suggestions, these attractions are explained more fully in the text.

When to visit

Any time of the year is good somewhere in the Southland. Summertime is more crowded, the desert is quite hot, and it's likely to be "smog season" around Los Angeles and environs. This is the time to enjoy the miles of white sandy beaches, dotted wih dramatic surfing areas, marinas, harbors, and noted coastal towns—Santa Barbara, Malibu, Santa Monica, Newport, Laguna Beach, La Jolla, and San Diego.

Desert parks and resorts are the goal of winter sun-seekers, while skiers head for the mountains.

Spring and fall provide the region's mildest weather and the choice seasons for most of the fairs and festivals. (For a calendar of monthly events, write the Greater Los Angeles Visitors and Convention Bureau, 505 S. Flower Street, Los Angeles, CA 90071.) Wildflowers carpet desert and higher elevations beginning in mid-February and lasting through June.

Since the sun season lasts all year, accommodations are not priced for a three-month "tourist season." Vacationers will find that dollars will stretch further in Southern California because many of its best-known features are free.

What to see

Entertainment centers are a part of the Southern California experience. Such magic words as "Hollywood" and "Rose Bowl" and "Sunset Boulevard" originated here. But don't overlook the natural attractions. Wilderness areas remain as they have for centuries—mountain peaks reach high above the roads and energies of man, lovely waterfall canyons elude all but the most probing eye, and the desert stretches for miles in sand and silence.

The Spaniards left their mark in California. Many towns grew up around the missions founded by Father Serra. A walk through San Diego's Old Town, Pueblo de Los Angeles, or the streets of Santa Barbara provides insight into the Spanish era's history and romance.

Southern California has something for everyone: from Marineland to missions; from the Hollywood Bowl concerts under the stars to the stars of Hollywood; from Sea World to sequoias.

How to get around

No matter how you arrive in Southern California (unless you drive your own car), you'll need some form of transportation to reach the many attractions in and around the major cities.

Never mind those hair-raising tales of L.A.'s freeway system. If you avoid the freeways at peak periods—7 to 9 A.M. and 4 to 6 P.M. weekdays—you will have no problem. Study a detailed map in advance, and stay in your own lane!

The Southern California Rapid Transit District operates a good bus system in Los Angeles, including a minibus service among points of interest in the downtown area. In Orange County, the Fun Bus whisks you to major attractions. From San Diego, you can take the Tijuana Trolley to the border city of Tijuana and back. Taxi service is good, but expensive; you'll find plenty of car rental agencies in each region.

Don't overlook tour facilities. In this land of multiple choices, sightseeing tours give background information and spotlight the high points of an area. They are usually good buys because they include admission prices (generally at reduced rates), where required.

Information for tourists and residents

Though this book is aimed primarily at the visitor and new resident, it includes information on possible discoveries for "back yard" vacations for those who have lived in Southern California for some time.

But if you are new to Southern California, no matter how you enter it—at its busy harbor, on its teeming freeways, or through its sprawling international airports—you'll sense immediately that this is a young and forward-looking region, a land with a well-grounded sense of the future. The past has been well protected, but not too many Southern Californians look back.

FESTIVALS & FESTIVITIES

The listings below provide a sampling of annual events and festivities of general interest to visitors. Dates change — it's advisable to check with the chambers of commerce of individual cities, or the Greater Los Angeles Visitors and Convention Bureau, 505 S. Flower Street, Los Angeles, CA 90071.

January
Palm Springs — Sled Dog Races, Aerial Tramway
Pasadena — Tournament of Roses Parade and Rose Bowl Football Game

February
Palm Springs — Bob Hope Desert Golf Classic and Desert Circus
Los Angeles — Chinese New Year, Chinatown; Mardi Gras, Olvera Street
Indio — National Date Festival
Kernville—Whiskey Flat Days

March
San Juan Capistrano — Fiesta de las Golondrinas (return of the swallows) at the mission
Buena Park—Gold Mining Contest

April
Blythe — Colorado River Country Fair
Del Mar — Jumping Frog Jamboree
Hemet — Ramona Pageant (through May)
Bakersfield—Heritage Days

May
Calico — Spring Festival
San Luis Obispo — La Fiesta
Bishop — Mule Days

June
Beaumont — Cherry Festival
Santa Barbara — Fishermen's Festival and Blessing of the Fleet
Ojai — Music Festival

July
Laguna Beach — Arts Festival and Pageant of the Masters (through August)
Lompoc — Flower Festival
San Diego — Mission Bay Sand Castle Contest
Del Mar—Thoroughbred Horse Racing

August
Newport Bay — Character Boat Parade
Los Angeles — Nisei Week, Little Tokyo
Long Beach—Sea Festival

September
Solvang — Danish Days
Pomona — Los Angeles County Fair
Julian — Wildflower Show

October
Borrego Springs — Desert Festival
Los Angeles — Double Ten Chinese Independence Day, Chinatown

November
Death Valley — '49er Annual Encampment
Hollywood — Santa Claus Lane Parade

December
Marina del Rey — Christmas Boat Parade
San Diego — Las Posadas, Old Town

Los Angeles

The West's largest city offers a great bill of fare for tourist and resident. Follow the steps of the Spaniards around Olvera Street in El Pueblo; enjoy star-studded performances at the Music Center; look up (or down) at L.A.'s new skyscrapers and subterranean shopping complexes; discover Griffith Park's secrets; and follow famous boulevards through Hollywood, along "The Strip," by the tar pits and Century City—all the way to the sea.

Big, bustling Los Angeles is a city in constant motion. The best overall view of the heterogeneous communities making up the metropolis of Los Angeles is from a plane, particularly at night. From nowhere else does the crisscrossing light pattern of the main street grid seem so extensive.

Sprawling inland from the Pacific Ocean over some 460 square miles, L.A. occupies as much land as the entire state of Rhode Island. The West's largest city is the focal point for one of the greatest population migrations in all recorded history. Over three million people call Los Angeles their home.

Why did they come? The Mediterranean climate was—and still is—the key. People found the year-round sun exhilarating; it stimulated the crops they planted. Citrus groves thrived; oil was discovered. Because they could operate all year, the cinema and aviation industries flourished, generating technological offspring—television and aerospace—that eventually outdistanced them.

L.A.'s genesis lives on in historic Pueblo de Los Angeles where cobblestoned streets and adobes mark its Spanish and Mexican roots. Just a few blocks away, Chinatown and Little Tokyo sweep visitors into different lands and cultures.

Architecture forms a large part of the city's heritage; it was the first major United States city to build *out* instead of *up*. Only recently have multistoried buildings changed the Los Angeles skyline.

Since the city has more cars than the entire state of New York, freeways play an important part in the Los Angeles lifestyle. Visitors find the freeway network a swift route among the multiplicity of attractions.

There's always pleasure to be found in Los Angeles. All you have to do is pin it down. You can sample the city in many ways: take in the basic natural gifts of sunshine and setting, or seek out the elaborate amusements of a city where entertainment is big business.

It takes a sense of humor to savor unpredictable, offbeat L.A. If you think museums and theaters are the measure of a city, you'll find some fine ones. But where else would you discover great art in a cemetery or look-alike replicas of once-trapped Ice Age creatures emerging from tar pits?

Getting there

Los Angeles has one of the largest and busiest airports in the country—Los Angeles International. Four other major airports in surrounding areas provide supplemental passenger service: Hollywood/Burbank, Long Beach, Ontario, and Orange County. You can make connections from one to the other by motor coach.

Within the airport, the Terminal Tram circulates every 10 minutes to all terminals. The charge is minimal for steps saved.

The city is also served by the nation's two big transcontinental bus companies (Continental Trailways and Greyhound) and by Amtrak rail service.

Settling in

First-timers and even those who haven't been to L.A. for a while may need some help in finding their way around

ON A CLEAR DAY, snow-capped San Gabriel range provides spectacular backdrop for city skyscrapers.

this large, ever-changing city. A few words of advice on touring and accommodations from those who know the area will make your visit much more enjoyable. The Greater Los Angeles Visitors and Convention Bureau offices at 505 S. Flower Street (Arco Plaza, Level B), Los Angeles, CA 90071, and 6801 Hollywood Boulevard (corner Hollywood and Highland), Los Angeles, CA 90028, offer free downtown and freeway maps, booklets, and current-event listings. (Some brochures are also available in the Theme Building at L.A. International Airport.)

The bureau's downtown office is open from 9 A.M. to 5 P.M. weekdays, 10 A.M. to 4 P.M. Saturday. Visit the Hollywood office weekdays between 9 A.M. and 4 P.M. (6 P.M. on Friday). The bureau's 24-hour Welcome Line phone number is (213) 628-5857.

Maps of greater L.A. are becoming more difficult to obtain; there may be a slight charge if you do find one. Motorists should come prepared with automobile club or Thomas Bros. maps.

Moving around

Once in Los Angeles, you can take guided bus tours of most major attractions. But if you plan any ambitious sightseeing, you will need a car.

Freeways are the lifelines of the city. Opinions vary as to whether they were designed by people of vision or madmen, but, at best, they get motorists long distances in astonishingly short periods of time. The often intertwining maze of routes may seem complicated at first, but a review of the freeway map on page 21 will help to simplify your driving. Try to avoid freeways during times of peak congestion—7 to 9 A.M. and 4 to 6 P.M.—when residents are traveling to and from work.

Touring Old Los Angeles

Los Angeles started as a Spanish village, then became Mexican, and finally Yankee. Today, the once somnolent Pueblo, aging but undergoing rebirth and restoration, is the nucleus of bustling districts. Close by, you can savor the sights and sounds, foods, and goods of Mexico and early California, the Orient, and the Mediterranean, all at the Civic Center edge of downtown L.A.

Pueblo de Los Angeles and vicinity

In 1781, 11 families recruited by the provincial governor, Felipe de Neve, concluded a 7-month colonizing expedition from Sonora, Mexico, to the banks of the Los Angeles River. They marked off the lots that gave birth to the Spanish village with the tongue-tangling name *El Pueblo de Nuestra Señora la Reina de Los Angeles* (the town of Our Lady the Queen of the Angels). Restoration of L.A.'s birthplace as a 44-acre State Historic Landmark is underway.

Walking is the best way to see El Pueblo. You can join a free guided tour departing from the visitors center (130 Paseo de la Plaza) hourly from 10 A.M. to 1 P.M. Tuesday through Saturday, or pick up a free map at the center and explore on your own.

The Plaza, once the center of activity for the whole town, is now closed to traffic and remains the heart of the Pueblo. On summer Sunday afternoons, the circular, lacy *kiosko* (19th century, iron-grilled bandstand) is the scene of open-air concerts of Mexican and Spanish music. Colorful fiestas are held throughout the year. Stroll around the square to view the varied topiary.

Southwest of the Plaza on Main Street stand three venerable structures: Masonic Lodge (dating from 1858); Merced Theater, the city's first; and Pico House—built over a century ago, it was the grandest hotel of its day. Under the theater and the Garnier Building an amazing labyrinth of basement shops and tunnels hid Chinese merchants during a period of oppression.

North of the Plaza, structures of interest include the Avila Adobe (see below) and Victorian-fronted Sepulveda House; a Siqueiros mural adorns nearby Italian Hall.

Old Plaza Fire House, on the Plaza at Los Angeles Street, is the restored station of Engine Company No. 1, the oldest Los Angeles fire station—serving from 1884 to 1897. Inside the two-story brick building is one of the first fire engines used in the city; the horse-drawn equipment was originally built in 1892 for the Chicago Columbia Exposition. Upstairs are the firemen's living quarters. The building is open Tuesday through Friday from 10 A.M. to 3 P.M., weekends from 11 A.M. to 5 P.M.

Plaza Church was first established as a chapel for the settlers in 1784. The diminutive church was originally only 18 by 24 feet. It was finally rebuilt in 1822 with proceeds from the sale of 7 barrels of brandy from Mission San Gabriel. In 1860 heavy rains nearly ruined the adobe walls, so the front was taken down and rebuilt with brick. In recent years other changes have been made, including the rebuilding of the bell tower to blend in with the church's original architecture. The door has the classic river-of-life design.

Olvera Street, a block-long, brick-paved pedestrian lane, is the greatest single magnet in the Pueblo and possibly the West's first pedestrian shopping mall. In its 50 years of existence, Olvera Street has developed its own distinct character, both Mexican and Californian, in shops, restaurants, color, and life. Visitors come, enjoy the experience, and return; the street is a continuous pageant. And its cheerful people are its greatest attraction.

Shop for candles, leather goods, silver jewelry, pottery, and Mexican candies. Or dine on good Mexican food with background music. The more Mexican way is to eat in one of the little food *puestos* along the street.

Watch the artisans at work. You may see a piñata being formed around a clay *olla* (you can have one made to order); wrought iron being fashioned; three players performing on one marimba; and candles, leather goods, blown glass, and pottery being made. Stalls and shops open at 10 A.M.

Avila Adobe, at 10 Olvera Street, is L.A.'s oldest dwelling (dating back to about 1818). During the American occupation of El Pueblo in 1847, it served as headquarters for Kearny, Stockton, and Fremont. Now restored, the house is a showcase of California living in the 1840s.

(Continued on page 15)

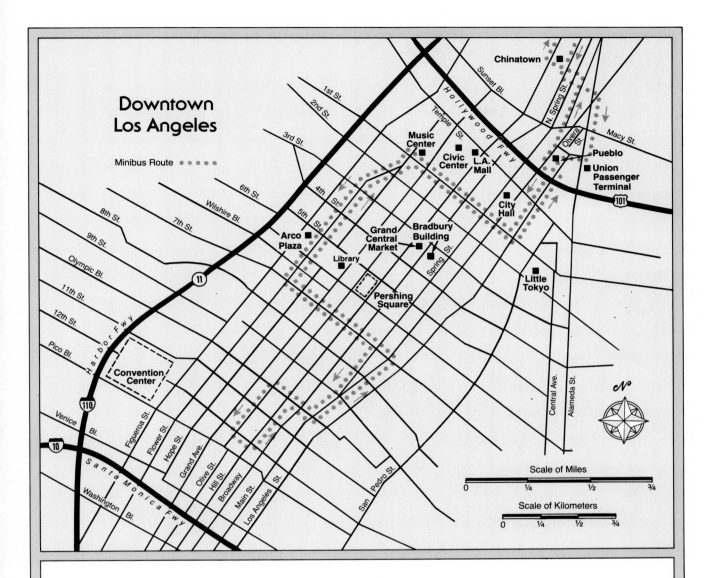

Downtown Los Angeles

Minibus Route • • • • •

Major Points of Interest

Civic Center (south of Hollywood Freeway)—panoramic city view from 27th-floor observation deck of City Hall; gardens, shops, restaurants, and Triforium in L.A. Mall around City Hall East

Pueblo de Los Angeles (north of Civic Center)—birthplace of L.A.; 19th century park restoration; Olvera Street, West's first mall with Mexican flavor

Chinatown—Little Tokyo (north and east of Civic Center)—smells, sights, and sounds of two cultures

Music Center (Grand Avenue at First Street)—L.A.'s cultural "in" place; Chandler Pavilion, Mark Taper Forum, Ahmanson Theatre

Arco Plaza (Atlantic Richfield and Bank of America twin towers)—home of Greater Los Angeles Visitors and Convention Bureau; interesting plaza sculpture and fountain; subterranean shops

Pershing Square (between Fifth and Sixth streets)—L.A.'s only downtown park; underground parking

Grand Central Market (Hill Street between Third and Fourth streets)—exotic food bazaar specializing in Mexican groceries

Bradbury Building (opposite Grand Central Market)—architectural landmark and background for movies and TV shows

DRAMATIC DESIGN marks glittering Chandler Pavilion (above), part of Music Center complex, and Double Ascension sculpture fountain (right) at Arco Plaza. Underneath lies subterranean shopping complex.

. . . Continued from page 12

The interesting church on the east side of the entrance to Olvera Street is La Plaza Iglesia Metodista (Methodist Church). Built in 1929, its architecture is in the Mexican tradition. Services are conducted in Spanish.

San Antonio Winery, east of El Pueblo at 737 Lamar Street, is another historic site. The spot where it stands was once in the heart of Old Town's vast vineyards (now completely urbanized). A visit to the last producing winery in L.A. includes a tour of bottling, aging, and tasting rooms. It's open Monday through Saturday from 8 A.M. Self-guided winery tours take about 20 minutes; picnic grounds adjoin the main cellar.

Union Passenger Terminal, one of the last great rail depots built in the United States, is approaching the half-century mark. Soaring interior spaciousness, white-stuccoed towers, arches, and passageways, and a red-tile roof make the attractive terminal at 800 N. Alameda Street (east of the Plaza) one of the city's landmarks.

You can begin a walking tour of cosmopolitan Los Angeles from this stately terminal. It is a good place to park (for a modest fee); from here you can walk to Little Tokyo, City Hall, the Plaza, and New Chinatown. Taken in that order, the round-trip walking tour is about 3 miles long. The minibus route (see page 13) follows much the same route.

Chinatown

"New" Chinatown opened in 1939 to replace the Chinatown ripped out for the Union Station. Located off North Broadway near College Street, this 2-block-long pedestrian mall has small, shop-lined lanes with names like Gin Ling, Sun Mun, and Lei Ling.

Although devoted to much the same kinds of enterprise as Olvera Street, New Chinatown has not aged as well. The emphasis here seems to lean more toward tourism, but in a few shops you can find some excellent Oriental wares. Two food markets offer a wide variety of foods, teas, and utensils; there are good Chinese restaurants. One confectionary is a deservedly popular shop.

Liveliest at night, the main mall is bright with lights and often bustling with crowds of after-dinner shoppers and sightseers. The most colorful season here is during Chinese New Year week in late winter. But special occasions throughout the year are likely to bring forth firecracker explosions and parades.

The most authentic Chinese section of the city is on North Spring Street, southeast of New Chinatown. Here you'll see Chinese markets, restaurants, a Chinese cinema, and a fascinating juxtaposition of Chinese and Spanish-language signs.

Dodger Stadium

North of Civic Center and adjacent to Elysian Park (a good place for a picnic before a game) is Dodger Stadium, home of L.A.'s first major league baseball team. The cantilevered structure has a seating capacity of 56,000. You park your car on the same level as your stadium seat. Baseball season generally runs from April to early October; for schedules, call (213) 224-1400.

Around Civic Center

The scene of much redevelopment in recent years, Los Angeles' Civic Center is separated from the Old Pueblo area to the north by the Hollywood-Santa Ana Freeway. First Street is the southern extremity, while Figueroa and San Pedro streets are the western and eastern boundaries, respectively.

City Hall

For years L.A.'s 32-story City Hall was the tallest building in Southern California; a ruling against other high-rises kept the city low-roofed until the late 1950s. Set on one side of the City Mall (probable former site of the Indian village of Yang-na, which antedated El Pueblo), the City Hall tower provides a panorama of the city on a clear day. From the observation deck on the 27th floor, you'll see Union Station to the north and, 15 miles distant, Mount Wilson.

To the northwest is Hollywood along the Santa Monica Mountains and, closer in, historic Fort Moore Hill. The beach cities along the Pacific Ocean are 16 miles to the west. To the south you'll see Los Angeles Harbor and possibly Catalina Island. The imposing peak to the northeast is Mount San Antonio. To the east and southeast are the city's industrial sections. The observation deck is open from 8 A.M. to 4 P.M. on weekdays.

The Los Angeles Mall, or City Mall, a handsomely landscaped complex of shops and restaurants, covers 2 blocks—from the Hollywood Freeway to First Street between Main and Los Angeles streets. Containing sunken gardens and subterranean parking, the mall is served by the downtown minibus.

The Los Angeles Children's Museum, within the mall at 310 N. Main Street, is designed just for children. Here they can paint and paste, dress up in costumes, and enjoy displays that invite touching and exploring. Open daily, the museum charges admission.

The Civic Center complex, a multilevel maze of buildings, shops, restaurants, gardens, sculptures, and waterfalls, is dominated by the Triforium: a 60-foot tower at Temple and Main streets that delivers music and a simultaneous light show through colored glass prisms. Performances are generally held around lunchtime or early in the evening.

The Music Center—L.A.'s cultural heart

The cultural "in" place of Los Angeles, the Music Center at First Street and Grand Avenue, is a $34.5 million complex specially designed to accommodate theatrical and musical presentations.

The Dorothy Chandler Pavilion, an elegant marble and black glass music hall, is the home of the Los Angeles Civic Light Opera and Philharmonic Orchestra. Completed in 1964, it was the first of the three-theater complex, linked on the surface by a landscaped mall and underground by a parking cavern. Acoustics are close to perfection anywhere in the 3,250-seat hall.

The pavilion provides a glittering setting for opera,

symphony, musical comedy, and dance performances. Check newspapers for current attractions. Free guided tours are available on some weekdays and Saturdays throughout the year; phone (213) 972-7483 for times and reservations.

Mark Taper Forum, intimate and innovative, is usually committed to experimental drama by the resident Center Theatre Group, lured away from its longtime U.C.L.A. home. Occasionally the 750-seat building is used for lectures, chamber music, and opera.

The building is linked to its larger companion, the Ahmanson Theatre, by a lofty colonnade that echoes the design of the Chandler Pavilion across the court.

Ahmanson Theatre, a spacious 2,000-seat auditorium, completes the triple complex of the Music Center. Dedicated to attracting first-class plays and musicals, it is operated most of the year by the Center Theatre Group.

Little Tokyo

A Japanese neighborhood bounded by Central Avenue and Los Angeles, First, and Third streets, Little Tokyo offers a bit of local color. Its redevelopment has brought new restaurants, gardens, and office buildings. Adjoining the boldly modern New Otani Hotel stands Weller Court, a collection of shops, restaurants, and plazas.

Highlighting the area's Japanese American Cultural and Community Center complex (San Pedro and Second streets) is the handsome Japan America Theatre. In addition to traditional *kabuki*, the theater presents Asian music and films, as well as Western concerts. A highly sophisticated sound system provides simultaneous English and Japanese translations of performances. JACCC Plaza, an acre of rock sculpture and fountains, fronts the theater.

During Nisei Week in early August, colorful pageantry stresses cultural achievements and traditions of ancient Japan. On the final Sunday night, the *Ondo* parade sing-songs through the streets.

Downtown Los Angeles

Los Angeles is a fine example of downtown renaissance. Height restrictions previously placed on tall buildings because of earthquake scares were removed in 1957, and the city is growing upward. Today's skyline is dominated by towering office buildings with rooftop dining, futuristic hotels, and "in-city" apartments where elegant 19th century Bunker Hill residences once stood.

At the outskirts of the downtown center area, between 11th and Pico streets off Figueroa, sprawls the heavily used Convention Center—two spacious buildings with easy access and acres of parking.

Getting around

Finding your way around the downtown area is relatively easy. Traffic isn't bad, except during weekday rush hours. A planned "People Mover" transit system will eventually link the Convention Center, shopping centers, and the financial district with the Civic Center and El Pueblo.

Tours on the minibuses operated by the Southern California Rapid Transit District show you a fair sampling of the downtown sector: the retail district, from Fourth to Eighth streets; the World Trade Center and big new-generation high-rises on Figueroa, from Seventh to Fifth; the historic Bradbury Building and Grand Central Market, near Third and Broadway; and the Music Center and monumental Civic Center, on First from Flower to Los Angeles streets. You can also visit the L.A. Mall, the Plaza and Olvera Street, Chinatown, and Little Tokyo.

Buses run at frequent intervals on a continuous loop route from 7 A.M. to 5:30 P.M. daily (until 4 P.M. Saturday) except on Sunday and holidays. Bus-stop signs indicate the route and your location; you can get a pocket-size map on board. It's quite a tour for 25 cents a ride (you'll need exact change). There's a 12-minute delay at one end of a round trip.

Walking is still a good way to see some of L.A.'s landmarks. Leave your car in one of the city's many parking lots. Or take advantage of the downtown walking tour offered by the L.A. Conservancy; make reservations a week in advance by calling (213) 623-CITY. (A $5.00 donation is requested.) Near the heart of working L.A., the buildings give you a sense of history: their achitectural styles reflect both the boom of the 1880s and the building boom of more recent years.

Spring Street, on the eastern side of your downtown exploration, is still a bulwark of financial dignity. The Pacific Coast Stock Exchange (618 S. Spring Street) has a visitors' gallery on the second floor; from here, you can get a first-hand picture of what's happening on the trading floor. The gallery's hours—7 A.M. to 1 P.M. Monday through Friday—coincide with those of the New York Stock Exchange. At 202 W. First Street, off Spring, you can tour the Los Angeles Times, the nation's second largest newspaper. Free guided walking tours are offered weekdays at 3 P.M.; children under 10 are not permitted. The Alexandria Hotel (Fifth and Spring) was once the hub of L.A.'s social life. Today, it's renovated as a cultural-historic monument; the stained-glass-domed Palm Court is worth a look.

Broadway, once the main retail street from Fourth to Eighth, is still bustling, and crowded—and often nerve-jangling on Sundays, when people pack the sidewalks (Spanish is heard as often as English here). The Grand Central Market, between Broadway and Hill and Third and Fourth, is a food bazaar that could exist only in a metropolis. The giant market, open from 9 A.M. to 6 P.M. daily except Sunday and holidays, displays items you may not find anywhere else in town. One stall contains 13 kinds of beans, peas, and lentils; another offers 20 varieties of tea. You can look over rare spices and chilies, rice in all grain sizes, different blends of olive oil, and all the ingredients for Mexican cookery. Many stalls have bilingual signs.

The Bradbury Building, across the street from the market at 304 Broadway, looks ordinary from the outside. Once you're inside, though, you'll see why this almost century-old structure is a city cultural-historic monument. Ornate iron railings line a five-story skylit interior; metal tracery decorates the open elevator cages. One of the prototype hydraulic elevators is still in use. Once a fashionable address for law firms, the building houses offices today. You can look around (for a fee) Monday through Saturday.

Seventh Street, west from Broadway, is still a major downtown retail street, with several large stores and shopping complexes. It was intended as a great artery to the west. But the need to grade the hill on which the Los Angeles Hilton was built slowed its development, and Wilshire overtook it as the main line.

Pershing Square, called Central Park until 1918, is L.A.'s only downtown park (bounded by Hill and Olive and Fifth and Sixth streets). Facing Fifth Street is a statue of Beethoven, a reminder that the park was once downtown's cultural center. You can park underneath or in nearby lots for a few dollars a day (less on Sunday). Weekdays are liveliest here; Saturday is good for shopping. Sunday morning is a good time to experience the deep canyons of downtown without crowds.

The Los Angeles Central Library, at Fifth and Hope streets, is part of the largest public library system in the nation. Built in 1926, the fortresslike structure was designed by architect Bertram Goodhue, who achieved fame as the architect of the 1915 San Diego Exposition. Now metamorphosed into Balboa Park, it touched off a wave of mission-style building in Southern California. Inside the library are detailed ceilings, pleasant gardens, an impressive second-floor rotunda, a mural-decorated History Room, and a wealth of books. It's open daily except Sunday and holidays; guided tours are available.

The Wells Fargo History Museum, in the company's headquarters at Fifth and Flower, includes a Concord stagecoach in the exhibition highlighting the bank's role in the "winning of the West." The free museum is open from 9 A.M. to 4 P.M. weekdays.

The World Trade Center, between Third and Fourth streets and Flower and Figueroa, is L.A.'s international business complex. Its two-level mall contains shops, restaurants, consulates, and a foreign currency exchange facility.

Plazas and shopping centers

Indoor shopping malls are at their best in the downtown area. Multitudinous stores and restaurants crowd multilevel centers, either above or below sculpture and fountain-studded plazas. Elevated walkways or under-street tunnels connect many buildings.

The Arco Plaza (connected by a footbridge across Fifth Street to the Bonaventure Hotel) is marked by a striking sculpture and pool on the street level. Underneath the twin towers of the Atlantic Richfield and Bank of America buildings lies one of America's largest subterranean shopping centers, lined with stores and restaurants and featuring fashion shows, concerts, and art exhibits on a regular basis. Here, too, you'll find the Greater Los Angeles Visitors and Convention Bureau, a Catholic chapel, and a post office.

The Broadway Plaza's two-level mall on Seventh Street, between Hope and Flower, is topped by the large Broadway flagship store and the Hyatt Regency Hotel.

At Crocker Center, between Grand and Hope and Third and Fourth streets, a three-story, glass-enclosed atrium houses shops and restaurants.

Several more centers, including the California Plaza (home of the Museum of Contemporary Art) atop Bunker Hill and the Pacific Plaza (between Seventh and Eighth streets, off Figueroa), will also feature department stores, shops, and restaurants.

A look at lodging

There's a fine choice of lodgings in downtown L.A. for travelers, conventioneers, and those who appreciate a central location. These hotels offer restaurants and night spots that attract visitors from all over the area. Some of the most impressive are listed below.

The Biltmore Hotel, across Olive Street from Pershing Square, harks back to another era. Untouched by the splendid modernization applied to the hotel's rooms and halls, the lobby is ornate in the grand manner, as stunning today as it was in 1923.

The Bonaventure Hotel, a new and striking downtown inn (between Fourth and Fifth streets and Flower and Figueroa), was designed by John Portman. Its five reflecting circular towers are your first step into a 21st century experience. Around the dramatic lobby atrium are five levels of shops. A ride in a glass elevator gives a good view of downtown, as do the rooftop restaurant and revolving cocktail lounge.

The Hyatt Regency, atop the Broadway Plaza, is a prime spot for one-stop shopping and landscape viewing. Its 26th-floor restaurant revolves, offering a good look at the downtown skyline.

The Los Angeles Hilton, on Wilshire and Figueroa, was one of the city's first high-rise hotels. Its convenient location and evening entertainment are perhaps more interesting than its architecture.

The Sheraton Grande (Figueroa Street, connected by pedestrian walkway to the World Trade Center) is L.A.'s newest complex of rooms, theaters, restaurants, gardens, and office buildings. You can take tea in the striking sunken lobby lounge.

South of Downtown L.A.

South and west of downtown Los Angeles lie several of the area's Olympic sports centers, two big museums, one of the country's best known universities, the international airport, and other scattered attractions. All can be reached from several freeways—the Santa Monica (Interstate Highway 10), San Diego (Interstate Highway 405), Harbor (State Highway 11), and Long Beach (State Highway 7).

Exposition Park

A meeting place for nature, ideas and experiments, history, and activity, 114-acre Exposition Park is bordered by Exposition Boulevard, Figueroa Street, and Menlo

and Santa Barbara avenues. A ramp from the Harbor Freeway takes you to Exposition Boulevard; the main entrance to the park is through the Memorial Gateway just west of the junction of Hoover and Figueroa streets.

In the center of Exposition Park, 16,000 fragrant rose bushes fill the Sunken Garden, a principal feature of the park's landscaping. The roses bloom from late spring through fall; all are identified.

The California Museum of Science and Industry, south of the Sunken Garden on State Drive, offers the opportunity for a do-it-yourself short course in basic science. It's a noisy museum: balls drop, a jet engine fires, a heart thumps. Some machines perform with soap bubbles and rubber balls. Others can be manipulated by a child to reveal the laws of orbiting bodies, to turn a car wheel or axle, or to play tic-tac-toe with an electronic brain that never loses. Throughout the museum you'll find gadgets that are fascinating and instructive.

Museum hours are 10 A.M. to 5 P.M.; it is closed only on Thanksgiving and Christmas. Admission is free. The main parking lot is behind the Hall of Health annex.

The Museum of Natural History is on the west side of the Sunken Garden. It's filled with Egyptian mummies, reconstructed dinosaurs, glittering exhibits of gems, and dioramas of animals in natural settings. Other displays depict Southern California life in the Indian, Spanish, Mexican, and American periods.

One-of-a-kind touches include such Hollywood memorabilia as William S. Hart's fan mail, Tom Mix's Stetson hat, W. C. Fields's billiard cue, and Mary Pickford's curls.

Open daily from 10 A.M. to 5 P.M., the museum is closed only on Thanksgiving and Christmas.

L.A. Memorial Coliseum, on the opposite side of the park from the museums, has an awesome seating capacity of nearly 95,000. The gateway to the park commemorates the Olympic Games. The stadium, built in 1928 and remodeled for the 10th Olympiad in 1932 and for the 1984 Games, covers 17 acres. The University of Southern California plays its home football games here; it's home for the Los Angeles Raiders pro football team, too.

Sports centers are numerous in this area. The modern indoor L.A. Memorial Sports Arena, in Exposition Park at the corner of Figueroa and Santa Barbara streets, has a seating capacity of 16,300. Collegiate and professional basketball, track meets, boxing matches (including the Olympic events), tennis tournaments, and special sports events and shows are held here.

Another outstanding sports center, the Forum, in Inglewood at the corner of Manchester Boulevard and Prairie Avenue, hosts Olympic and professional basketball and ice hockey, as well as ice shows, track meets, tennis, and boxing events. The Forum seats 18,600.

Southern California also boasts the first world-class velodrome in the western states. Built at the California State University Dominguez Hills in Carson, it was completed in 1983 for pre-Olympiad development of U.S. cyclists. The campus is east of the intersection of the Harbor and Santa Monica freeways.

University of Southern California covers several blocks along Exposition Boulevard opposite Exposition Park. Founded in 1876 by the Southern Conference of the Methodist Episcopal Church, it's the largest private university in California. Its architecture is a fine integration of old and new; notice especially Doheny Library and the campanile. U.S.C. is noted for its Department of Cinema, the oldest (1929), largest, and one of the most respected in the country.

Towers of Simon Rodia

In Watts, at 1765 E. 107th Street (Century Boulevard exit from Harbor Freeway, State 11), a group of unusual towers soar as high as 104 feet above the ground, a strangely beautiful symbol of a man's ambition "to do something big." The man was Sabatino (Simon) Rodia, an Italian tile setter who spent 33 years single-handedly building the towers. Rodia wired steel reinforcing rods together into a lacy structure, stuccoed them with cement, then studded the cement with broken bits of glass, tile, pottery shards, pebbles, and seashells.

After completing his work in 1954, Rodia quietly left town, and the future of the towers became uncertain. But the public became interested in preserving this forerunner of pop art. The towers' fate was settled when the steepest one was subjected to a "pull test" before television cameras and didn't budge.

You can visit the towers daily. An adjacent art center sponsors cultural events, exhibits, and classes.

Hollywood Park Race Track

Just east of the San Diego Freeway (I-405) at Century Boulevard in Inglewood, picturesque Hollywood Park features thoroughbred racing Wednesday through Sunday from mid-April to late July and from early November until late December. Harness racing goes on from mid-August to late October. Post time for the thoroughbred races is 2 P.M.; for harness racing, 7:30 P.M. The race track is famous for its beautifully landscaped infield.

Morning workouts (from 7 to 10 A.M. during the season) are open to the public. Activities are described over the public address system by a racing expert.

North of Downtown L.A.

Just north and east of the downtown area, off the Pasadena Freeway (State Highways 11/110), you'll find a garden oasis and several spots of historical interest.

Lawry's California Center

Expanded from offices and a seasoning preparation plant, Lawry's handsome shopping complex offers a restaurant, wine shop and cellar, antiques, cookware, pottery, and plants. You can enjoy lunch, cocktails, or dinner—all in a setting of lawns, trees, and flowers.

The complex is open daily except major holidays. Shop hours vary according to the season. Lunch is served from 11 A.M. to 3 P.M.; dinner is served in the evening from May to November.

(Continued on page 20)

SUNSET BOULEVARD drive gives you a look at Griffith Observatory (left) on Mount Hollywood. To the north, sun lights up tennis courts (below) in Griffith Park. Farther west you drive by colorful Beverly Hills park (above).

. . . Continued from page 18

Lawry's plant can be toured weekdays only; free 45-minute guided tours start at 11:30 A.M., and at 1:30 and 2:30 P.M. For those who want to improve their culinary skills, Lawry's offers a schedule of cooking classes. Subjects range from the basics of food preparation to the esthetics of gracious serving. The fee covers both cooking demonstrations and the food you'll sample. For further information and reservations, call (213) 225-2491.

A hint of L.A.'s history

Though you'll find a scattering of historical monuments, museums, and parks in and around L.A., these three attractions are so conveniently located that they can become the focus of a single outing.

Heritage Square (east side of the Pasadena Freeway, Avenue 43 exit) is the beginning of the city's Victorian home preservation and restoration program. Several homes reflecting L.A.'s lifestyle from 1865 to 1914 now stand on this square. Guided tours are usually offered the first two Sundays of each month from 11 A.M. to 3 P.M. (there's a small donation).

Lummis Home (west side of the Pasadena Freeway, Avenue 43 exit), or El Alisal, is the two-story "castle" and surrounding 3 acres that belonged to Charles Fletcher Lummis, founder of the Southwest Museum (see below). The house—never completed—was Lummis's lifelong project.

A native of Massachusetts, Lummis created the slogan "See America First"—and put his belief into practice by walking over 3,000 miles to reach Los Angeles. Here, he became the first City Editor of the Los Angeles Times. Two plaques on the walls of El Alisal list his achievements; one seals the crypt containing his ashes. Now a state park, the house and grounds are open Wednesday through Sunday from 1 to 4 P.M.

The Southwest Museum, at 234 Museum Drive, is north of the Lummis home. Established by Charles Lummis, it contains one of the country's outstanding displays of Western Indian artifacts. Of particular interest are the portraits and basketry.

Though there's a hillside parking lot above the building, it's more interesting to park below the museum and enter through a tunnel lined with dioramas showing American Indian life. An elevator whisks you up to the museum building and exhibits. The museum is open Tuesday through Sunday from 11 A.M. to 5 P.M.; admission is free.

L.A.'s Famous Streets

One of the best ways to see Los Angeles is to get off the freeways and drive its celebrity boulevards: Wilshire, Santa Monica, Sunset, and Hollywood. Each presents a different facet of city life. Almost every attraction in the western section of L.A. is on or near these thoroughfares. Two of them stretch from downtown Los Angeles to the ocean; one—Hollywood Boulevard—ends in the hills after taking you through the heart of Hollywood, filmland's one-time glamour spot.

Wilshire Boulevard

Stretching 16 miles from the city's center to the ocean, Wilshire Boulevard is one of the world's prestige streets, often compared to New York's Fifth Avenue. Launched in the 1920s with the opening of "Miracle Mile" (La Brea to La Cienega avenues), it soon began accumulating high-class shops, department stores, business firms, smart apartment houses, and plush restaurants. If you have time, you will want to stop at attractions along the way and explore interesting side streets. But even if you just keep driving, you will pass places closely identified with the growth of this city, along with some of the most interesting examples of new commercial architecture in the United States. Several well-known hotels have a Wilshire Boulevard address, starting with the downtown Los Angeles Hilton and including the farther-out Ambassador, Beverly Hilton, and Beverly Wilshire.

MacArthur Park, bisected by Wilshire Boulevard just west of Alvarado Street, was long known as Westlake, a country park at the westernmost edge of the city. Renamed for General Douglas MacArthur in 1942, the 32-acre park has a small lake and pleasantly landscaped grounds. Popular with the summer lunch group, it sports an open-air theater for Shakespearean and musical performances.

The Ambassador Hotel comes into view on the left soon after you cross Vermont Avenue. Set far back from ever-burgeoning Wilshire Boulevard amidst 27 protective acres of parklike grounds, the venerable old structure has long been a Los Angeles landmark. Fresh appearing after an extensive face lifting, it still exudes an atmosphere of elegance.

Some of the best-looking buildings along this section of Wilshire are the insurance companies, banks, and churches. The Old World architecture of the Wilshire Boulevard Temple (with the largest Jewish congregation in the world) and the Masonic Temple contrasts sharply with the contemporary style of St. Basil's Catholic Church.

Miracle Mile, locally renamed Mid-Wilshire, begins at La Brea Avenue and stretches for several miles to La Cienega. You'll recognize it by its median landscaped with palms. Though not as glamorous as in its heyday over 50 years ago, this section does have some outstanding attractions.

Hancock Park is one of the few remaining patches of greenery along Wilshire Boulevard. This is the site of the Rancho La Brea Tar Pits, where Pleistocene-era animals were trapped some 40 centuries ago. The collection of prehistoric animal skeletons that was found here is displayed in the George C. Page Museum on the park grounds, almost directly above the engulfing tar. Visitors can see films of the discovery of these remains and learn what life was like in the Los Angeles Valley over 14,000 years ago. The museum is open from 10 A.M. to 5 P.M. Tuesday through Sunday (except major holidays); there's an admission charge.

In Pueblo days, the Spaniards used *brea* (tar) from these pits to waterproof their roofs. Not until 1905 was it discovered that the bubbly, black pits had entombed such creatures as mastodons, dire wolves, and imperial

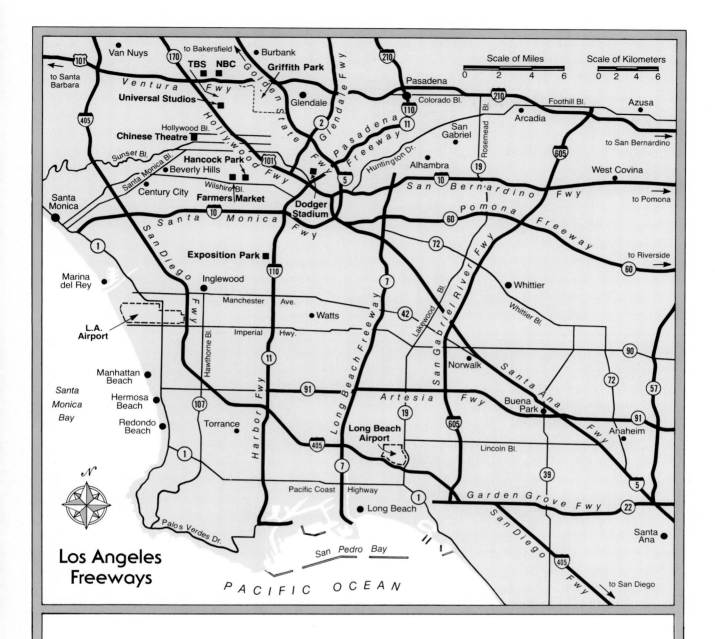

Los Angeles Freeways

Major Points of Interest

Studio tours—behind-scenes peek at television and movie studios; largest tours at Universal, Burbank Studios (TBS), and NBC

Griffith Park (off Golden State Freeway)—L.A.'s superpark: zoo, Travel Town, Fern Dell, Griffith Observatory, Greek Theater

Chinese Theatre (Hollywood Boulevard)—celebrated movie house with forecourt of footprints and signatures of stars

Beverly Hills (Wilshire Boulevard)—hotels, restaurants, galleries, and shops of celebrities

Century City (Santa Monica Boulevard just west of Beverly Hills)—city of tomorrow on former movie lot; ABC Entertainment Center

Farmers Market (Third Street and Fairfax Avenue)—giant market-restaurant-gift shop complex started by farmers in Depression

Hancock Park (Wilshire Boulevard)—La Brea Tar Pits, site of prehistoric animals' entrapment; Page Museum; L.A. County Museum of Art, one of greatest U.S. art museums

Exposition Park (off Harbor Freeway)—California Museum of Science and Industry, Natural History Museum of L.A. County, U.S.C.

PAINTING *receives earnest examination (left) from art patron at Los Angeles County Museum of Art. Shopping at Farmers Market often includes meeting a friend for lunch (below).*

mammoths that came to drink at the ponds 13,000 to 40,000 years ago, only to be caught and trapped in the seeping tar. Today, a strange, life-sized scene of the re-created ancient animals—including fiberglass imperial mammoths with tusks 12½ feet long—brings a touch of prehistory to busy Wilshire Boulevard. At the observation building in the northwest corner of the park, you can see the asphalt-laden water still bubbling and some animal bones still enmeshed in the tar. Scientists are still digging, hoping to find small bones and microfossils overlooked in the original digs of 1906-1915, and perhaps new evidence of Ice Age man.

Los Angeles County Museum of Art is the largest art museum built in this country in over 30 years. It is housed in three gleaming pavilions on a 3-foot-thick concrete slab atop the tar pits in Hancock Park. The reflecting pool that surrounded it has become a major sculpture garden, dominated by a monumental Rodin bronze of Honore Balzac. A latecomer in the art-collecting field, the museum has acquired some well-known works of art and is particularly rich in impressionistic paintings.

The Ahmanson Gallery, dominant pavilion in this imposing complex, houses the museum's permanent collections in separate galleries on four floors extending out from a lofty skylit central court. Collections, ranging from ancient treasures to futuristic experiments, are arranged chronologically.

On the upper level that connects the three buildings is the B. G. Cantor Sculpture Garden, a popular meeting place featuring works of famous sculptors. You can lunch at the cafeteria in the nearby Leo S. Bing Center, which has facilities for films, lectures, concerts, and temporary exhibitions. The third pavilion, the Hammer Wing, is the home of changing exhibits.

The art museum is open Tuesday through Friday from 10 A.M. to 5 P.M., and on weekends from 10 A.M. to 6 P.M. The admission charge is moderate.

Farmers Market is keynoted by its familiar white clock tower that rises above West Third Street and Fairfax Avenue and gives the busy neighborhood the air of a midwestern farming community. Words above the tower entrance read simply, "An Idea." The idea was to help Los Angeles-area farmers during the worst years of the Depression by letting them use a vacant field at the edge of the city to market their wasting crops.

The Farmers Market idea not only helped the 18 original farmers, but also grew into a giant market-restaurant-gift shop complex covering 20 acres and serving 20,000 visitors and shoppers daily all year. Although tour buses pack the parking lots around noon, most people here are from L.A.

Some of the original farmers and their families are still associated with the market, maintaining their widespread reputation by selling fresh food from all parts of the world. Here you can enjoy a tray of delicious food from any one of the market's 26 kitchens serving food from six countries. This is also the place to go shopping without a list, letting impulse be your guide through the tempting displays. You can buy a puppy, a fish, or an exotic bird here—but leave your pet at home. No animals are allowed to roam the premises.

The market is open Monday through Saturday from 9

A.M. to 6:30 P.M. during the winter; it stays open somewhat later during the summer. Activity begins to slow down around 5 P.M. One restaurant offering varied entertainment is open until 2 A.M. For a map listing each merchant in the market, stop at the office just inside Gate No. 1. With the map, you can chart a course through the busy aisles that will take you past every stall and shop. With so many things to see and buy, a walk among the stalls takes about an hour. Allow plenty of extra time to visit the shops.

La Cienega Boulevard's loose Spanish translation, "the watering hole," is an apt one. Located about a mile past Fairfax Avenue, this is "Restaurant Row." The boulevard is more glamorous at night, when diners congregate in eateries on both sides of the street to enjoy some of L.A.'s best food.

Art galleries also abound on this fabled boulevard. The gallery row between Melrose Avenue and Santa Monica Boulevard hosts popular Tuesday evening promenades during which strollers can wander through shops or just gaze in the windows. Hospitality may include a glass of wine or a few hors d'oeuvres.

Just east of La Cienega, at 6505 Wilshire Boulevard, you can visit the Martyrs Memorial & Museum of The Holocaust. Free guided tours are available weekdays and Sunday afternoons, except for major public and Jewish holidays.

Beverly Hills comes into view when you cross San Vincente Boulevard. The city's boundaries roughly extend from San Vincente west to Century City and Benedict Canyon Drive, and from Olympic Boulevard on the south to the hills above Sunset Boulevard on the north. But though Beverly Hills is surrounded by L.A., it has never surrendered its identity: there are no billboards, and buildings are lower. At the busy intersection of Olympic Boulevard and Beverly Drive is a "Monument to the Stars" honoring those who fought for the community's preservation when annexation to Los Angeles seemed likely.

Shop prowling is one of the city's main attractions for visitors. Beverly Hills is the place where New York stores open branches, fashion imports converge, and dining is cosmopolitan. Perhaps because this is the center of the affluent community, variety seems wider and specialities more specialized. Here more than elsewhere, shops project a heightened sensual appeal; even the most appealing goods play second fiddle to imaginative display. And where else would you need an appointment just to shop?

Wilshire Boulevard boasts many big stores, but *the* shopping street is 3-block-long Rodeo Drive—the third side of the triangle formed by Wilshire and Santa Monica boulevards. Though stores here provide a valet parking service for recognized customers, it's best for strollers to park elsewhere. Check with the Beverly Hills Visitors Bureau, 239 S. Beverly Drive, for maps and locations of shops. Be sure to take a look at the architecturally unique Rodeo Collection, a recent shopping enclave.

Prefer to stay close to the action? Visit the Beverly Hilton or Beverly Wilshire hotels, the city's largest.

Beyond Beverly Hills, Wilshire takes you past the exclusive Los Angeles Country Club; 18-hole golf courses line both sides of the boulevard.

Westwood Village, mecca for college students and a rather quaint community in its own right, nestles at the foot of the University of California, Los Angeles campus. Stop for a walk through the village and explore its inviting shops and eating spots.

Like a village within a village, Westwood's old Masonic Club, now called Contempo Westwood, is well entrenched as a shopping, dining, and arts center. Here you'll find the 500-seat Westwood Playhouse. Contempo Westwood is on La Conte Avenue across from the U.C.L.A. campus.

U.C.L.A. has grown in one generation from a cluster of four Romanesque hilltop buildings to a complete city of learning. The mammoth campus covers 422 acres of terraced hillside.

A major force in the city's cultural life, U.C.L.A. is a leader in drama, music, medicine, and the arts. The interesting architectural forms of the buildings are complemented by the fountain in front of Franz Hall, the Japanese Gardens, 8 acres of Botanical Gardens, and 4½ acres of 20th century art in the Franklin D. Murphy Sculpture Gardens. Of particular interest are the Dickson Art Center and the Museum of Cultural History.

For campus tour reservations, stop by the Visitor Center at 100 Dodd Hall or call (213) 825-4338. Free campus maps are available at parking kiosks; parking is free on Sunday. You can reach U.C.L.A. by turning north off Wilshire onto Westwood Boulevard.

Palisades Park in Santa Monica is the terminus for Wilshire Boulevard. Stretching for almost 2 miles along the cliff top, the park offers perhaps the most beautiful and familiar view of Santa Monica Bay. On a clear day you can see the Channel Islands, and on almost any day you can see the Santa Monica Mountains reaching out into the ocean to form the northern crescent of the bay. This corridor of green lawn, flowers, and tall palm trees is a pleasant area for a stroll or a picnic.

Before you explore the park, stop at the Tourist Information Center on Ocean Avenue just south of Santa Monica Boulevard and ask for a brochure. It will point out such features of interest as the sundial, the camera obscura, the totem pole, some of the trees and memorial plantings, and the park's seven monuments.

Santa Monica Boulevard

Originating in Silver Lake, the district east of Hollywood, Santa Monica Boulevard parallels Wilshire Boulevard heading north for a stretch, then turns south and cuts through Beverly Hills and across Wilshire on its way to the ocean. Though not particularly noted as a scenic thoroughfare, it does pass some interesting sights. If you have driven out Wilshire Boulevard, it's an alternate route back to Los Angeles or on to Hollywood.

Hollywood Cemetery, on Santa Monica Boulevard between Van Ness and Gower streets, is the final resting place for some legendary Hollywood film stars. Silent film star John Gilbert is buried here, as are Douglas Fairbanks and many others. This is where the mysterious lady in black paid her visits to Valentino's grave.

Paramount Studios, one of the few still left in Hollywood, is south of the cemetery. It is not open for tours.

The Mormon Temple, a monumental white edifice high atop a hill on Santa Monica Boulevard (a few blocks east of the Santa Monica Freeway), is the largest temple of the Mormon faith (Church of Jesus Christ of Latter-day Saints). The gold-leaf figure of Angel Moroni on top, once visible 25 miles out to sea, is now getting lost among the high-rises. You can tour the grounds but may not go inside the temple. Movies shown at the Visitor Information Center take you on a tour of the interior. The center is open from 9 A.M. to 9:30 P.M. daily.

Century City—a panorama of broad thoroughfares, sky-reaching buildings, green parks, and plazas—is a futuristic supercity being built on land once owned by a major movie studio. Turn onto the Avenue of the Stars from Santa Monica Boulevard (just south of Wilshire) to visit this trend-setting city within a city.

Based on the master plan of architects Welton Becket and Associates, Century City seems slightly larger than life. Traffic within the giant blocks is designed for the pedestrian; all parking on this 180-acre site is underground.

The land from which Century City rises was once the ranch of Tom Mix before it became the back lot of Twentieth Century-Fox Studio. In 1961 it was sold to the Alcoa Company for construction of a major new urban center in Los Angeles. Although the movieland sets were demolished, more than $1 million was invested in saving and replanting the unique studio tree collection.

Spread out like an oversized Japanese fan, Century City has as its crown jewel the 800-room Century Plaza Hotel, designed by architect Minoru Yamasaki. Surrounded by landscaped grounds and resembling New York City's Rockefeller Center, it was the choice for the Presidential State Dinner honoring the first astronauts to reach the moon.

The ABC Entertainment Center, across the street from the Century Plaza Hotel, features the large Shubert Theatre, a setting for Broadway productions on the West Coast, as well as for other legitimate theater performances. There are also two first-run cinemascopic theaters. Twin 44-story triangular office towers rise in the background. Shops, restaurants, and clubs complement the theaters and face the plaza. The center is open daily, from morning well into the night. For information on a 1-hour multimedia tour, call (213) 553-0626.

Twentieth Century-Fox, one of the oldest and most prestigious movie studios in the industry, stands on one corner of the Century City property. Work still goes on here (television series and independent productions), and some movie sets are still standing. The studio fronts onto Pico Boulevard; from here, you can get a fairly good view of the prop lot (part of the lot can also be seen from the Century Plaza Hotel windows). The only way to get inside the studio is to take the 2-hour walking tour offered by Gray Line Tours; call (213) 481-2121.

Sunset Boulevard

Gloria Swanson immortalized this street in the film *Sunset Boulevard*. She even lived on the famous thoroughfare (across from the Beverly Hills Hotel). Her home is gone, but other stars live nearby.

There's still a magic to the name "Sunset Strip," although its character has changed. Even if you're not a star-gazer, Sunset Boulevard is an interesting drive. Beginning at El Pueblo downtown, it proceeds through Hollywood and wanders along the foothills of the Santa Monica Mountains for 25 miles to its intersection with the Pacific Coast Highway.

The boulevard intersects with the canyon roads that cut across the mountains to the San Fernando Valley. "Hideaway" homes are built along these winding roads. Perhaps the best known residential area is exclusive Bel Air.

Angelus Temple and Echo Park are just south of Sunset Boulevard on Glendale Boulevard. Although Angelus Temple is visually unprepossessing, in the 1930s it presented one of the greatest shows in Los Angeles—a nightly, slightly edited version of the life of Aimee Semple McPherson, complete with full cast and scenery. Aimee, a self-appointed faith healer, is gone, but the temple lives on.

South of the temple is Echo Park, a pleasant haven of greenery complete with a small lake for boating in a sylvan setting. It is notable for its lotuses which flower in July. Sometimes stocked with fish, it's the meeting place for small children.

Hollywood flavor is not seen along Sunset. You'll catch it on the next main street north: Hollywood Boulevard (see at right). You will see bulky buildings housing film, television, radio, and recording studios, plus a concentration of camera shops.

Sunset Strip in its heyday was one of the plushest stretches of the boulevard. Within this 20-block area were a trio of famous nightclubs: Trocadero, Mocambo, and Ciro's. Fans gathered here to watch the comings and goings of the movie colony. With the gradual demise of Hollywood as a film center, the Strip has exchanged its Rolls Royce culture for a Volkswagen one.

There's still action at night, but it centers on the young and hip strolling in and out of the numerous loud, gaudy lounges and glorified hamburger stands. The view over L.A. is still good, but people don't seem to notice; they're too distracted by the colorful costumes and the theatrical billboards.

Sunset Plaza is an oasis of delightful small stores just past La Cienega. You can buy and browse among boutiques and art galleries, eat at some very good restaurants, or sit at a sidewalk cafe and "people-watch."

A mile past Sunset Plaza, you reach the end of Sunset Strip. Suddenly the towering buildings are replaced by the gracious green spaces surrounding the lovely homes of residential Beverly Hills in one of the most dramatic urban transitions to be seen.

"Where do the stars live?" is a frequently asked question here. Street-side vendors will provide you with addresses (not particularly accurate) for a price. You can also pick up a brochure on the stars' homes from the Sunset Plaza merchants or from the Greater Los Angeles Visitors and Convention Bureau in downtown L.A.

Lionel Barrymore's former home and garden is now Butterfield's Restaurant (8426 Sunset Boulevard) below the Strip. On the hill above Sunset Boulevard and Doheny Road stands Greystone Mansion—a "castle" which cost Edward Doheny of Teapot Dome notoriety $4 million to build. Because of its tremendous size, the mansion later became a white elephant on the market. Eventually purchased by the city of Beverly Hills, the gardens around the house are open daily except holidays from 10 A.M. to 5 P.M. A series of concerts takes place here during the summer; information on times and tickets is available from the Beverly Hills Visitors Bureau at (213) 271-8174.

The Beverly Hills Hotel (at Beverly Drive and Sunset Boulevard) enjoys a lush, green 16-acre setting across from a park. This pink palace, set back from a busy intersection (also the entrance to Coldwater Canyon), looks like a stage setting. Not camera shy, it has been used in films many times. It has also been home to a multitude of famous personalities at one time or another.

Will Rogers State Historic Park will expose you to the wit and personality of humorist Will Rogers. At the main house (filled with mementos of the "cowboy philosopher's" busy life) of this Pacific Palisades estate, a curator is on hand to tell you about the paintings, Navajo rugs, lariats, saddles, and other objects.

In the stable area, you'll still find polo ponies in the corrals and exercising and roping rings. Riding and hiking trails circling the low hills above the ranch houses invite exploration. The park is open every day except major holidays. Admission is free; there is a small fee to see the main house (open from 10 A.M. to 5 P.M.). No picnicking or camping is permitted on the grounds. The entrance road to the park is located at 14235 Sunset Boulevard.

Self-Realization Fellowship Lake Shrine is one of the hidden treasures along this route. A small natural lake, fed by springs, it is set in a garden that almost succeeds in shutting out the traffic noise of busy Sunset Boulevard. Look for the shrine at 17190 Sunset Boulevard in Pacific Palisades, just up from the coast highway.

The fellowship is devoted to yoga. Its miniature park, dedicated to all religions, is open free of charge to everyone daily except Monday from 9 A.M. to 5 P.M. You walk a lakeside path past shrines, along garden slopes, and past a small houseboat, being rewarded with vistas of gazebos, a chapel in a windmill, and a waterfall.

Hollywood Boulevard

A comparatively short street, Hollywood Boulevard is perhaps the best known of all L.A.'s thoroughfares because it leads directly to the place most people visit first—Hollywood. Pedestrian-looking architecture? Perhaps. But Hollywood Boulevard still manages to retain a little of the sparkle of yesteryear.

Look at the hills to the north. Those large letters spell out the name of the town. Look underfoot. The bronze stars studding the sidewalk mark the names of the film, radio, and television actors who gave the name "Hollywood" its special romance.

Barnsdall Park, once the haughty stronghold of Olive Hill at Hollywood Boulevard near Vermont Avenue, ceased to be forbidden ground when the city of Los

Angeles inherited it from the late Aline Barnsdall in 1927.

Hollyhock House, one of Frank Lloyd Wright's early achievements, sits atop the summit. Extensively restored in 1975, it's now open to the public for touring from 10 A.M. to 1 P.M. Tuesday and Thursday, and noon to 3 P.M. Saturday and the first and third Sunday of each month. Visitors pay a moderate fee.

Here also is L.A.'s handsome Municipal Art Gallery, first major art gallery to be built in the city since 1965. Opened in 1971, it replaces a smaller pavilion also designed by Wright.

This two-story gallery, designed by architect Arthur Stephens, harmonizes well with the other buildings on the hill: Hollyhock House and the Junior Arts Center. The gallery does not have a permanent collection but presents a series of changing exhibitions. Films and dramatic and musical performances take place in the 300-seat auditorium. The gallery is open from 12:30 to 5 P.M. Tuesday through Sunday; guided tours start at 2 P.M. There's a small admission charge.

For one week in the summer, an All-City Outdoor Art Festival exhibits sculptures, paintings, and other works of art.

Hollywood and Vine may disappoint you. At first glance the boulevard looks like any Main Street of any town. But look north on Vine Street at the Capitol Tower, a circular-shaped structure appropriately resembling a stack of neatly piled records. If you make reservations 3 weeks in advance, you can take a 45-minute tour of the record-making facility, in addition to getting a peek at a recording studio. Write Capitol Tower, 1750 N. Vine Street, Hollywood, CA 90028, for further information.

Also on Vine (just south of Hollywood Boulevard) is the Brown Derby Restaurant, where celebrity gazing competes for attention with the tempting cuisine. The Huntington Hartford Theater, among the best in Los Angeles, is at 1615 N. Vine Street; the grand art deco showcase, Pantages Theatre, stands at 6233 Hollywood Boulevard.

The Hollywood Wax Museum, near Highland Avenue, has life-sized figures of movie personalities, presidents, and historical personages. In the Chamber of Horrors, you'll see the coffin used in the movie *The Raven* and a scene from *The House of Wax* with Vincent Price. A recent addition is the Oscar Movie Theatre, showing a film that spans more than 40 years of Academy Award winners and presentations. The accompanying sound track contains the best songs of each era. On Friday and Saturday evenings, and on Sunday afternoons you can enjoy live stage shows. The theater is open daily from 10 A.M. to midnight (until 2 A.M. on weekends); admission price varies, depending on age.

Grauman's Chinese Theatre still survives, despite a name change. Sid Grauman was a real showman. First he built the Egyptian Theatre, a replica of a palace in Ancient Thebes, on the south side of the boulevard. Then he outdid himself by creating the Chinese Theatre, a model of a Chinese temple with imported Oriental pillars, across the street (6925 Hollywood Boulevard).

The many hand, foot, hoof, and face prints, along with the signatures of well known stars imprinted in the concrete courtyard of this celebrated movie house (now Mann's Chinese Theatre), trace the history of Hollywood cinema since the theater opened in 1927.

The Hollywood Bowl, built in a natural amphitheater in the Cahuenga Hills, grew from a simple bandstand in a weedy dell into an open-air concert theater with seating capacity of 20,000. The bowl's natural acoustics are responsible for its success; modern technology is trying for even better amplification. The "Symphonies Under the Stars," its noted summer series, features the Los Angeles Philharmonic Orchestra. The most notable annual event is the pre-dawn pilgrimage to the bowl for the memorable Easter sunrise service.

The bowl is on the west side of Highland Avenue, north of the Hollywood Boulevard intersection.

Mulholland Drive, within the city, then Mulholland Highway beyond, winds along the summit backbone of the Santa Monica Mountains, L.A.'s own mountain range. Driving its whole 55-mile length starting from the Hollywood Freeway in Cahuenga Pass is one of the easiest ways to get a view of the wilderness so threatened by urban pressure. The only longitudinal route along the Santa Monicas, this highway is one of the traditional scenic drives in Los Angeles.

At Topanga Canyon, you can follow winding Topanga Canyon Boulevard down to the ocean, emerging just east of Malibu, or continue on through the mountains, ending up at Leo Carrillo State Beach. You can also reach the sea on Malibu Canyon Road. The road past Topanga Canyon Boulevard is slow and the countryside almost wild.

You can get onto Mulholland Drive from the Hollywood Freeway in Cahuenga Pass, or you can avoid some of the tortuous course through residential areas by joining it farther west, at Laurel Canyon, Coldwater Canyon, Benedict Canyon, or Beverly Glen. Or enter Mulholland Drive from the San Diego Freeway.

Griffith Park

Griffith Park is a superpark, once the largest municipal park inside any city in America. Comparable in area with the cities of Beverly Hills and Santa Monica, on a fine weekend it may attain a population midway between the two (58,000).

Straddling the eastern end of the Santa Monica Mountains, the park was begun over 80 years ago with a gift to the city of some 3,000 acres by Colonel Griffith J. Griffith. The gift included a trust fund used since for the acquisition of more land and for building the grand old Griffith Observatory and Greek Theater.

Although rising to just 1,625 feet at the summit of Mount Hollywood, the mountains in the park are steep and rugged. Such topography has helped to preserve nearly three-fifths of the land in a nearly natural state. Until the era of the bulldozer, it was simply too vertical for conventional city-park development. Most of the mountain heartland remains a sort of domesticated wilderness.

The perimeter of Griffith Park is very accessible. To the north is the Ventura Freeway, to the east the Golden

TOP VISITOR ATTRACTIONS
*include film festivals at ABC
Entertainment Center (above) on the
Avenue of the Stars in Century City.
The waters "part" (right) for tram
trips through Universal Studios'
back lot.*

State Freeway, and to the west the Hollywood Freeway. Both Western and Vermont avenues enter the southern park edge. Western leads to Fern Dell and the Nature Museum, Vermont to the Bird Sanctuary and Greek Theater; both reach the Observatory. Well-marked freeway exits lead to other points of interest.

Griffith Observatory, high on a promontory, commands a vast panorama, spectacular at night. The observatory's large dome contains a 500-seat planetarium theater; two smaller domes are for telescopes and the Hall of Science. Visiting hours vary by season; generally, the observatory is open from around noon until 10 P.M. daily. Admission to the museum is free, but you will pay for theater shows (children under 5 aren't admitted).

Greek Theatre, at 2700 N. Vermont Avenue, seats 4,500 people for drama, music, and dance performances in a natural canyon amphitheater. Check local newspapers and city guides to find out what's playing.

Fern Dell is reached through the next canyon to the west, another access to the upland. Called Western Canyon, its road begins off Los Feliz Boulevard just east of the end of Western Avenue. You'll find Fern Dell to be a natural, spring-fed fern bower with a collection of exotic ferns. Here you can walk a half-mile past waterfalls and terraced pools.

A good place to start exploring the park is the Fern Dell Nature Museum. Its exhibits describe plant and animal life in the park and some of the area's geological features. On weekends you can attend free showings of travel and nature movies in the museum. Its hours are from 1 to 5 P.M., Wednesday through Sunday; admission is free.

Griffith Playground means business. Intense recreational activity concentrates in the flatland along the eastern and northern edges of the park. The southeastern tip is one of the liveliest parts of the park, at least when a soccer game is in progress. Here, along Riverside Drive south of Los Feliz Boulevard is Griffith Playground, which contains a swimming pool, tennis courts, playing field, and other activities. Across Riverside Drive are the Cultural Arts Center and the Mulholland Fountain, a memorial to the father of the Los Angeles Aqueduct.

North of Los Feliz Boulevard, Riverside Drive becomes Crystal Springs Drive. After passing a miniature train ride, a children's pony ring, and one of three nine-hole golf courses, you'll come to the venerable 1926 Spillman merry-go-round, still one of the best of its era. This is also the site of a nature center and park headquarters. Beyond are two 18-hole golf courses.

Los Angeles Zoo (exit on Zoo Drive at the junction of the Golden State and Ventura freeways) draws more people than any other park attraction. First all-new zoo of its size to be built in modern times, it features over 2,000 birds, mammals, and reptiles in 113 acres of attractive grounds. Moats and natural settings replace bars and cages. Among the most popular zoo spots are the Children's Zoo and the Koala House. You can walk (mostly uphill) or take a tram to see the five continental areas.

You'll pay an admission fee plus an extra charge for the tram; parking is free. The zoo is open daily (except Christmas) from 10 A.M.; picnic areas are nearby.

Travel Town, at the northwest corner of the park, is home for antique trains and airplanes. Youngsters enjoy the ride; rail buffs enthuse over the rolling stock. The free exhibit is open daily except Christmas.

The Equestrian Center, at Riverside Drive and Main Street, lies across the river from Train Town. Here you'll find a training area, jumping course, and indoor arena; you can also rent horses and ride along 53 miles of park bridle trails. Weekend activity is intense.

HUNTING FOR CELEBRITIES

People-watching is Los Angeles' most popularly practiced spectator sport. Residents and tourists are equally avid participants in a game—most appropriately titled "star-gazing"—that can be played at any hour of the day or night.

Since Los Angeles and environs abound with entertainment and sports world luminaries, sightings of famous faces have been recorded throughout the area.

However, if your observation time is limited and your curiosity piqued, you might visit a few of the haunts favored by these celestial beings, or drop by places where they shop and work.

Most of the well-known faces hide out in the hills above Hollywood, in the canyons of Bel Air, around the crest of the Santa Monica Mountains, in Beverly Hills, or farther west near Pacific Palisades and Malibu. Tours past some celebrities' homes are offered (see facing page).

Even celebrities go out to shop and eat lunch. Try the eateries around the various studios. Farmers Market is close enough to CBS for a lunch break.

Some expensive restaurants are frequent haunts of stars. You'll have to buy a meal for the dubious chance of glimpsing your favorite, and reservations are a must. A sure way to be asked to leave is to bother a star inside the restaurant.

The following eating and sipping spots are among current favorites. In Los Angeles: Jimmy's (201 Moreno Drive), L'Ermitage (730 N. La Cienega Boulevard), Ma Maison (8368 Melrose Avenue—unlisted number, 655-1991), Matteo's (2321 Westwood Boulevard), Morton's (8800 Melrose Avenue), Spago (8795 Sunset Boulevard), and Trumps (8764 Melrose Avenue). In Beverly Hills: La Scala (9455 Santa Monica Boulevard), Le Bistro (246 N. Canon Drive), and Trader Vic's (Beverly Hilton Hotel).

WORLD OF ENTERTAINMENT

Movie making in Los Angeles is the great fascination of visitors, but many residents consider it old hat. These same residents, however, often know little more than the average tourist about how to see "the industry."

Below is a rundown of studio tours, television facilities, and ways to see something of the stars—their homes, their footprints, and how they look (in person and in wax).

Movie studios

The motion picture industry's sound stages are scattered over an area that includes not only Hollywood but also most of its neighboring cities.

Universal Studios (Lankershim Boulevard just north of the Hollywood Freeway) offers elaborate tours. Over a million people a year enjoy a ride through the studio's 420-acre lot on guided, candy-striped trams that pass by TV and sound stages, false front sets, stars' dressing rooms, warehouses, and labs. You'll experience a flash flood, a shark attack, and The Battle of Galactica, and watch live shows.

During the summer, tours run daily from 8 A.M. to 6 P.M.; the rest of the year they operate weekdays from 10 A.M. to 3:30 P.M., weekends from 9:30 A.M. to 4 P.M. VIP tours (for 6 or more) are expensive, but may give you a chance to dine with a celebrity in the commissary. For specific information, call (213) 877-1311.

Burbank Studios (Warner Bros., Columbia Pictures, and several independents) offers an intimate view of movies and TV. You are taken through the lot in vans and on foot, observing whatever is going on in the day's production schedule. You may or may not see actual filming; nothing is scheduled for the tour. Often you'll walk quietly on either a sound set or recording stage. You'll tour prop and special effects shops and a historical back lot.

The cost is fairly high (especially if you reserve lunch in the Blue Room), and children under 10 aren't allowed—but you'll see things you won't see anywhere else. Two-hour tours are offered on weekdays, by reservation, at 10 A.M. and 2 P.M. (There are two additional tours during the summer). Enter at the Hollywood Way gate just off the Ventura Freeway. Call (818) 954-1744 for information.

Television studios

Many popular TV shows originate here, and you can be part of the audience if you first get advance tickets, offered free by most studios. The Greater Los Angeles Visitors and Convention Bureau, 505 W. Flower Street, Los Angeles, CA 90071, has a limited number available.

For tickets to a specific broadcast, it is necessary to write several months in advance to the broadcasting network from which the program originates. Enclose a stamped envelope, giving your address in the L.A. area. Tickets will not be mailed to out-of-state addresses.

Ticket requests should be mailed to: ABC, Guest Relations and Ticket Office, 4151 Prospect Avenue, Los Angeles, CA 90027; CBS, Ticket Division, 7800 Beverly Boulevard, Los Angeles, CA 90036; and NBC, 3000 W. Alameda Avenue, Burbank, CA 91523.

NBC Television Studio tours depart daily (except holidays) for a 1-hour behind-the-scenes look at set construction, special effects, make-up, and wardrobe; you'll also see how you'd appear on camera. Don't expect to watch a show being taped—for this, you'll need studio audience tickets (some available early in the day at the studio). For information on tour cost, call (818) 840-3537. The studio is located at 3000 W. Alameda Avenue (visible from the Ventura Freeway at the Buena Vista exit in Burbank).

Wax, footprints, and star trips

If you've been to a wax museum, you may have loved or hated it; the figures recall certain characters and movies accurately, but obviously they're not real. Six Flags Movieland, 7711 Beach Boulevard, Buena Park, is about the best (see Orange County chapter for details). Hollywood Wax Museum, 6767 Hollywood Boulevard, competes for the tourist who wonders where the stars are if they're not on the boulevard.

At Mann's Chinese Theatre, 6925 Hollywood Boulevard, foot, hoof, and palm prints of the stars have been collecting tourist stares for over 50 years. The forecourt is always open.

A rib-tickling tour by Starline Sightseeing Tours leaves from the front of the theater for drives past stars' homes. Gray Line Tours offers a 2-hour walking tour of the Twentieth Century-Fox lot as well as looks at Hollywood and Beverly Hills; call (213) 481-2121 for information. Hollywood Fantasy Tours (1721 N. Highland Avenue) provides an in-depth look at Hollywood's past, present, and future.

Hollywood on Location provides information about filming around L.A.; for a fee, they'll provide movie and show names, shoot times and locations, names of stars, and maps to sites. Call (213) 659-9165 between 3 and 5 P.M. for an idea of the next day's activities. Pick up the package around 9 A.M. the next morning from the offices at 8644 Wilshire Boulevard.

CROWDS THRONG to L.A.
area's wide sandy beaches.
Lifeguards staff stations, ready
to rescue swimmers, surfers
from tugging tide.

An impressive dimension is added to Los Angeles by an array of beaches and mountains ringing the L.A. Basin.

Southern California beaches are hardly a discovery. If you've ever been caught in a coast highway traffic jam on a summer Sunday afternoon, you know that the shoreline of the Los Angeles city region is perhaps the greatest summer recreational resource in California. What is surprising is the variety of ways you can enjoy the coastal area. Ranging in topography from wide, sandy stretches with gentle waves to narrow, rocky strips with explosive surf, these beaches invite every aquatic pleasure: swimming, boating, fishing, surfing, scuba diving, snorkeling. Though the shoreline is mainly urban, on a few stretches you can be amazingly alone.

Three high mountain ranges separate Los Angeles from desert lands to the north and east, forming an imposing backdrop for the teeming city. The San Gabriel, San Bernardino, and San Jacinto (page 89) ranges rise abruptly to peaks over 10,000 feet. At low elevations, the frontal slopes of these mountains are closed because of fire danger from July 1 to the first rainfall (usually in November). But in winter, residents head for the hills for snow fun: belly-thumping down the slopes on improvised sleds at such resorts as Lake Gregory, Lake Arrowhead, and Big Bear—easily reached from the valley floors.

The Santa Monicas, a fourth mountain range, march right into the Pacific Ocean west of the city, their rocky tops forming the offshore Channel Islands. Where mountains and beaches meet at Point Mugu, this chapter begins, tracing the metropolitan coastline first east, then south. Then the chapter shifts its focus to the attractions in or near the three mountain ranges surrounding Los Angeles.

Along L.A.'s Beaches

Southern California's beaches see action every month of the year. The huge Los Angeles population makes full use of the sea as a coolant when summer heat builds. Water temperature is around 67°F. from July until fall. Air temperature at Santa Monica will reach an average maximum of about 75°, even as the temperature in inland Pasadena rises ten degrees higher.

Winter weather is cyclic, with clear, warm air and a glassy sea often following a blustery rainstorm. Although few swimmers brave the 55° water for a dip, wet-suited surfers, surf kayakers, wind-surfers, and lightweight-catamaran sailors turn out in force.

Here are some highlights of a coastal tour of Los Angeles County from Santa Monica Bay in the west to Long Beach Harbor in the south.

West of Santa Monica

The south slope of the Santa Monica Mountains drops abruptly to the sea on the first section of this east-west Los Angeles area beach tour. Its western half is rocky headlands and coves; it runs to good swimming beaches at the eastern end. Point Mugu to Malibu has the cleanest ocean along the metropolitan coast, offering

Beaches and mountains at L.A.'s front and back doors lure escapees from city living. Long stretches of sand and water — dotted with fishing piers, marinas, museums, and shopping complexes — invite exploration. Mountain ranges provide summer and winter fun. Valley cities like San Fernando, Van Nuys, Burbank, Glendale, Pasadena, and Riverside include family amusement centers, gardens and parks, and museums in or near their boundaries.

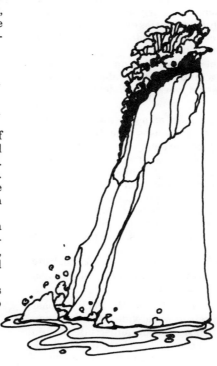

clear water, healthy kelp beds, the best shore and offshore fishing and diving, and some very good surfing.

Variety of activity and topography marks the beaches west of Santa Monica Bay. You can camp at Point Mugu State Park and at Leo Carrillo State Beach, venture up into the hills, sand-ski, and try your luck at gliding from bluff to beach. Facilities vary, but lifeguards are on duty during the summer.

Zuma Beach, just west of Point Dume off State Highway 1, is L.A.'s largest county-owned beach. An excellent swimming beach (except for occasional summer riptides), it offers ample parking for about 2,500 cars (at a small charge) and modern facilities.

Dume, next door, is a long, steep-sided finger of sandstone pointing prominently to the south. Flocks of pelicans and cormorants perch on rocks a few hundred yards offshore; meanwhile, flocks of surfers are hurtling toward broad, sandy beaches or paddling away from them. Swimming is good; so are the tidepools.

Santa Monica Bay: Home of surf and stars

Along this crescent-shaped bay, almost all the coast is sandy with wide beaches. About half of it is set aside for public use, and used it assuredly is: its total annual visitor count numbers about 50 million. Day-use parks usually offer excellent swimming, good surfing, sunbathing, and beach play. Hang gliding is good at two spots: Dockweiler and Torrance beaches. (The latter discourages the sport during the crowded summer season.) Although the beaches are fairly similar with sandy stretches below high bluffs, facilities differ. Some charge admission; others do not. Lifeguards are generally on duty during the peak season.

In 1983, winter storms destroyed or damaged some of the area's fishing piers (and a few private residences); but repair and restoration work got underway almost immediately.

Malibu has long been known as a "getaway" spot for movie and TV stars; their houses line the road for several miles and perch precariously on the cliffs above it. Zonker Davis Accessway, one of many new public-access footpaths along the coast, links Santa Monica Bay and the Pacific Coast Highway, threading between Malibu residences and passing a restaurant.

Malibu Lagoon, a 35-acre state beach with a ⅔-mile ocean frontage, offers good swimming (one area is for surfers only). Restrooms, concessions, and parking are along the highway.

At Malibu's private pier, you'll find sportfishing boats, an excursion boat, and a restaurant; you can fish from the pier if you have a license.

J. Paul Getty Museum, at 17985 W. Pacific Coast Highway in Malibu, received worldwide attention upon Getty's death in 1976. An American industrialist (often called the richest man in the world), Getty left the bulk of his estate to the museum, ensuring its future expansion. At present, several hundred million dollars are represented in his collection of rare tapestries, Greek and Roman statuary, Louis XV and XVI furniture, and valuable paintings by Italian and Dutch masters.

The museum itself is a replica of the Villa Papyri (a large villa at Herculaneum destroyed by the eruption of Vesuvius in A.D. 79); about $17 million was spent in its construction.

From June through September, the museum is open from 10 A.M. to 5 P.M. Monday through Friday; from October through May, hours are 10 A.M. to 5 P.M., Tuesday through Saturday. There's no admission charge, but you'll need a parking reservation. Call (213) 459-8402 at least a week in advance of your visit.

Will Rogers State Beach, at the intersection of the coast highway and Sunset Boulevard, is beneath the Pacific Palisades (so close that slides have forced several relocations of the highway a few feet south, into some badly needed parking lots). Lifeguards and restrooms are provided on the beach, and restaurants line the highway nearby. The beach is the scene of the lifeguards' annual December games.

Santa Monica

At Santa Monica the shore turns southerly for a splendid sweep of 20 miles of almost wholly accessible, broad, sandy beach encompassing eight public beaches, five fishing piers, and two small craft harbors. Then it rounds the Palos Verdes Peninsula for 15 rocky miles as the road rides high above the cliffs before losing itself among the channels of two big harbors—Los Angeles and Long Beach.

Santa Monica State Beach, adjacent to Ocean Avenue, has been the most frequented of the bay beaches since the 1860s. It has picnic tables, fire rings, and playground equipment, and is handy to restaurants.

Santa Monica Pier, hard hit during the 1983 storms, is now on the way back to its former glory. It's a gathering place for tourists as well as locals, for bathing-suited beachgoers and more fully clad sightseers. The pier, the esplanade below, and the cliffside park above are colorful, and bustling. Some activities are free—you don't have to pay to fish from the pier, or to watch surfers, volleyball players, and amateur acrobats at what used to be Muscle Beach. For a fee, you can go out on a fishing party boat.

Body builders work out at an arena just south of the Venice Pavilion and Windward Avenue. Ocean Front Walk (a paved footpath that runs from Santa Monica to the harbor channel at Marina del Rey) borders one side of the weight pen.

Venice—California's answer to Italy

Perhaps one of the most unusual beachfront communities in the West, Venice-by-the-Sea was the dream of Abbot Kinney, a wealthy Easterner, who, in 1892, induced the Santa Fe Railroad to extend its tracks to these 160 acres of sand dunes and salt marsh. Here he built his dream city of homes, hotels, interconnecting canals plied by a fleet of gondolas, amusement halls, and a large Chautauqua auditorium. Unfortunately, engineering mistakes caused the canals to deteriorate. Venice began to decline, and oil developments ended the dream.

The pier, at the foot of Washington Street, is organized for round-the-clock fishing. Bays at short intervals expand its perimeter to a length of about 400 yards.

(Continued on page 35)

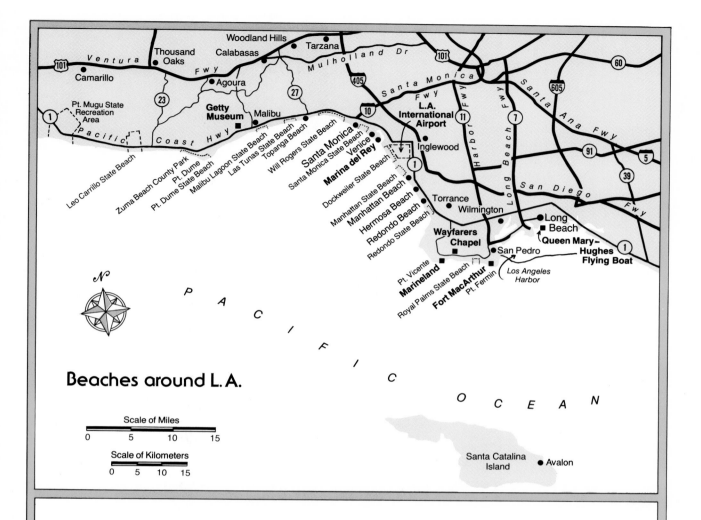

Beaches around L.A.

Scale of Miles

0   5   10   15

Scale of Kilometers

0   5   10   15

Major Points of Interest

J. Paul Getty Museum (Malibu) — replica of ancient Roman villa houses priceless statuary, furniture, paintings

Santa Monica — splendid public beaches, fishing piers, boat harbors, waterfront carnival

Marina del Rey — home port for over 10,000 boats; Fisherman's Village houses shops, restaurants, galleries; take harbor cruise

Palos Verdes Scenic Drive — 15 miles of varied spectacular marine and mountain views; see Wayfarers Chapel

L.A. International Airport — area's largest air terminal; shuttle service to downtown, connections to outlying airports

Marineland (Palos Verdes Peninsula) — water zoo and oceanarium; watch whales, seals, and dolphins perform; Sky Tower offers sea view

Los Angeles Harbor — maze of channels, inlets, and islands covers 50 miles of waterfront; takeoff site for Catalina Island; deep-sea fishing; shopping at Ports O' Call nautical village

Long Beach — naval center and major port; good swimming, boating, fishing. Shoreline Village shops; two former Spanish ranchos now open for tours

Queen Mary (Long Beach) — fabled British ocean liner; tour decks, shops, museum; dine and sleep aboard

Spruce Goose (Long Beach) — Howard Hughes' Flying Boat, world's largest wooden plane, on exhibit next to Queen Mary and LondonTowne

Catalina Island — getaway island 21 miles offshore; tour Avalon, island interior; take boat trips to seal colony and undersea gardens; overnight accommodations, good boating and swimming

ARCHITECTURAL CONTRASTS,
*Wayfarers Chapel (right) in Palos
Verdes, and J. Paul Getty Museum
(below) in Malibu, are open to
visitors. Call ahead for museum
parking space.*

Marina del Rey

It's easy to believe that Marina del Rey, home port for more than 10,000 boats, is the largest manmade pleasure boat harbor on the Pacific Coast.

One of the most dramatic waterfront scenes in the world is the huge armada of boats of all types heading out to sea or parading placidly up and down the main channel.

New shopping centers abound in Marina del Rey; new motels and hotels face beach and waterfront.

Harbor cruises leave Fishermans' Village—a Cape Cod collection of shops, restaurants, and art galleries—every hour. The harbor cruise gives you a close-up look at many celebrities' boats, as well as Chinese junks, catamarans, antique and classic craft, and old, square-rigged Scandinavian schooners.

Large public launching ramps allow boat owners to truck or trailer in their boats. Power and sailboat rentals are available for marina cruising and for offshore deep-sea fishing.

The famed Marina del Rey waterfront restaurant row is one of the largest concentrations of casually elegant eating places in the Greater Los Angeles area.

Manhattan, Hermosa, and Redondo

At this trio of beaches you'll find more youthful beach aficionados per square yard than almost anywhere else along the coast. Both Manhattan and Hermosa beaches have public fishing piers. Much like other piers in the region, each has a bait and tackle shop, rest rooms, and a snack bar for the comfort of anglers.

Redondo State Beach adjoins a marina complex (King Harbor) of restaurants, motels, yacht clubs, and boat facilities. Next to it are the shops and restaurants that line two piers extending out over the water, giving a good view of the 1½-mile beach.

Palos Verdes to Long Beach

Following the scenic drive around the Palos Verdes Peninsula is a pleasant alternative to continuing on the coast highway. You pass several interesting tourist attractions, as well as many ocean overlooks. You're on your way to the busy ports of Los Angeles and Long Beach. Attractive seaside shopping, good fishing spots, a marine museum, and the imposing ocean liner *Queen Mary* are only some of the ocean-front attractions. You'll also find some historical surprises.

The plush Palos Verdes Peninsula, below Point Conception, is the most prominent projection on the coastal map—about 15 miles of rocky shore with a few sandy beaches. Informal access at several points has been made by tidepool probers, rock fishermen, skin divers, and surf scanners. A spectacular scenic drive through this area—along Palos Verdes Drive—is one traditional attraction of the Los Angeles region. The road begins in parklike Palos Verdes Estates and ends in Point Fermin Park in San Pedro. In between, it follows the rugged cliff top for a 15-mile stretch, offering you varied and spectacular views of the sea and mountains.

Other parts of the drive take you through beautiful residential areas and flower fields; there are ocean view turnouts at several spots. You'll pass such points of interest as the Point Vincente Lighthouse, Marineland Oceanarium, and the Wayfarers Chapel (overlooking Abalone Cove).

Less frequented is the relatively isolated seacoast 100 feet below the cliffs. Since accessibility to this shore is limited by tides, all of the beach areas are hard to explore in one day. Newspapers publish exact times of tides for each day. Fires and overnight camping are prohibited.

Point Fermin Park offers a place to picnic and watch the hang gliders. The Old Point Fermin Lighthouse (built in 1874 of lumber brought around Cape Horn) is restored, but it's not open to the public. Overlooking Point Fermin, the buildings of old Fort MacArthur's Upper Reservation house the gallery of the Angel's Gate Cultural Center (3701 S. Gaffey Street). At the gallery, you can shop for crafts (it's open weekends from 1 to 4 P.M.). The center also holds a children's theater and workshops for local artists and craftspeople; an amphitheater is planned for the future. Before you head up the hill to the center, stop on the road below to view the striking Korean bell.

Royal Palms State Beach, 2 miles northwest of Point Fermin off Paseo del Mar (extension of Western Avenue), offers one of the few places to swim on the south coast of the peninsula. Space and facilities are limited.

Wayfarers Chapel is set on a hill at Portuguese Bend (a mile east of Marineland), looking out over the ocean and Palos Verdes Drive. Glass walls, redwood beams, and a white-rock campanile bearing a gold cross make this a striking structure. The grounds are set with plants mentioned in the Bible. The chapel is open daily from 11 A.M. to 4 P.M.; Friday and Saturday tours start at 12:30 and 1 P.M. Swedenborg Reference Library and Museum is located just east of the chapel.

Architect Lloyd Wright (son of Frank Lloyd Wright) designed the unique chapel for the Church of the New Jerusalem as a memorial to Emmanuel Swedenborg, but it is intended as a place of worship and meditation for people of all faiths.

Marineland: An aquatic show

Marineland, a water zoo at the southwest tip of the peninsula, is actually a four-ring sea circus. Though the aquariums and sea collections are impressive, entertainment is the first purpose of this recently renovated and newly landscaped Palos Verdes show place. Here's a rare opportunity to see a "killer whale" leaping 18 feet out of the water to grab a fish from the teeth of its trainer, a dolphin jumping through a fire-ringed hoop, or a sea lion crooning a tune.

Visitors can play with the dolphins, observe sea lions in a natural cove, even go snorkeling among waters teeming with fish. You can observe animals under treatment at the Marina Animal Care Hospital, using a two-way microphone to discuss their prognosis.

One ticket admits you to the Oceanarium, shows, and exhibits; there's an extra charge for the Baja Reef snorkeling adventure. Parking is free. During the summer, Marineland opens daily at 10 A.M.; the box office closes at 5 P.M. Winter hours are 10 A.M. to 4 P.M., Wednesday through Sunday. For exact operating schedules, phone (213) 541-5663. Shows run in repeating cycles.

If you're not already on Palos Verdes Drive, the best approaches are the Hawthorne Boulevard exit from the San Diego Freeway, and Gaffey Street south from the end of Harbor Freeway and right on 25th Street.

Los Angeles Harbor: An aquatic freeway

The Port of Los Angeles and the Port of Long Beach share the world's largest manmade harbor. Its maze of channels, inlets, and islands covers 50 miles of developed waterfront, shielded by a 9-mile breakwater. Newest of the major western ports (started in 1889), Los Angeles is a leader in total tonnage processed and in modern handling techniques. It is the center of the country's seafood canning industry. The Port of Los Angeles includes the Terminal Island, San Pedro, and Wilmington districts.

Soaring 185 feet above the harbor's main channel is the Vincent Thomas Bridge, a replacement for an auto ferry. This handsome suspension bridge connects San Pedro with Terminal Island, location of most of the harbor's large shipping berths and warehouses. Under the bridge's western end is the Catalina Terminal, where ferries and seaplanes depart for Catalina Island. You'll pay a small toll to cross the bridge.

The area off Harbor Boulevard in San Pedro flanks the main channel of Los Angeles Harbor and makes dock-watching a breeze. There's a little park where Sixth Street runs into Harbor; at its south end is the Los Angeles Maritime Museum, where you'll see detailed models of the supertankers *Aurora* and *Torrey Canyon*. The museum is open from 9 A.M. to 4 P.M. weekdays and from 12:30 to 4 P.M. on weekends; admission is free. There's a small observation deck.

Fort MacArthur, near the harbor entrance, once helped protect the harbor. Headquarters of the 47th Artillery Brigade, it's also an air defense center.

Cabrillo Beach, just south of the fort, is usually crowded with people, cars, and boat trailers. You'll find picnic tables and barbecue pits. In addition to a still-water beach inside the breakwater, there's a surf beach on the ocean that's popular with fishermen. On the harbor side are a public boat launching ramp and a fishing pier paralleling the breakwater. The free Cabrillo Marine Museum, across from the beach at 3720 Stephen White Drive, offers L.A. Harbor and maritime lore in general. There you can look at seashells, ship models, marine specimens, and navigation equipment. The museum is open from 12 to 5 P.M. Tuesday through Friday, and from 10 A.M. to 5 P.M. Saturday and Sunday.

Ports O'Call Village, an extensive shopping complex, faces the harbor's main channel at Berth 77 on Harbor Boulevard. There's a lot here: restaurants, import shops, and craftspeople combine with harbor tour boats and nautical memorabilia. You can hover over the harbor in a helicopter or shoot to the top of a sky tower— and when a crisp day brings on the urge to head out to

sea, an hour-long cruise on the *Buccaneer Queen* may be the answer.

Banning Park is located on the Pacific Coast Highway 2 blocks east of Avalon Boulevard. General Phineas Banning, a fabled host who founded the town of Wilmington, built a 30-room colonial showcase in 1864 and landscaped it with acres of beautiful gardens. Now restored, the mansion is a museum exhibiting furnishings from the last century. The home and grounds are open to the public daily. On Wednesday, Saturday, and Sunday, free tours are offered at 1, 2, 3, and 4 P.M.

Long Beach: A city on the rise

Long important as a naval base, major port, and manufacturing center, Long Beach is again surfacing as a major resort and recreational area. California's fifth largest city is linked to Los Angeles (21 miles to the north) by the Long Beach Freeway. The Pacific Coast Highway and San Diego Freeway cut east and west through the city. Direct flights to the Long Beach Airport avoid the Los Angeles traffic.

Thanks to thoughtful planning, Long Beach is no longer known as the "Coney Island of the West"; today, it's one of Southern California's most attractive, progressive communities. An extensive 421-acre redevelopment project has changed the whole face of the city, from the downtown center to the harbor. An attractive pedestrian mall and boardwalk runs from downtown Long Beach Plaza (and the amphitheater adjoining it) to the shoreline.

The city's transit system is California's most sophisticated. A several-block-long stretch of First Street— between Pine Avenue and Long Beach Boulevard—is for buses only. Lining the "bus mall" are brightly lit passenger shelters, where video information systems display up-to-the-minute routes and schedules for transportation throughout the city, as well as to L.A. and Orange counties.

The redevelopment program includes the restoration of some of the city's more historic buildings; but it's the new business and residential high rises that have really changed the Long Beach skyline. Even the oil drilling rigs that dot the harbor have been cleverly concealed behind facades on palm-studded, manmade islands.

Along Ocean Boulevard, across from the city's municipal offices, stands the handsome Convention and Entertainment Center—the site chosen for two of the 1984 Olympic events (volleyball and fencing). Here you'll find the Terrace Theater (home of the symphony, civic light opera, and grand opera), the more intimate Center Theater, and the Arena.

Farther east, at 2300 Ocean Boulevard, the Museum of Arts is quartered in a charming turn-of-the-century house. The museum and adjoining bookstore and gift shop are open Wednesday through Sunday from 1 to 5 P.M. Visit nearby Bluff Park Historic District for a look at several blocks of carefully preserved early 1900s residences.

At the waterfront, imaginative harborside development has resulted in new parks, marinas, tourist-oriented shopping complexes, and hotels. On the water

side of the Convention and Entertainment Center is Shoreline Park, a 100-acre aquatic playground with fishing platforms, picnic sites, and a recreational vehicle park. Next door, lushly landscaped Rainbow Lagoon Park boasts paddle boats and biking paths.

Shoreline Village, at the foot of Pine Avenue, resembles an early 1900s seaside hamlet. Specialty shops and restaurants cover 7 acres along the water. A ride on one of the hand-carved Looff carousel animals (vintage 1906) is sufficient reason to make the trip.

Every year in March, the Toyota Grand Prix is held along Shoreline Drive. The nerve-jangling, ear-popping race attracts visitors from all over the world. For information, contact the Long Beach Area Convention and Visitors Council, 180 E. Ocean Boulevard, Suite 150, Long Beach, CA 90802; or call (213) 436-3645.

Across the channel looms the regal *Queen Mary*. Near the retired Cunard liner, and perhaps almost as famous, is Howard Hughes' "Spruce Goose"—the world's largest wooden airplane, now housed under the world's largest clear-span aluminum dome. Little LondonTowne, a replica of an English village, sits beside the two attractions.

The *Queen Mary* is open daily for tours and dining; you can even sleep aboard, in staterooms run as a hotel. Three-hour guided tours (10 A.M. to 4 P.M.) cover the bridge, engine room, officers' quarters, and upper decks. If you prefer, stroll the venerable ship on your own, peeking into some of the shops and enjoying a meal in one of the on-board restaurants.

A 1½-hour water tour departs from the bow of the *Queen Mary*—daily during summer, Thursday through Sunday the rest of the year. Times vary; call (213) 547-0802 for a schedule.

On a visit to the Hughes Flying Boat (open daily 10 A.M. to 6 P.M.), you can enter the enormous plane and peer into the cockpit, see a cutaway engine display, and view films and memorabilia from Hughes' aviation career.

You'll be charged admission to both the *Queen Mary* and the "Spruce Goose"; prices are reduced for combination tickets.

To reach both attractions, exit the Long Beach Freeway at Harbor Scenic Drive and follow the signs, or cross the Queen's Way Bridge from Shoreline Drive.

Along the beaches inside the harbor breakwater, there's almost no surf, making the 5½-mile arc of white sand attractive to swimmers and sunbathers. Between Redondo and Park avenues, the Belmont Fishing Pier extends out into the harbor. At Alamitos Bay, you'll find marinas, restaurants, yacht clubs, and a couple of on-the-water shopping complexes—Seaport Village and Marina Pacifica Mall. On Naples Island, you can dine in a restaurant, picnic in a park, or take a gondola ride along the waterways.

Two Spanish ranchos evoke the past. Rancho Los Cerritos, at 4600 Virginia Road, is one of the finest of the L.A. area's restored adobes. Built in 1844, the delightful Spanish-style house was once surrounded by acres of rolling hills and lush grazing land. You can still view the original garden today; some of its trees are over a century old. Los Cerritos is open Wednesday through Sunday from 1 to 5 P.M.; there's no admission charge.

Rancho Los Alamitos, located atop a knoll, has become a city museum-park. A visit to the ranch will transport you back over a century: the adobe's history goes back to 1806. Once owned by Jose Figueroa, an early California governor, it was a working cattle ranch until 1953. The Bixby family (donors of the property) left the house equipped with family possessions that span many generations.

Free, 1-hour guided tours are given between 1 and 4 P.M. Wednesday through Friday, and from 10 A.M. to 5 P.M. Saturday and Sunday. To reach the adobe, take Palos Verdes Avenue south from the San Diego Freeway. At the intersection of Anaheim Road you'll see a "private road" sign; just keep going 1 more block to Bixby Hill Road, then turn left to the entrance.

Catalina Island: A nearby getaway

Once a hideout for buccaneers and smugglers (though only 21 miles from shore) and the site of an unusual aquatic gold rush, Santa Catalina Island has been a popular visitor destination ever since 1887, when the resort town of Avalon was opened and steam service started from the mainland. Except for Avalon, the 21-mile-long island consists of mountainous wilderness and calm coves.

Crossing the sea. Just getting to Catalina is an enjoyable experience. You'll have your choice of conveyances—from sleek turbo jets to whirling helicopters, from stubby amphibian boats to modern excursion vessels. Boats depart year-round from terminals at San Pedro and Long Beach; from April through October, there's a boat from the Balboa Pavilion at Newport Beach. The sea crossing takes about 2 hours.

For fares and schedules, call Catalina Cruises at (213) 775-6111 or (714) 527-7111, Catalina Express at (213) 519-1212, or (in season) Catalina Passenger Service at (714) 673-5245.

If you fly to Catalina, you'll get there in only 20 minutes. Seaplanes leave from the Long Beach Airport; helicopter service is available from Long Beach and San Pedro.

For all travel information, call the Catalina Island Chamber of Commerce at (213) 510-1520.

Avalon is still chiefly geared to the pedestrian, but motor traffic is increasing; tour vehicles line up to greet debarking steamer passengers. Shops and restaurants along Crescent Avenue offer good souvenir shopping. The visitor information and services center on the Green Pleasure Pier makes a good first stop.

Still the landmark to visitors arriving in Avalon Harbor is the fortress-like Casino—really a movie theater topped by a vast, open ballroom. On the first floor is the Catalina Museum.

Exploring the island can be a short or long-term experience. On a half-day stop you can combine a trip on a glass-bottom boat with a scenic tour of the Wrigley residence and your choice of a Casino tour or a coastal cruise (summer only).

If you're staying for a full day or overnight (be sure to make reservations), you'll have time for further explorations of the island's coastline or interior.

Around L.A.'s Mountains

Our tour of the mountains encircling the Los Angeles region extends from the San Fernando Valley in the west to the Upper Santa Ana River Valley in the east. We begin with the westernmost Santa Monica Mountains, move on to survey the San Gabriel Mountains and their environs, and end by exploring the recreationally rich San Bernardino Mountains.

Along the way you'll find many diverse parks, gardens, resort areas, and landmarks, as well as some of Southern California's most famous smaller cities. In or near these mountain chains are such familiar names as Griffith Park, Burbank, Pasadena, San Marino, Mount Wilson, Pomona, and Lake Arrowhead.

In these mountains, sportsmen can hike and ride over hundreds of miles of trails, try their luck in the stocked streams of national forests, and hunt for various wildlife. Motorists and sightseers can take scenic walks, picnic, explore a wilderness area, or drive through picturesque thoroughfares. Angeles National Forest, a giant preserve in the San Gabriel Mountains, includes nearly a fourth of the area of Los Angeles County.

Santa Monica Mountains

Los Angeles has a mountain range in its midst. Even those who have never heard of the Santa Monicas by name probably know Griffith Park, Mulholland Drive, and Sunset Boulevard, all within or bordering this island of emptiness that reaches into the heart of L.A.

The Santa Monicas are unusual among American mountains in that they run east and west: 47 miles from the Los Angeles River to the Oxnard plain. Some of the best beaches in the northern section of the Los Angeles coast abut the Santa Monicas.

In a drive through the Santa Monicas, you can see Griffith Park; three great canyons (Sullivan, Rustic, and Topanga); the Claretian Seminary (former palatial estate of King Gillette of razor blade fame); and Tapia County Park. You'll also see familiar gorges and rock formations at Malibu Creek State Park, formerly the 20th Century-Fox movie ranch; the Paramount Ranch (now a park, once a location for movies and TV); Lake Sherwood (one of six impoundments of Malibu Creek and tributaries open to the public for a fee); and Malibu Canyon and Point Mugu on the coast.

Griffith Park now has an extensive system of hiking and bridle trails. Inquire at the park ranger office on Griffith Park Drive. Will Rogers State Historic Park also has trails for horses and hikers that ascend to good view points.

San Fernando Valley

The San Fernando Valley section of Los Angeles (220 square miles bounded by the Santa Monica, Santa Susana, Verdugo, and San Gabriel mountains) only 60 years ago comprised open wheat fields, farms, and a few small towns. Since the area was annexed by the city of Los Angeles, it has grown to a population of over a million. Despite the valley's tremendous growth, there are still charming remnants of its past and some ap-pealing oases of the present. You can reach the valley from downtown Los Angeles on the Hollywood or San Diego freeways. From the north, you enter on the Golden State Freeway (Interstate Highway 5); from the west, on the Ventura Freeway (U.S. Highway 101).

Famous landmarks of Southern California history have been preserved in and near the valley. You'll find the original San Fernando Valley mission, some famous stagecoach stops and movie sites, and, to the north, the site of Southern California's gold discovery. Parks and gardens in the valley are varied. Two of the most familiar are Forest Lawn, an unusual cemetery in Glendale, and Valencia's Six Flags Magic Mountain, a family amusement park.

To simplify the location of these historic landmarks, we have organized the section from west to east. It starts where you would arrive in the valley on the Ventura Freeway, from the west, and on the Golden State Freeway, from the north; continues through the middle of the valley; and ends in the Arroyo Seco foothills.

At the western end of San Fernando Valley, three historic sites and one movie location bring back the past.
- *Newbury Park's Stagecoach Inn*, built in 1876, has seen action as a country hotel, stage stopover, military school, Scottish gift shop, and finally, the stately museum it is today. Part of a 4-acre park, the grounds also contain a collection of carriages, stagecoaches, and wagons. Nearby, a small Chumash thatched hut, an adobe, and a homesteader's cabin represent early California's three cultures. The inn is open Wednesday, Thursday, Friday, and Sunday. Admission is free. From the Ventura Freeway, exit left on Lynn Road to Ventu Park Road; turn right and look for the sign on your left.
- *Simi Valley's Strathearn Historical Park* centers around a residence that's actually two structures: a pre-1800 adobe with a grand two-story Victorian attached to its south side. The residence is full of turn-of-the-century furnishings, most of which belonged to the Strathearn family. In the yard, a lineup of antique ranching equipment awaits inspection. Here, too, you'll find the original Simi Valley Library and an 1880s Colony House, one of 12 prefabricated houses moved (in pieces) to this area from Chicago.

Strathearn Park is open Sundays from 1 to 4 P.M. Admission is free. From the Ventura Freeway, take Topanga Canyon Boulevard north 7 miles to State Highway 118. Drive west to Madera Drive near the freeway's end, then south on Madera to Strathearn Place.
- *Wildwood Park in Thousand Oaks* was the location for more than 300 movie and TV westerns. As you enter the park, look to the cliffs at your right—smoke signals were often filmed rising from these crags. A mile into the park are Stagecoach Bluffs; from here, film crews rolled countless wagons into the canyon below. From the Ventura Freeway, take Lynn Road north 2.2 miles and turn west on Avenida de los Arboles.
- *Calabasas* was a stage stop a century ago, days out from Los Angeles on the road to Monterey. Fifty years ago it was the last stop in the San Fernando Valley for motorists heading west on U.S. 101. Today it is by-passed by the Ventura Freeway, and its visitors are those who deliberately seek it out.

(Continued on page 40)

WATER-ORIENTED
DESTINATIONS include Avalon
Bay at Catalina (above) and Long
Beach's mighty Queen Mary (right).
Dome covers Howard Hughes'
"Spruce Goose"; LondonTowne lies in
foreground.

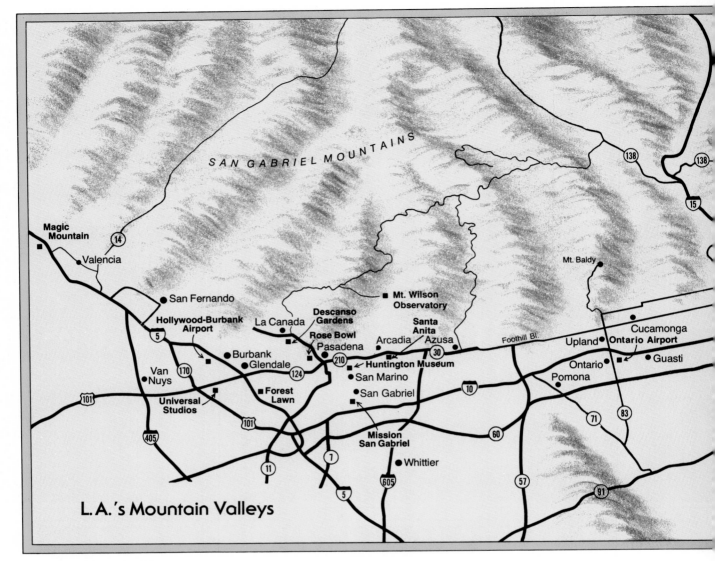

L.A.'s Mountain Valleys

. . . *Continued from page 38*

The gem of Calabasas is the Leonis Adobe. Tucked away among tall trees, this ranch house is a monument to Miguel Leonis, a contentious Basque land baron who played a colorful part in the region's history. Restored and furnished, it is open from 1 to 4 P.M. on Wednesday and weekends. A small donation provides maintenance. Take the Mulholland Drive-Valley Circle Boulevard exit from the Ventura Freeway.

Los Encinos State Historic Park (16756 Moorpark Street, Encino) is the place where the valley's recorded history began over 200 years ago. The Portola party stopped here, beside an Indian settlement built around a spring that's still flowing. Here, the bustle on the boulevard seems far away. Encircled by old olive trees and tall grevillias are turn-of-the-century sheep ranch buildings and the 1849 Osa adobe. Some of the rooms in the Osa adobe are furnished; recorded voices describe their contents. Los Encinos is open Wednesday through Sunday from 10 A.M. to 5 P.M. Expect a small admission charge.

Six Flags Magic Mountain, located near the Golden State Freeway in Valencia, features "white-knuckler" thrill rides, as well as more gentle rides, top-name entertainment, and other attractions.

You can take a bouncing, splashing dash on a log through a water flume that climaxes with a 90-foot plunge into Whitewater Lake. Try a ride on a runaway mine car around and through narrow passageways, a water-jet boat called "El Bumpo," or a skydiving ride called "Freefall." Among the park's five roller coasters are the world's largest wood double-racer and the largest steel coaster ever built. Small fry will enjoy the petting zoo—a miniature animal farm.

All this is part of a 260-acre family amusement park, the Southland's newest. The entrance fee includes unlimited use of rides, attractions, and entertainment (food, games, and shopping aren't included). Open daily from 10 A.M. to 11 P.M. (to midnight weekends) during the summer, the park is open weekends only the rest of the year.

40 AROUND L.A.

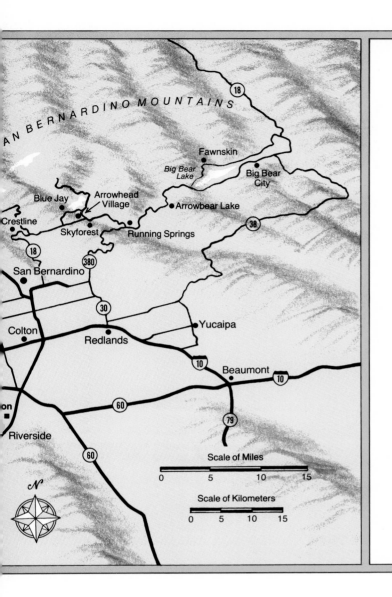

Major Points of Interest

Magic Mountain (Valencia)—260-acre family amusement center; top summer-night entertainment

Descanso Gardens (La Canada)—acres of camellias and rose gardens offer year-round blooms; Japanese tea pavilion

Rose Bowl (Pasadena)—stadium for New Year's football game; tour Football Hall of Fame inside

Norton Simon Museum (Pasadena)—controversial architecture; superb collection of art, sculpture, paintings, medieval tapestries

Forest Lawn (Glendale)—memorial park noted for statuary, church replicas, art works

L.A. State and County Arboretum (Arcadia)—see plants from every continent of the world; take guided tram trip through outstanding plantings; historic buildings

Santa Anita Race Track (Arcadia)—thoroughbred horse racing December to mid-April on well-landscaped grounds; no charge for watching morning workouts and touring stables

Huntington Library (San Marino)—also art gallery ("Blue Boy," "Pinkie") and botanical gardens on 200-acre estate

Mission San Gabriel (San Gabriel)—restored mission was once known for ancient vineyards; unique architecture and paintings attract visitors

Mission Inn (Riverside)—tour landmark hotel housing treasures from 1875

Rim of the World Drive (San Bernardino Mountains)—scenic route to Lake Arrowhead and Big Bear resort areas

William S. Hart Park, northwest of the valley at the junction of Newhall Avenue and San Fernando Road in Newhall, was originally Horseshoe Ranch—property of William S. Hart, Western star of the silent screen. He left the 253-acre estate to Los Angeles County, with instructions that it be preserved as a park.

The original ranch house at the bottom of the hill contains mementos of the star's motion picture career and is flanked by a corral filled with gentle livestock for the delight of children. Shaded picnic areas are nearby. Hart's home atop the hill, a Spanish-Mexican style mansion called "La Loma de Los Vientos" (Hill of the Winds), houses historical weapons, American Indian artifacts, Western art (including paintings by Charles Russell and Frederic Remington), and other Western Americana. A herd of bison roams the hills.

The ranch is open from 10 A.M. to dusk daily; free mansion tours run every hour between 10 A.M. and 5 P.M. weekends, and between 10 A.M. and 3 P.M. Wednesday through Friday. There's no admission charge. A free shuttle service brings visitors from the park entrance.

Placerita Canyon State and County Park memorializes the golden dream of Don Francisco Lopez. In 1842—6 years before the Sutter's Mill gold strike—this weary shepherd stopped for a nap under an oak tree near what is now Newhall. As the story goes, Lopez dreamed of gold as he slept. When he awoke, he was hungry and pulled up a clump of wild onions growing nearby. Gold nuggets clung to the roots—the first glimpse of an $80,000 deposit. The gold is gone now, but the tree—called the Oak of the Golden Dream—still stands in this small park about 5 miles east of Newhall, off U.S. Highway 14.

The park is a pleasant place for a picnic or a hike (you can pick up a trail map at the nature center). Scenes for the Cisco Kid movie series were filmed here.

Mission San Fernando is the focal point of the valley's oldest settlement. Founded in 1797 by Father La-

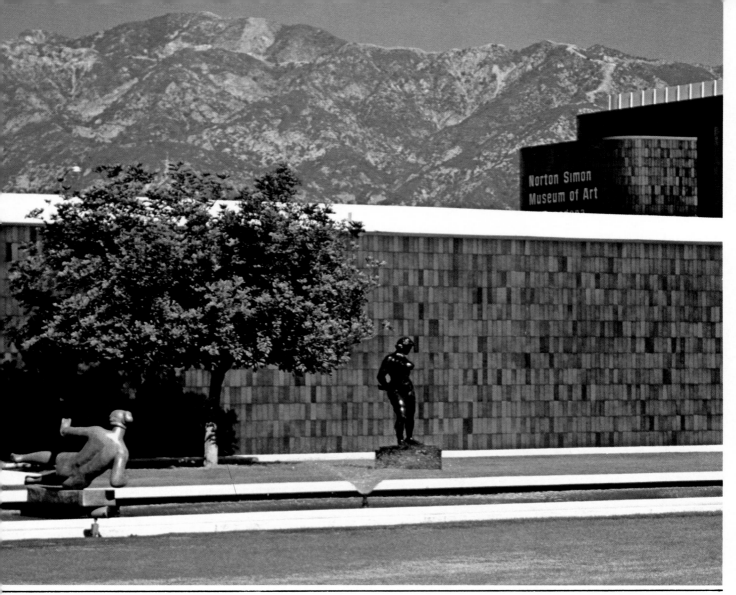

ART AND GARDENS attract tourists to the San Gabriel Valley. Sculpture garden (above) is part of Pasadena's Norton Simon Museum of Art. Teahouse (right) sits among Descanso Gardens in La Canada.

suen, California's 17th mission was known for its hospitality (it was a Butterfield Stage stop) and its fine cattle. The mission subsequently served as headquarters for Governor Pico, and later for Colonel Fremont during the Mexican-American War. Allow at least an hour for the well-marked walk through the extensive buildings and grounds. Located on San Fernando Mission Boulevard between the San Diego and Golden State freeways, the mission is open daily from 9:30 A.M. to 5 P.M. A small donation is requested.

Across the street in Brand Park is the Memory Garden, with a statue of Father Serra. From there, go south on Columbus Avenue 2 blocks to the YMCA field for a look at the Andres Pico Adobe. Its exterior shows how a typical adobe house grew. The oldest portion was built about 1834 by former mission Indians; later in its long career, lean-to rooms and a second story were added.

Forest Lawn in Glendale, east of Griffith Park, is the first of the extraordinary Forest Lawn Memorial Parks (open to visitors from 9 A.M. to 5 P.M. daily). These superbly landscaped 206 acres form what is probably the best known, most visited, and most controversial cemetery in the world. There are no tombstones here; instead, you'll see an unusual collection of statuary, memorials, shrines, and replicas of famous churches. The collection includes reproductions of Michelangelo's sculpture and of the famous "Last Supper" stained-glass windows. Forest Lawn is also the home for the world's largest religious painting, "The Crucifixion," which is 195 feet long and 45 feet high. The park's entrance is on Glendale Avenue, northeast of the terminus of Glendale Boulevard at San Fernando Road.

Forest Lawn-Hollywood Hills, noted for its patriotic theme, features a Court of Liberty with a 175-foot Birth of Liberty Mosaic, a Monument to Washington, and a Lincoln Terrace. The Hall of Liberty Museum and various churches house historical memorabilia. A free patriotic movie is shown daily. Forest Lawn-Hollywood Hills is located at 6300 Forest Lawn Drive.

Additional art treasures may be viewed at Forest Lawn-Covina Hills and Forest Lawn-Cypress.

Burbank — where entertainment begins

Satirized for years as "beautiful downtown Burbank" on a television show, this city is really the center of the movie and television industry. Film studios are based here and stars live nearby in the Toluca Lake area. The Hollywood-Burbank Airport is one of the busiest in Southern California, and even the formerly drab downtown section has become a delightful shopping mall.

Burbank is one place where you can tour the studios (see page 29). Universal City (the world's largest studio), Burbank Studios, and NBC Television Studios offer guided tours.

San Gabriel Valley

The San Gabriel Valley is certainly the most lush, in terms of greenery, and the most plush, in terms of wealth and architecture, of the three Los Angeles area valleys. It contains the oldest valley settlements in the L.A. region, some of the area's finest museums and estates, and some of the oldest architecture and gardens.

Pasadena, the *grande dame* of the area, is perhaps best known for the colorful Tournament of Roses Parade and Rose Bowl game held on New Year's Day. But primarily it is an attractive residential community with stately trees and old buildings at the base of the San Gabriel Mountains. Driving through the quiet streets, you'll find many places of architectural interest, including the Gamble House at 4 Westmoreland Place, one of the best-known works of architects Charles and Henry Greene. The house is open for 1-hour guided tours (for a fee) from 10 A.M. to 3 P.M. on Tuesday and Thursday, and from noon to 3 P.M. one weekend a month; call (818) 793-3334 for further information.

• *The Pasadena Historical Society Museum*, at 470 W. Walnut Street (across Orange Grove from Gamble House), is another example of the gracious mansions that once lined the streets. Guided tours are from 1 to 4 P.M. Tuesdays and Thursdays; donations are requested.

• *The Tournament House*, at 391 S. Orange Grove Boulevard, contains Rose Bowl memorabilia. From February through September, free ½-hour tours are offered on Wednesdays between 2 and 4 P.M.

• *The Pasadena Library*, a grand-manner City Hall, and the Civic Auditorium are all set in a row along a short stretch of Garfield Avenue. All were built between 1925 and 1932 to become the heart of a formal civic center, a plan which never materialized. Around the remodeled Civic Auditorium, the Pasadena Center, with its shops, meeting rooms, and landscaped gardens, provides a focal point for access to the civic center.

• *The Norton Simon Museum* (at Orange Grove and Colorado boulevards), one of the most important new museums of art in California, symbolizes the new architectural look coming to Pasadena. The cornerless, tile-clad museum baffles design critics, but most admit that its positioning and classic setting are superb. The collection ranges from Indian and Southeast Asian sculpture to European old masters, impressionist and modern paintings, and medieval tapestries. Galleries and gardens display sculpture. The museum is open Thursday through Sunday from noon to 6 P.M.; there's a modest admission charge for anyone over 12.

• *Brookside Park and the Rose Bowl* in its center cover more than 500 acres in Arroyo Seco Canyon. Here you'll find picnic areas, playgrounds, hiking trails, a swimming pool, and a municipal golf course, in addition to the famous Rose Bowl. Seating 100,000 spectators, the stadium is the home of a climactic intersectional football game played every New Year's Day. During the rest of the year, it is the site for other football games, political rallies, civic events, and, on the second Sunday of every month, a gigantic swap meet. The stadium entrance is on Rosemont Avenue.

• *Descanso Gardens*, at 1418 Descanso Boulevard in La Canada, was formerly a private estate and is now 165 acres of magnificent beauty any time of the year. From late December through March, the vast collection of camellias is in bloom. A Japanese tea pavilion is nestled here in a camellia forest.

The beautifully landscaped historical rose garden features species planted in chronological order to demonstrate the development of modern hybrid tea roses. The peak of the blooming season is May and early June. Through the archway opposite the historical roses are group plantings of each of the All-American Rose Selection winners chosen since the program began in 1940. Unlike many of the old roses, these specimens bloom from May until December. Descanso Gardens is open from 9 A.M. to 4:30 P.M. daily except Christmas. Take a guided tram tour between 1 and 4 P.M. Tuesday through Friday, or between 11 A.M. and 4 P.M. on weekends.

Huntington Library, Art Gallery, and Botanical Gardens inspire many superlatives. Located at 1151 Oxford Road north of Huntington Drive in San Marino, the home and 200-acre estate of Pacific Electric tycoon H. E. Huntington were willed to the public, so you may visit them without charge. The Art Gallery in the mansion is composed of seven large and fifteen small galleries. Acknowledged as best in the country, the 18th century British art collection exhibited here includes "Sarah Siddons as the Tragic Muse," "Blue Boy," and "Pinkie."

In the library (a large, white classical building), you'll see selections from the outstanding collection of half a million volumes of rare books and 5 million manuscripts, some as old as eight centuries. Among the fascinating works are a Gutenberg Bible, a "First Folio" of William Shakespeare's plays, Benjamin Franklin's hand-written autobiography, and George Washington's genealogy in his own hand.

The acres of rural and formal gardens on the estate have a number of highlights: the desert garden, the palm garden, two types of Japanese gardens, the circular Shakespearean garden with a bust of the poet and flowers and shrubs mentioned in his works. Also included are the herb garden, the first commercial avocado grove in Southern California, and an orange grove—but not a producing one.

Huntington is open to visitors Tuesday through Sunday from 1 to 4:30 P.M.; tours are offered at 1 P.M. weekdays. L.A. County visitors need Sunday reservations. Donations are requested.

Mission San Gabriel, fourth mission to be dedicated in California (1771), was moved to its present site 9 miles east of Los Angeles in 1775. Its location at the crossroads of three well-traveled trails (now 534 Mission Drive in San Gabriel) made it a busy place. It was once known for its extensive vineyards and winery, the oldest and (at one time) the largest in the state. The mission's winery helped to finance the Plaza Church in the Pueblo of Los Angeles.

Architecture of the church is unlike that of other missions: the facade is on a side wall, and there are Moorish-capped buttresses and long, narrow windows, reminiscent of a cathedral in Cordova, Spain, where the mission's main builder received his training. Notable attractions include its bells and early California religious and historical treasures. The tradition-minded Claretian Fathers restored the mission and maintain it today, conducting masses every Sunday. Mission San Gabriel Arcángel is open to the public daily except for major religious holidays, from 9:30 A.M. to 4:30 P.M. There's a small admission charge.

Los Angeles State and County Arboretum, at 301 N. Baldwin Avenue, between Huntington Drive and Colorado Boulevard, includes 127 acres of plants grown in every continent of the world. The Demonstration Home Gardens, jointly sponsored by the Arboretum Foundation and *Sunset* Magazine, display take-home ideas in garden design. Peacocks roam the grounds, and historic buildings date from the time the property was Rancho Santa Anita. Guided tram tours leave from the entrance during mid-day. Hours are from 9 A.M. to 5 P.M. daily.

Santa Anita Race Track is just across Baldwin Avenue from the arboretum. During the thoroughbred horse racing season from December 26 to mid-April (with a special meet in October), throngs of racing fans jam the 500-acre track. Well-landscaped grounds include nearly one million special Santa Anita pansies in peak bloom for the season. The track entrance is on Holly Avenue. Gates open at 11 A.M.; general admission is $2.25. There is a parking fee. During the season you can watch morning workouts and tour the stables without charge.

San Gabriel Mountains

Stretching from seaward slopes to the Mojave Desert, the San Gabriel Mountains form the northern border of the Los Angeles area. The most accessible of high mountain ranges near Los Angeles, these mountains have been called the city's mountain playground, offering back-country hiking and riding, camping, picnicking, wilderness areas, and short walks to scenic waterfalls.

You can see some of the high country by car, but the best is seen on forest trails leading to the heights. The middle high country (or mid-range) is reached by the Angeles Crest Highway, the eastern high country by San Antonio Canyon Road. Both are within an hour's drive from the edge of Los Angeles. For information and maps, write to Angeles National Forest Supervisor, 150 Los Robles Avenue, Pasadena, CA 91101.

Angeles Crest Highway, State 2, originates in La Canada and connects the most popular sites and activities in the San Gabriel Mountains. At Vista, one of the picnic areas on the range crest, you may catch sight of bighorn sheep. Many climbers move up to this higher country when the fire season closes the front range. Of the crest peaks, Mount Williamson and Mount Islip are the shortest hikes from the highway and the two easiest to climb. Vincent Gap, 5 miles from Big Pines, is the starting point of popular hikes to the old Big Horn (an introductory walk of 3 hours with very little climbing). Mount Baden-Powell, a steep, 4-mile trip each way, is second perhaps only to Old Baldy as a worthy climb.

Mount Wilson Observatory, reached by the Mount Wilson Road which leaves State 2 at Red Box, is world renowned for the 100-inch, 100-ton Hooker telescope camera and its magnificent views. The observatory is open free of charge from 10 A.M. to dusk daily. It lies beyond Mount Wilson Skyline Park, which has a picnic area and children's zoo. Admission is $2 per car.

San Gabriel Wilderness, an area set aside to preserve the wild, rough mountain country, requires accomplished hiking skill and good maps to explore. Automobile sightseers can sample the flavor of this area on a drive of about 70 miles from La Canada to Azusa on State 2 and 39. You will enjoy panoramic rim views (especially at Jarvi Memorial Vista) across to rugged Twin Peaks and down into awesomely steep Devil's and Bear canyons.

Pomona-Walnut Valley

Along the base of the San Gabriel and San Bernardino ranges is a valley usually designated as Pomona-Walnut by weather forecasters. Vineyards are losing out to urban pressures in what was once one of the great wine-producing areas. You can still visit about six of the wineries in the Cucamonga-Guasti area.

Pomona, a center for horses and higher education, is also the site of the huge Los Angeles County Fair every September. Largest county fair in the nation, it underscores an often overlooked fact: the urbanized Los Angeles area is still a significant agricultural producer.

At 2 P.M. on the first Sunday of October, November, and each month from January through June, you can watch an Arabian horse show at Cal Poly near Pomona. The shows have been held since 1925, when the campus was still part of the Kellogg ranch.

Rancho Santa Ana Botanic Gardens, on Foothill Boulevard just west of the turnoff to Padua Hills, is devoted exclusively to native California plants. A short, well-marked nature trail, beginning near the giant sequoias west of the administration building, takes you past a cone collection, home demonstration garden, and through woodland, rock, dune, and desert areas. Try to see it in the spring when the California poppy is in bloom. It is open daily from 8 A.M. to 5 P.M.

The San Bernardino County Museum shouldn't be missed. You'll see a mixture of animal, vegetable, and mineral exhibits, as well as the largest egg collection in the U.S. Located at 2024 Orange Tree Lane in Redlands, the museum is open Tuesday through Saturday from 9 A.M. to 5 P.M. and Sunday from 1 to 5 P.M. Next door is the Edwards mansion, a classic example of Victorian architecture. (The mansion is now a restaurant.)

Historical countryside

If you drive from L.A. to the mountains or desert through Riverside, Perris, and Hemet, expect to see some historical countryside. Allow time along the way for such attractions as California's first navel orange tree, the famous Mission Inn, and Mount Rubidoux — site of an annual Easter sunrise pilgrimage.

Riverside is the birthplace of California's multimillion dollar navel orange industry. One of two original trees brought from Brazil in 1873 is still bearing fruit (at the corner of Magnolia and Arlington streets); the other, transplanted to the courtyard of the Mission Inn by President Theodore Roosevelt in 1903, died in the late 1920s, but the trunk is still preserved.

The Mission Inn, modeled after the California missions, is a stunning sight. Begun as an adobe cottage in 1875, it grew to become one of the showplaces of the countryside. Covering a square block bounded by Sixth, Seventh, Main, and Orange streets, this resort hotel houses many treasures, including the Patio of the Fountains, the Garden of the Bells, and the St. Francis Chapel. One-hour tours leave the lobby twice daily on weekdays and three times a day on weekends.

Ramona Bowl focuses on Indian history in the Hemet and San Jacinto area, where the local residents have been staging California's greatest outdoor play, *Ramona*, since 1923. It is generally held on three successive weekends starting in late April. Early reservations can be made after January 31 by requesting an application from the Ramona Pageant Association, Box 755, Hemet, CA 92343; enclose a stamped envelope.

San Bernardino Mountains

Highest of the mountain ranges surrounding Los Angeles, the San Bernardinos are another part of the mountain barrier between coast and desert. Past them are two major automobile routes: Cajon Canyon north to the Mojave Desert and San Gorgonio Pass east to the Coachella Valley. Peaks are high: Mount San Gorgonio (called Old Grayback because of its high expanse of naked granite) is 11,502 feet; many peaks on the south face reach over 10,000 feet. The San Bernardinos are rich in history, scenery, and recreation.

From Interstate Highway 15 you can get into the mountains on scenic Rim of the World Drive; the interstate also provides an easy "back door" to both the San Bernardino and San Gabriel mountains.

Rim of the World Drive (State Highway 18) is the famous route leading to the best-known locations in the San Bernardino Mountains. The scenic road winds up to elevations of 5,000 to 7,200 feet. As you start your ascent from San Bernardino, note the "arrowhead," a natural landmark on the mountain face.

For spectacular views along your way, take short side roads up to fire lookout stations on top of Strawberry Peak (most accessible), Keller Peak, and Butler Peak. Rim of the World Drive takes you near Crestline, Lake Gregory (site of an old Mormon settlement and today a favorite swimming destination), Blue Jay, Lake Arrowhead, Running Springs, Arrowbear, Big Bear Lake, and other small mountain resorts.

Lake Arrowhead is a manmade recreation lake and all-year resort, offering water sports and beautiful scenery. A marina has water-ski instruction, boat rentals, and swimming and fishing areas. You'll find a golf course, theaters, abundant restaurants, motels, stores, and private cabins here. At the south end of the lake, the resort center village is a picturesque, Alpine-style town but also contains a bit of bustling civilization, especially on weekends. The resort is open in the winter for skiers.

Big Bear Lake, farther east, is another resort development and scenic spot for water activities. In the village on the west end of the lake are motels, shops, and restaurants, many with lake views. Staying in the village, you can walk to theaters, a bowling alley, and an ice rink. South of Big Bear, manmade Cedar Lake, complete with an old waterwheel and mill, was the locale for the first technicolor movie.

Nearby Snow Summit ski resort runs its lifts in the summer for views of the lake and mountains at an 8,300-foot elevation. Good ski areas abound in the area; most are along the south shore. Depending on the weather, the season runs from November to March. From the mountain ridge south of the lake, you can look across Barton Flats to the vast white dome of San Gorgonio, summit of a snowy wilderness that is a goal for rugged hikers and backpackers.

Orange County

Mickey Mouse, a gathering of wax stars, free-roaming lions, and a berry farm with theme park — this is part of Orange County, center for family fun and fantasy. Orange groves may be scarce, but the swallows still return to Capistrano; surfboards jockey for the high "comber"; brightly colored sails weave in and out of Newport and Dana Point marinas; and Laguna hosts a time-honored art festival.

Once little more than a sleepy agricultural county scented by orange blossoms, Orange County was transformed by the magic wand of Walt Disney in the 1950s into one of the largest tourist meccas in Southern California.

Today, Orange County possesses the greatest aggregation of manmade amusements to be found anywhere. In addition to renowned Disneyland, the county boasts three major theme parks and several specialty attractions. The area has become a sort of spread-out, continuous world's fair.

But there's more. There's the great Golden Coast — extending from north of Huntington Beach (surfing capital of the world) through the seaside communities of Newport and Balboa and the art colony of Laguna south to San Clemente. This generous stretch of beach world produces many of Southern California's famous golden tans.

Among the rolling hills on the former Irvine Ranch is a University of California campus, part of a dynamic master-planned community. You'll also find remains of mission days at San Juan Capistrano, where the famed swallows return annually to visit.

Visitors return again and again to Orange County. There are always new additions to the amusement parks or new restaurants and shops to browse. You can't see it all in a day or even several days. You'll find many attractive, moderately priced hotels and motels clustered around the inland amusement parks and also along the beach highway.

During the summer — peak tourist season — most places you visit will be crowded. Summer temperatures rise to the high 80s and up inland; at the ocean it's much cooler, but beach space is often at a premium. In winter, you'll have plenty of elbow room, but amusement park hours are shortened and it's likely to be cold along the shore. Still, a visit to Orange County at any time of the year guarantees a fun-packed vacation.

A Mecca for Diversion

The possibilities for adventure in Orange County are unlimited: peer from inside your car as a lion climbs on the hood to examine you, eat a slice of boysenberry pie while strolling the streets of a ghost town or listening to Wagon Camp music, gaze at crocodiles squirming in their mud baths, or watch Dorothy and her friends tread the "yellow brick road." This is only a sampling of the many attractions centered in this region. And, most surprising of all, none of the above-mentioned adventures happens in Walt Disney's "Magic Kingdom," a major amusement area that alone would bring fame to any county.

Threaded by freeways, the area is accessible from anywhere in Southern California. You can drive, take a bus, or fly directly to Orange County.

By car from Los Angeles, take the Santa Ana Freeway (Interstate Highway 5) or the San Diego Freeway (Interstate Highway 405), which joins I-5 south of Lion Country. North and southbound freeways (Long Beach, San Gabriel River, Orange, and Newport) connect with the coast highway and freeways north of Orange County.

NEWPORT'S BUSY BAY is best seen from boat deck. Catch a cruise at venerable Balboa Pavilion, harbor's focal point.

The easiest route from the east is along Interstate Highway 10 (San Bernardino Freeway) to the Riverside Freeway (State Highway 91).

Bus transportation is both national and local. Orange County is served by Trailways Bus Service and Greyhound, both of which operate with national schedules. Trailways has terminals in Santa Ana and Laguna Beach. Greyhound has stations in Santa Ana, Anaheim, Laguna Beach, and Fullerton for through, not local, traffic. (You can't take Greyhound from Los Angeles to any Orange County town closer than San Clemente.)

The Southern California Rapid Transit District has direct service from its main Los Angeles terminal (located at 6th and Los Angeles) to Disneyland, Knott's Berry Farm, and the Movieland Wax Museum.

Airlines serve Orange County from major California cities. From Los Angeles International Airport, you can take commuter flights or helicopter rides to Fullerton Airport and to John Wayne/Orange County Airport in Santa Ana. The flight takes about 25 minutes.

You can also fly directly to Orange County on Air Cal, American, Frontier, Imperial, PSA, Republic, and Western. For further information on these flights, see your travel agent or airline representative. An airport coach service makes daily scheduled runs from Los Angeles International Airport to Anaheim, and from Anaheim to John Wayne/Orange County Airport. Limousines and taxis are also available for hire.

Once you're there, check with your hotel or the visitors and convention bureau (see below) about rental cars and the numerous sightseeing services.

Orange County has one of the best transit systems in Southern California. Buses cover every area of the county, and booklets with maps are distributed widely. Any city hall, large hotel, or civic center will have them. You can pick them up at the Convention Center in Anaheim. For a moderate fee, you can ride The Fun Bus from all major hotels and motels to and from major attractions in Orange County and Los Angeles. Phone (714) 635-1390 for details.

Two other commuter buses offer service between local hotels and regional shopping centers: the City Shopper (also goes to Crystal Cathedral) and the Anaheim Express. Check with your hotel for schedules.

Tourist World

Consider time and money when you plan a foray into Orange County's amusement centers. You'll need both.

Many major attractions are clustered around Buena Park, 20 miles southeast of Los Angeles and just a tempting 5 miles from Disneyland in Anaheim. Amusement centers, special-interest museums, a glass cathedral, an alligator farm—even if you have unlimited stamina, you'll never see them all in one day. Farther south, there's a lion park you won't want to miss. In this entertainment mecca, a full weekend only allows you to scratch the surface.

Tour companies offer limited-time visits to major attractions. If you prefer a more leisurely pace, go on your own—but bring a good map to help you get around.

Anaheim Convention Center

Located at 800 W. Katella Avenue (directly across from Disneyland), the convention center makes a good first stop for your Orange County tour. Here, the Anaheim Area Visitor & Convention Bureau offers free information on lodging, restaurants, and attractions. Call the Visitor Information Line at (714) 635-8900 for a 2½-minute recording giving attraction hours and information relating to sports and special events.

The sporting life

Sports events draw many visitors to the area. In addition to water-oriented activities along Orange County's beaches (described later in the chapter), you'll find plenty of tennis courts (including Tennisland Racquet Club, 1 block from Disneyland) and more than 20 public golf courses.

Anaheim's two professional sports teams play at the Anaheim Stadium, 2000 S. State College Boulevard, just north of the Santa Ana Freeway. The California Angels' baseball season begins in April and runs through September. The Los Angeles Rams, Anaheim's football team, play from August through December.

At Los Alamitos Race Course (4961 Katella Avenue, Los Alamitos), quarter horse races are held nightly except Sunday, from May to August and from November to January. Harness races take place from February to May. Thoroughbreds race from mid-October to November during the Orange County Fair.

The Orange County International Raceway in Irvine is a drag strip for autos, motorcycles, and go-carts. Call (714) 552-5514 for current race information. To get there, head north off the Santa Ana Freeway at Moulton Parkway. In Costa Mesa, motorcycles race every Friday evening from April to October at the Orange County Fairgrounds, 88 Fair Drive. Midgets compete at the El Toro Speedway, 23001 S.E. Valencia.

Let's go shopping

Orange County's shopping facilities range from waterfront browsing to the latest in air-conditioned malls to quaint villages. For great gifts, try The City in Orange, Anaheim Plaza, and Westminster malls—and be sure to include a stop at South Coast Plaza, one of the county's busiest (and largest) shopping show places. Across the street, South Coast Plaza Village contains even more stores.

Along the waterfront are Old World Village in Huntington Beach, super-chic Fashion Island and Lido Marina Village in Newport Beach, and Laguna Beach's one-of-a-kind shops. Check with the Anaheim Area Visitor & Convention Bureau for brochures.

Performing Arts Center

The curtain will rise on the Orange County Performing Arts Center in the autumn of 1985, ushering in the area's first major theater complex. Situated on 5 acres adjacent to South Coast Plaza in Costa Mesa (Bristol exit from I-405), the center will include two theaters and multi-level parking.

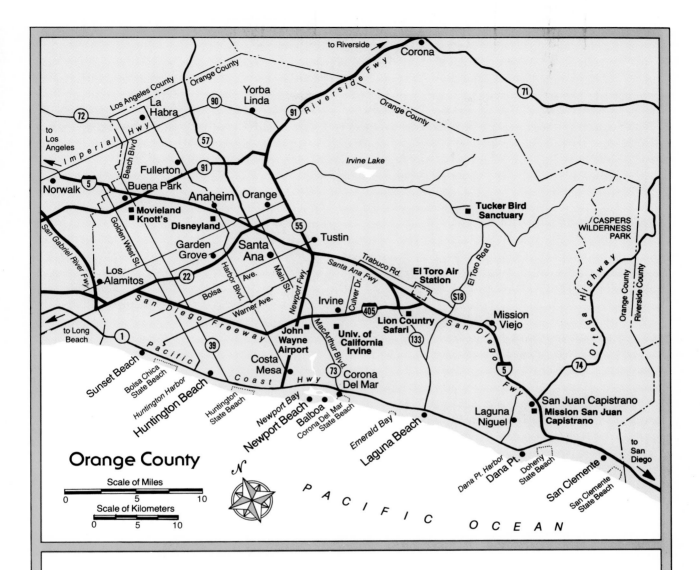

Orange County

Scale of Miles
0   5   10

Scale of Kilometers
0   5   10

Major Points of Interest

Movieland (State 39, Buena Park)—best collection of Hollywood stars in wax; horror in the Black Box; star hand and footprints

Knott's Berry Farm (State 39, Buena Park)—one-time berry farm turned theme park; old-time nostalgia, new rides, shows, music

Disneyland (Santa Ana Freeway to Anaheim)—seven "lands" of make-believe; new rides; fireworks display summer evenings

Lion Country (Moulton Parkway off San Diego Freeway)—take a safari in your car past lions and other animals in "African plains"

Huntington Beach—surfers' "capital"; good Pismo clamming

Newport Beach—boating playground; Newport Center shops, restaurants, art museum

Balboa Peninsula—colorful community of shops and homes; Balboa Pavilion, famous landmark; Balboa ferry ride between Balboa Island and peninsula; dory fleet goes to sea daily for fishing

Laguna Beach (on Pacific Coast Highway south of Newport Beach)—Southland's prominent art colony, summer resort, lovely beach

Dana Point Harbor—the only Southern California marina landscaped as park; picnic facilities, bike trails, restaurants, still-water beach, fishing pier

San Juan Capistrano (off San Diego Freeway)—home of "Father Serra's Chapel" in California's 7th mission; stop by renovated railroad station

MICKEY MOUSE (right) leads parade down Disneyland's Main Street while Dorothy and friends (below) invite you along Movieland's yellow brick road. Plummeting rides (below right) are only part of Knott's Berry Farm's family entertainment complex.

Disneyland–
Best-known Park of All

The father of "theme parks" springing up around the country, Disneyland has been world-renowned for over 20 years for its combined use of technology and imagination to control the environment and to achieve illusion. Disneyland is at its best in creating a three-dimensional illusory experience you move through, most masterful of which is the Haunted Mansion. A disembodied head speaking from inside a glass sphere, a ballroom full of transparent dancers, and spirits perching on the back of your moving chair are all part of the hair-raising experience.

In Disneyland, an enjoyable ride becomes a trip into history, space, fantasy, or a foreign land. An entire area becomes a reproduction of a well-known fairy tale.

Disneyland even undergoes marked seasonal changes outdoors when only subtle changes have occurred in the weather, producing Easter blooms in spring, flashing autumn colors after Labor Day, and displaying brilliant poinsettias at Christmas time. The park has truly become what Walt Disney intended: a place enjoyed by adults as well as children, actually drawing more of the former than the latter.

On your first park visit, consider the 2½-hour small-group guided tour, which will introduce you to all seven "lands" in the Magic Kingdom. The tour costs about $4 more than the Passport alone (unlimited admission ticket to all events), but it offers a good overview of the park, making it easier to return to attractions you'd like to experience again.

Main Street 1890 in Home Town, U.S.A. is your first stop in the park. The colorful Disneyland Band, known for its showmanship as well as its musical skill, often marches here—in front of the nostalgic old ice cream parlor and silent movie house, or in the Town Square and depot (departure point for the Disneyland Railroad's park tour). At the opera house, see the Walt Disney Story, climaxed by the animated show "Great Moments with Mr. Lincoln."

Adventureland offers a jungle boat ride and safari in alligator, gorilla, and elephant territory; the opportunity to climb the treehouse of the shipwrecked and industrious Swiss Family Robinson; and a visit to the "enchanted" Tiki Room.

New Orleans Square, with the Mississippi steamwheeler, Blue Bayou Restaurant, exciting Pirates of the Caribbean ride, and eerie Haunted Mansion, evokes the glamour of the French Quarter of this Louisiana city.

Frontierland, the haunt of Tom Sawyer and Davy Crockett, is your target for a ride on the sailing ship "Columbia" or on the riverboat "Mark Twain" (both pass Tom's island). Take a raft across the river and explore Fort Wilderness, or steam across the land on the Big Thunder Mountain Railroad's runaway train.

Bear Country features a Country Bear Jamboree with such characters as Swingin' Teddi Barra, and offers canoes you can paddle along the rivers of America.

Fantasyland—that make-believe world of Peter Pan, Alice in Wonderland, and other storybook characters—is reached by crossing a moat and entering Sleeping Beauty's Castle. Recently renovated, this "land" now resembles a Bavarian village; existing rides have been lengthened and changed, and new ones have been added. You can still enjoy your old favorites—but don't miss trying Pinocchio's Daring Journey, Snow White's Scary Adventures, and the other recent additions.

Tomorrowland requires continuous renovation to keep up with advances in the exciting world of science. It now offers a monorail, a submarine voyage, a Mission to Mars, an Adventure through Inner Space, and a Peoplemover. Towering over Tomorrowland is Space Mountain, a rocketing race through the galaxy.

Each land has restaurants and refreshment stands, musical entertainment, shops, services, and free exhibits. You won't see all of Disneyland in a day, so either return again or plan ahead, being very selective for your only visit. Disneyland changes continually—whenever inspiration and imagination ignite.

Daytime or evening can be equally engrossing in Disneyland. In the summer, music of the Dixieland band is prominent in the night air, and name bands entertain. Multicolored fireworks light the sky at 9 P.M. every night. You'll spend a lot of time waiting along the parade route to see such popular evening attractions as the Electric Parade meandering through the park.

Disneyland is less crowded in winter (as well as in the fall and early spring). Lines are shorter, and streets offer you more strolling room. It's also cooler then, but there's less entertainment.

Open daily from 9 A.M. to midnight (to 1 A.M. Saturday) from mid-June to September, the park is closed Monday and Tuesday in the winter season (September through February). Winter hours are from 10 A.M. to 6 P.M. Wednesday through Friday, and from 9 A.M. to 7 P.M. on weekends. From March to mid-June, the park is open 10 A.M. to 6 P.M. weekdays, 9 A.M. to 9 P.M. weekends. To get to Disneyland, take the Santa Ana Freeway to the Harbor Boulevard exit in Anaheim. There's a parking charge.

The Disneyland Hotel

Across the street is Disneyland Hotel—the largest hotel in the county. It's connected to the park by a fast monorail from Tomorrowland. Your monorail ticket allows you to stop off at the hotel for a visit.

More than a hotel, this 60-acre resort complex features 14 theme restaurants and lounges, a marina, and a multitude of shops. On the full-size marina, a floating barge features outdoor entertainment. Seaports of the Pacific, a waterfront bazaar, is set among lush tropical gardens, waterfalls, and a palm-laden beach. Koi swim around in their own pond, and twice nightly the pulsating Dancing Waters and Lights Fantastic Show fascinates visitors.

Need some exercise? You can swim in one of three pools, rent a pedalboat, or take advantage of nearby Tennisland's courts.

You don't have to be a guest to enjoy the marina activities and evening show. The hotel is also a good spot for watching Disneyland's nightly fireworks.

Knott's Berry Farm

Knott's, at 8039 Beach Boulevard in Buena Park, is the oldest of the county's amusement parks. It began in 1920 as a berry farm with a little roadside shed where the Knott family sold their produce. A restaurant was added in the early '40s; it attracted such crowds that founder Walter Knott decided to provide guests with amusements while they waited for Mrs. Knott's chicken dinners.

From these humble beginnings, the farm has grown into a 150-acre combination "ghost town," theme park, and restaurant and shopping center—still operated as a family enterprise.

Five theme areas offer everything from Wild West shows to Snoopy. Most of the 165 rides, shows, and attractions are concentrated on one side of Beach Bouelvard, but some spill across the street to an area with lagoons and a full-scale reproduction of Independence Hall, built with handmade bricks and featuring a Liberty Bell (authentic down to the crack).

Everything is designed for family enjoyment, from the vaudeville show in the Calico Saloon (where the strongest drinks served are sarsaparilla and boysenberry punch) to the Good Time Theatre, a 2,150-seat, air-conditioned showcase for top stars.

Ghost Town, an authentic reproduction of a mining town, started it all. Here you can ride "shotgun" on a stagecoach, pan for gold, or ride an ore car through a mine or a "log" down a water flume. Passengers on the Denver & Rio Grande—a real, smoke-belching narrow-gauge train—will be suitably affrighted when gun-firing bandits enter the car.

At Fiesta Village, you can shop, watch Mexican artisans, take a stomach-gripping swoop on Montezooma's Revenge, and enjoy a Mexican meal.

The Roaring '20s, featuring bumper cars, old Model A Fords, and a large game arcade, provides a tongue-in-cheek look at an uninhibited period of American history.

Knott's Airfield salutes the days of early aviation with a collection of awesome thrills including the Corkscrew and the 20-story Parachute Sky Jump; you'll find soapbox racers here, too.

Camp Snoopy, opened in 1983, is set among tall trees, waterfalls, streams, and a large lake. Bobbing pontoon bridges, swaying suspension bridges, and a sky-high playground hung from the treetops add to its appeal. At the Old Wooden Mill, you'll find a fun house, one of 30 attractions in this area.

Ride a steamboat, stern-wheeler, train, balloon, mule-powered carousel, roller coaster, or pony. Slides and tunnel shoots invite squeals. Snoopy strolls through his kingdom, greeting guests and posing for photos.

The entrance fee to Knott's Berry Farm includes unlimited use of all rides and adventures except panning for gold and the shooting gallery. During the summer, the park is open daily until midnight (later on weekends). Winter hours are 10 A.M. to 6 P.M. Monday, Tuesday, and Friday; 10 A.M. to 10 P.M. Saturday; and 10 A.M. to 9 P.M. Sunday.

Additional Attractions

Several inland visitor destinations are clustered around Knott's in Buena Park. Others are scattered around the towns of Garden Grove, Santa Ana, Costa Mesa, and Laguna Hills. It's a diverse collection, ranging from alligators, horses, and lions to airplanes, cars, wax images, and a cloud-reflecting church.

California Alligator Farm

Reptiles in residence are one of Southern California's most venerable tourist attractions. The California Alligator Farm, located in a 2-acre junglelike park across La Palma Avenue from Knott's, houses more than 100 species. All five orders of reptiles are represented, but the emphasis is on crocodilians.

Alligator and snake shows are held several times daily throughout the year.

Six Flags Movieland

Just a few minutes' drive north from Knott's, at 7711 Beach Boulevard, is the Six Flags Movieland—the biggest gathering of celebrities in the world. Featured are over 230 wax likenesses of Hollywood stars in scenes from memorable movies and television shows. Here you'll find more glitter and glamour than in Hollywood, and you'll encounter more stars than on the busiest day at any studio lot: Judy Garland and friends in *The Wizard of Oz*; Sophia Loren in *Two Women*; Clark Gable and Vivien Leigh in *Gone with the Wind*; Paul Newman and Robert Redford in *Butch Cassidy and the Sundance Kid*. One warning: Don't get carried away and touch any of the figures. If you do, you'll trigger an alarm system.

When you join Vincent Price in the Black Box, you'll also experience the thrill of such horror movies as *Halloween*, *Altered States*, and *Alien*. Or stroll along Backlot Boulevard, on restored sets from some of Hollywood's best-remembered movies. On your way to the California Plaza, an outdoor restaurant, you'll walk past hand and footprints of some of today's stars.

Movieland is open daily from 9 A.M. in the summer, from 10 A.M. in the winter.

The Kingdom of the Dancing Stallions

Across the street from Movieland, at 7662 Beach Boulevard, one of the area's newer attractions offers daily musical performances featuring 37 white Spanish dancing stallions with elaborately costumed riders. You can even get a close-up view of the magnificent horses in a solid brass stabling area. For show times, call (714) 546-4366.

Crystal Cathedral

A tall glass edifice stands at Chapman and Lewis streets in Garden Grove. It's the Crystal Cathedral, home of the Reformed Church in America. Free, hour-long tours of the glass-paned church and grounds include a look at one of the world's largest pipe organs.

Tours are offered between 9 A.M. and 4:30 P.M. Monday through Saturday, between 12:30 and 4:30 P.M. Sunday.

A look at planes and cars

Movieland-of-the-Air, at the John Wayne/Orange County Airport, contains one of the country's largest collections of antique aircraft. More than 50 airplanes (many originals) are on display in this museum. Open daily from 10 A.M. to 5 P.M. during the summer, it's closed Monday and Tuesday during the rest of the year.

The Briggs Cunningham Automotive Museum, at 250 E. Baker Street in Costa Mesa, is one of the finest in the world, focusing on some 100 cars that were industry leaders in performance, looks, and technical features. Featured are a 1927 Bugatti, a Hispano-Suiza, and other sports, racing, and classic cars. The museum is open from 9 A.M. to 5 P.M. Wednesday through Sunday.

Lion Country Safari

Extending the range of the tourist-park district southeastward is Lion Country Safari, a 300-acre wild animal preserve where people are "caged" in automobiles while animals roam free. You drive through country populated by one of the world's largest assemblages of African animals, all rambling through natural surroundings. Eight preserves keep incompatible beasts separated.

The safari ends at an entertainment center, offering bird shows in an amphitheater and a junior jungle where children may pet small exotic animals and play in a tree house. On the jungle river boat trip, you'll see exotic birds close at hand and an island full of chimps; another jungle ride takes children past animated animals. You can also rent a hippo pedal boat for a ride on Lake Shanalee.

The park's operating hours vary according to season. It's open daily from 9:45 A.M. to 5 P.M. in summer, until 3:30 P.M. during the rest of the year. Car windows must remain closed, and convertibles are banned. Animals are most active during the cooler hours, on rainy days, and at feeding times.

Adjacent to the San Diego Freeway at the Moulton Parkway offramp, you'll see no-nonsense signs giving would-be gate crashers this terse warning: "Trespassers will be eaten."

Irving Meadows Amphitheatre, on the grounds, presents evening weekend concerts; for information, call (714) 855-6111.

The Present...

The northwestern section of Orange County is crowded; you'll find little evidence of the bean fields that once flourished for miles. As urban sprawl spread southeastward, "instant cities" sprang up, land sites decreased, and people began to fear this once-beautiful countryside would suffer the fate of surrounding areas.

Irvine Company—owners of an 83,000-acre ranch comprising one-fifth of the area of Orange County—in 1960 retained William L. Pereira to prepare a broad, general plan for the land, designed to stop or at least to integrate the urban sprawl. Within this framework, the Irvine Company planners, working with other consultants, prepared a more detailed plan. A comprehensive look at the total environment, the plan established building and population density limits and provided greenbelt areas, effective traffic flow, and esthetic balance. Billboards, overhead power lines, and TV antennas were forbidden. Both shopping centers and wildlife preserves were included in the mountains-to-ocean scheme. Still being modified to conform with state and regional planning commissions, the plan is a model for the rest of the country.

The University of California at Irvine enjoys the unique advantage of being developed within the master plan. Its 1,500 acres (over twice the area of U.C.L.A.) are the focal point of the city of Irvine, which one day will incorporate some 53,000 acres of the ranch. By the turn of the century, the community is expected to have 100,000 people, the university 27,500 students.

...and the Past

Where are all the orange trees? Many are gone, though a few groves survive on the Irvine Ranch and some still hold out around the Santa Ana area. And faint traces of a distant past still linger among the mission ruins at San Juan Capistrano. Other historical attractions also exist, and looking for them is part of the fun. The Diego Sepulveda Adobe (1900 Adams Avenue in Anaheim) stands on old Indian grounds.

The Orange County Experience, a very special historical tour that includes stops for freshly squeezed orange juice at the old Irvine headquarters and for wine atop a Dana Point bluff, is operated by a history professor. Designed for small groups, the tour provides a 4½-hour dip into the past and a glimpse of what's ahead for Orange County. For details, call (714) 680-3556.

For a tour on your own, visit Heritage Hill Park in El Toro—the county's first historic park, comprising an original adobe and three restored turn-of-the-century buildings. From I-5, take the Lake Forest Drive exit east for 2 miles, then turn left on Serrano Road. Tours are given at 11 A.M. and at 2 and 3 P.M. daily; the park is open from 8 A.M. to 5 P.M. Just down the road is Serrano Creek Park. A 1½-mile jogging trail runs through its towering eucalyptus grove; shaded tables invite picnicking.

The Charles W. Bowers Memorial Museum, in Santa Ana, offers a look into Southern California's past. The mission-style structure has galleries devoted to natural history, archeology, early and contemporary California art, and artifacts of the Southwest. Here you will find an extensive collection of early Spanish and Mexican documents, among them deeds to area ranchos.

The Bowers Museum, at 2002 N. Main Street, is just south of the Main Street offramp from the Santa Ana Freeway. Hours are 10 A.M. to 5 P.M. Tuesday through Saturday, noon to 5 P.M. Sunday. Admission is free; donations are accepted.

Venerable San Juan Capistrano

The village of San Juan Capistrano has been a favorite stop for travelers ever since its mission was founded in 1776, the year of American independence. About midway between Los Angeles and San Diego, it's by-passed by I-5. Even so, its streets fill up on weekends and holidays with people who come to see the picturesque mission, shop, eat, or break up a longer journey.

The town is small enough to cover on foot. Horseback riders from nearby rural communities and cyclists in from the lightly traveled old highway are part of the traffic. On the street you still hear the Spanish language, and you can see the influence of Mexico in the restaurants, the craft and fashion shops, and in the building design.

Architecture. The sweep of California history is displayed in the architecture of San Juan, from the mission and adobes of the Spanish and Mexican eras to the Egan house and the railway station dating from the late 19th century. Nondescript buildings remain from the time San Juan was a farm with a main highway running through it. Now, with architectural controls in effect, some handsome new structures are appearing in the mission district.

The most impressive structure is the new parish church at the northwest corner of the mission grounds. Though built in the likeness of the original "Great Stone Church," it's considerably larger. A dramatic bell tower rises 104 feet above the ground. Across the street is the architecturally striking public library, oriented around a central courtyard with a reflecting pool, stream, and fountain.

On the main street, south of the mission, are almost all the adobes—some still family occupied, some converted into businesses, some in ruins. All are labeled. Just around the corner from the train depot is Los Rios Street, a charming pocket of the past. The city's historical society is housed in the O'Neill Museum, a restored 1880s house. The well-furnished museum is open Tuesday to Friday from 9 A.M. to 1 P.M., and Saturday and Sunday from noon to 3 P.M. Admission is free.

You may want to sample the shops along Camino Capistrano, where you can buy goods both old and new: Navajo rugs, pottery, saddles, Indian jewelry, and Western wear.

Mission San Juan Capistrano is the great attraction of San Juan Capistrano. The mission was founded in 1776 by Father Junipero Serra. The seventh in the California mission chain, it was completed in 1806 after a decade of work, but much was destroyed in an earthquake only 6 years later.

A small admission charge takes you through the gates. For another small fee you can rent cassettes to guide you through the legendary ruins and restored gardens. Fluttering white pigeons splash in the mossy fountain; they're so used to visitors that they may eat out of your hand. Past the fountain, broken, ivy-covered walls are all that remains of a stone church that was once the most magnificent in the mission chain. Today, the ruined walls hold the mud nests of the legendary swallows of Capistrano.

Four bells, saved when the original bell tower collapsed, today ring out in a campanile. Behind the campanile are a small tranquil garden, a fountain, and the mission museum.

Having survived the rigors of neglect and time, the modest mission chapel is believed to be the oldest church in California. The adobe chapel, called "Father Serra's church," is the only extant place where he is known to have said Mass. Inside, the 300-year-old giltwork *reredos* (altarpiece) from Spain was added during the mission's restoration in the 1920s.

Outside you may stroll through a shady arcade (a remnant of the original mission) and along flower-bordered paths past ivy and rose-covered walls. Other buildings and excavations of tallow vats and working parts of the mission are open to visitors. The mission grounds are open from 7 A.M. to 5 P.M. daily.

The legend of the swallows of San Juan Capistrano is known through stories, songs, and poems. Supposedly, the swallows return to their nests every year around St. Joseph's Day; actually, the majority of cliff swallows do return on March 19, but some of the group also arrive a little earlier or later. The swallows leave their mission nests for an unknown southern destination around October 23 (date of the death of the patron saint of the Mission, St. John of Capistrano).

The town's 1894 rail station is on the Amtrak line between Los Angeles and San Diego; both northbound and southbound trains stop here five times daily. Part of the depot is now a restaurant.

It is also a museum of railroad memorabilia. On the roofed loading platform you sit on old-time depot benches or on an old shoeshine stand while waiting for a table. A freight-weighting platform holds a combo at night. A caboose, boxcars, and a dining car now house shops and eating space.

Caspers Wilderness Park

Another bit of old California, this park is reached 7 miles in from San Juan through the lovely pastoral land beside the Ortega Highway (State Highway 74). Here the county has set aside a 5,500-acre former ranch as a wilderness preserve. You can picnic free beside the highway or in a meadow farther into the park for 50 cents, or you can camp for $2.

Caspers Park is a hiker's and horseback rider's park, with almost no development, including water—so bring your own. You walk beside the creek of Bell Canyon—which flows in winter—through grassy meadows, into oak and sycamore woodlands, up through chaparral to low ridges for a view of the mountains and the sea.

Tucker Wildbird Sanctuary

Just past the charming old town of Modjeska (named for the great actress who lived nearby) is a beautiful oasis of trees, flowers, plants, and wildlife, operated by California State University at Fullerton. You can walk along a lovely stream and listen to the birds sing. The sanctuary is open from 9 A.M. to 4 P.M. daily except Mondays; a small donation is requested for upkeep.

Getting into the back country is done by following narrow roads along gentle hillsides. The ride is best in spring.

PIGEONS PERCH *on fountain (left) at Mission San Juan Capistrano during their sojourn. No bars separate you from animals (below) at Lion Country Safari.*

BED & BREAKFAST—SOUTHERN CALIFORNIA STYLE

Bed and breakfast inns may not have originated in the Southland, but the area soon discovered their appeal and added unique touches to attract travelers. Some inns are just a stone's throw from beaches, some are located in historic homes or buildings, and others resemble intimate hotels. All offer breakfast; most provide wine or "high tea" upon guests' arrival. Flower-filled courtyards and fruit or plant-filled rooms remind vacationers that Southern California is a horticultural center.

Part of the small hostelries' charm is the opportunity to learn about the area from the host or other guests. It's a good way to exchange ideas on restaurants, modes of transportation, or "must sees." Inns seem to attract a compatible crowd.

A sampling of inns appears below. Plan to make reservations well in advance of your trip; some of the long-established hostelries are soon completely booked for summer weekends. For rates and additional information, write or call the inn directly.

Britt House, 406 Maple St., San Diego, CA 92103; (619) 234-2926: Beautifully restored Victorian; 8 rooms and cottage, each with distinctive decor; most share baths. Delicious afternoon tea; breakfast served in rooms or parlor. Parking is on the street; you'll need change for meters during the day.

Rock House, 410 15th St., Del Mar, CA 92014; (619) 481-3764: Turn-of-the-century house overlooking ocean was home, church, gambling parlor, and hotel; 8 rooms, 2 with private bath, 1 with fireplace. Breakfast in sunny dining room, afternoon wine tasting; nonsmokers only.

Carriage House, 1322 Catalina St., Laguna Beach, CA 92651; (714) 494-8945: Imaginatively furnished New Orleans-style colonial; 6 spacious suites with kitchens and baths; more suites on Spanish-style property a block away. Breakfast in Grandma Bean's Dining Room off lush courtyard; children and pets accepted.

Eiler's Inn, 741 S. Coast Highway, Laguna Beach, CA 92651; (714) 494-3004: Turning its back to busy highway, inn offers 11 small rooms and 1 suite (all with private baths) around central courtyard. Buffet breakfast, afternoon tea; sun deck; library.

The Old Seal Beach Inn, 212 Fifth St., Seal Beach, CA 90740; (213) 430-3915: Garden entrance sets tone for French Mediterranean ambience; 22 rooms with private bath (some with kitchens). Breakfast room; swimming pool; 1 block from ocean.

The Parsonage, 1600 Olive St., Santa Barbara, CA 93101; (805) 962-9336: Queen Anne Victorian originally built as parsonage for Trinity Episcopal Church in 1892; 5 rooms, 3 with shared baths; restored with period furnishings, original redwood interior; location between downtown and foothills offers panoramic views, convenient shopping, touring.

Valerio Manor, 111 West Valerio St., Santa Barbara, CA 93101; (805) 682-3199: 1904 Colonial-Federal house, once a boarding school, then a sorority; 5 rooms, one with private bath; parlor with fireplace. Croquet; pick-up service from train station, airport; bikes for rent.

The Bath Street Inn, 1720 Bath St., Santa Barbara, CA 93101; (805) 682-9680: Century-old Victorian blends near-downtown location with country inn feeling; 6 rooms on 3 floors, some with private baths. Free bikes; pick-up service.

The Glenborough Inn, 1327 Bath St., Santa Barbara, CA 93101; (805) 966-0589: Turn-of-the-century house (4 rooms, shared baths, fireplace, hot tub) and 1880s cottage (4 rooms, private baths, New Orleans-style garden). Evening wine in the parlor.

The Old Yacht Club Inn, 431 Corona Del Mar, Santa Barbara, CA 93103; (805) 962-1277: Built in 1912 as private residence, temporary yacht club in 1920s; 1½ blocks to beach; 5 rooms with shared baths. Big breakfast, dinner by arrangement; bike rentals.

Union Hotel, 362 Bell St., Los Alamos, CA 93440; (805) 344-2744: 1880s way station for stage route was destroyed by fire, rebuilt in 1915, then abandoned. Third incarnation open 3 days a week: 12 rooms, 2 with private baths; swimming pool; Victorian gazebo; hideaway spa; full breakfast.

The Rose Victorian Inn, 789 Valley Road, Arroyo Grande, CA 93420; (805) 481-5566: Lawn with arbor and gazebo surrounds former pioneer rancher's home; 9 rooms on 3 stories, 5 with private baths; restaurant, bar.

Heritage Inn Bed and Breakfast, 978 Olive St., San Luis Obispo, CA 93401; (805) 544-7440: Built in 1904 and twice relocated, one-time boarding house is city's longest-established bed and breakfast inn; 8 rooms with shared baths; bicycles available.

The Country House Inn, 91 Main St., Templeton, CA 93465; (805) 434-1598: Rambling, gracious 1886 home in placid town; 6 rooms with shared baths. Continental breakfast; convenient for wine touring.

Along the South Coast

Orange County's coast has two faces. The shore of the Los Angeles plain, as far south as the Balboa Peninsula, has the heaviest-use beaches. The more picturesque bluff coast begins at Corona del Mar, with a rocky shoreline dotted with small-coved beaches. This coast is the summer resort capital of Orange County, with most activity centering around the county's north end (on beaches that are not the most attractive part of the coastline).

Watch your driving along these beaches, for cars park wherever there's an available inch of space, and it's not uncommon to see a horizontal surfboard with legs attached dashing across the highway between bursts of traffic.

Terrible storms battered the coastline in early 1983, sweeping away beaches, destroying the Seal Beach pier, and rupturing Huntington Beach's pier. The sand has returned, though, and the piers will soon be repaired or replaced.

Seal Beach abuts the Los Angeles County line and is just south of Long Beach. Along the inland side of the highway, the coastal route from this point south almost to Huntington Beach bears the constant reminder of the oil industry—with operating pumps, refineries, and storage tanks. But modern technology has enabled the beach towns and parks to continue serving the populace with no greater inconvenience than a lingering odor of petroleum.

Seal Beach and Sunset Beach (just south of Seal Beach) are beach towns in the full sense of the word. The coast highway follows along just behind the rim of sand, lined on either side with refreshment stands and places offering any kind of beach gear for sale or rent. At Seal Beach, summertime surfing takes place early or late in the day between the pier and jetty areas.

Sunset Beach has a marina (reached from the coast highway) and an aquatic park (west on Edinger Avenue from Bolsa Chica Road), as well as a launching ramp and space for parking car trailers.

Bolsa Chica State Beach is 6 miles long, but only the northern end—a 3-mile-long strip between ocean and highway—is lined with sun-lovers in the summer and on warm weekends the year around. This part of the beach is an extension of the general shoreline, a 300 to 360-foot-wide strand of sand adjacent to the highway; it has fire rings (common to several beaches in this region), rest rooms, and lifeguards. Exclusively a day-use park, it closes at midnight.

At the southern end, steep cliffs between the road and the beach make access difficult. Some trails and one stairway near 16th Street penetrate the bluffs. A biking path and walkway extends the entire length of the beach. Clamming, diving, and fishing are popular here; grunion runs occur between March and August.

On the landward side of the highway across from the beach is Bolsa Chica Ecological Reserve, a series of spreading salt marshes that provide a landing site on the Pacific Flyway.

Huntington Beach

In 1901 Philip Stanton organized and helped settle a town site on the coast of Shell Beach. The new town,

---

ART FESTIVALS IN LAGUNA BEACH

Laguna Beach is a city created by artists. Attracted by her curving bay setting, one of the most picturesque sections of the Pacific Coast, they came to capture the magnificent, unspoiled beauty of the sea and land on canvas, and remained to form the nucleus of a town. From their first humble art shows has grown one of the oldest and most exciting spectacles in the state—the Festival of Arts and Pageant of Living Masters. Launched out of Depression desperation, the show now attracts some 300,000 spectators annually.

From mid-July to late August, the entire city is alive with art. In addition to the more famous exhibition, you can browse through two other art shows, all running simultaneously: Art-A-Fair, a traditional exhibit of arts and crafts, and the zany Sawdust Festival, an unstructured, unjuried, and uncensored art show.

The Festival of Arts and Pageant of Living Masters is an ambitious cultural festival.

From noon until 11:30 P.M. daily, visitors stroll through a tree-shaded park among booths displaying works by local artists in all media.

Children can take a fling at creativity in an art workshop—smocks, paints, and canvases are provided. A marionette show plays in a little theater. At 8:30 P.M. the Pageant of Living Masters begins. Masterpieces of painting, sculpture, and tapestry are re-created by living models in a 2-hour tableau. Staging, lighting, costumes, and commentary add to the effect.

So popular is this evening performance that tickets are sold out months in advance. You can get an application form for next year's show while you're there or write (several months in advance to be sure of tickets) to Festival of Arts, 650 Laguna Canyon Road, Laguna Beach, CA 92651. Prices include the admission fee to the grounds.

Parking is limited, so plan to arrive early. Park along Laguna Canyon Road or (for a fee) in a lot across the street from the grounds.

SECLUDED COVE *below bluff*
near Laguna Beach expands
when tide goes out, accommo-
dating both watcher and walker.

named Pacific City, was intended to rival Atlantic City on the East Coast. In 1902, Henry E. Huntington of Pacific Electric Railway bought a controlling interest in the project and renamed the community.

The beach is famous today, but not for the same reasons as its East Coast counterpart. To intrepid surfers world-wide, it's "the capital"—home of the summer international surfing competition—where they can tackle some of the greatest combers along the coast. Most of the surfing activity centers around the Huntington Pier site (at the foot of Main Street). If you want to get a good look at man and board, come early in the morning or later in the evening (after the swimmers and sunbathers have gone).

You won't be alone, even on a foggy morning, for here flock the fishermen, outfitted with folding stools, tackle boxes, and lunch sacks, to settle in for a long peaceful day. When the weather is less calm, a good place to fish is at the flood control levee of the Santa Ana River. A trail along the riverbank ultimately ends at Yorba Linda, many miles inland.

The state beach, stretching for 2 miles south of the pier, is spectacular on summer nights, when its 500 fire rings are ablaze with bonfires.

Newport Beach and Balboa

The opulent homes, handsome yacht clubs, and mast-studded harbor you see here would appear to have little connection with Newport's salty past, when the town was literally a "new port" between San Diego and San Pedro. Yet some of its original character still remains, or is being recultivated, if you look carefully.

In 1863, Captain S. S. Dunnels pushed the sidewheeler *Vaquero* past the mud flats into the harbor at the mouth of the Santa Ana River, unloaded lumber from San Diego, and picked up a cargo of produce from the inland fields, marking the beginning of a prosperous trading era. James and Robert McFadden bought that boat and landing in 1888, contracted for another steamer, built a long wharf on Newport Bay, and laid out a town. This was the beginning of Newport Beach.

Balboa Peninsula no longer boasts of sidewheelers, but thousands of boats still use the harbor. Pleasure craft of every description are anchored in channels dredged from former flats on land created by the dredging and planted with homes. It's the biggest yachting harbor on this section of the coast, berthing some 8,000 boats. Whatever land is left sells by the square foot—perhaps one of the reasons this area is called the Gold Coast.

Most of the tangible glimpses of yesteryear are on Balboa Peninsula (on the ocean side of Newport), a long skinny sandspit stretching out to sea, the tip of which is called Balboa.

If you turn south on Via Lido at the north end of the peninsula, you cross a humpbacked bridge leading to Lido Isle, a posh residential area dredged up from the harbor's bottom. Almost every waterfront home has a boat at its back door.

For a new look in shopping centers, start at Lido Village, a cluster of former apartments transformed into a labyrinth of shops and patios against the seawall. This is one of the more unusual cityscapes in California:

street and sidewalks are paved in brick and are outfitted with street lamps, trees, bedded and hanging flowers, benches, and bike racks. Fountains grace the walkways. It takes some looking, upstairs and down, to find the more than 75 shops, ranging in scope from a yacht dealer to boutiques specializing in intimate apparel.

On the peninsula is the site of McFadden's Pier (west of the intersection of Balboa and Newport boulevards). The original pier was destroyed by fire and rebuilt as a fishing spot with tackle shops at its foot. But many buildings around the area date back to the original waterfront days and are now being restored as Cannery Village, a charming conglomeration of boutiques, restaurants, boatyards, and antique shops. One cleverly converted warehouse, The Factory, has over 30 tiny shops under one roof.

The dory fleet which works from the beach adjoining the pier is the last of its kind on the West Coast. Each day at dawn, fishermen shove off in their small wooden boats, working alone 5 to 10 miles out to sea to set trawl lines with thousands of baited hooks for rockfish, halibut, mackerel, flounder, sea trout, and sand dabs. With luck, the fishermen head for shore by midmorning, helping one another through the surf onto the beach, where the area quickly turns into one large, open-air fish market. To the delight of camera-clicking customers, this picturesque fleet has now been designated an historic landmark.

The Newport beach, extending 5¼ miles, is narrow at the northwestern edge and broadens farther south and east. There are fire rings near Balboa Pier, farther out on the peninsula. The largest parking areas are at Palm and Balboa boulevards and at 26th Street. Surfing is popular in the morning in the Newport Pier area, in late afternoon from 30th Street west, and all day at the mouth of the Santa Ana River.

The peninsula's jetties supposedly tamed what was once considered some of California's best surf. But a rock extension of the jetty created a phenomenon called The Wedge, where large breakers are further amplified into a maelstrom. Expert body surfers challenge the waves even during the winter.

Balboa Pavilion, focal point for the Newport Beach playground area for over three-quarters of a century, once was the terminus of the big red streetcar line, Pacific Electric, from Los Angeles. It also served as a bath and boathouse for stylish bathers in ankle-length bathing togs. Since then, the venerable pavilion, with its much-photographed cupola, has been the scene of many "firsts," including the first Surfboard Riding Championship Races in the U.S. in 1932. The Tournament of Lights yachting celebration, held in December, began here in 1908.

When the Big Band sounds echoed across the nation in the 1940s, the pavilion resounded to thousands of dancing feet as the Balboa Peninsula became known as the place that gave birth to a dance that swept the nation—the Balboa Hop.

Recently redecorated, the pavilion still preserves its original 1905 look. It has a restaurant, gift shop, and banquet room; it also serves as headquarters for fishing charters, whale-watching cruises, and harbor excursions, and as the Newport terminal for Catalina tours. At a nearby dock, you can rent all types of water craft.

Harbor cruises are perhaps the best way to see Newport Bay. You won't get a look at all of Newport's 13 square miles (2 of which are underwater), but you will see its small islands and blufftop subdivisions. Harbor cruises leave from the "Fun Zone Dock" near the ferry landing—about 20 daily in the summer, fewer on weekends the rest of the year. On a 45-minute narrated cruise (moderate charge for adults and children), you'll see waterfront homes of motion picture and television stars and many of the boats berthed in the area. For a 4-hour evening cocktail cruise, complete with dancing and live entertainment, you'll pay a bit more.

Balboa Ferry has little three-car ferries (the last on the southern coast) which have been transporting residents and vacationers between the peninsula and Balboa Island since 1919 (45 cents for cars, 15 cents for walk-on passengers). Instituted by a petition signed by the entire island population (then 26 strong), the ferries are still the most interesting way to get to Balboa Island, connected now by a two-lane bridge and road from the coast highway.

Balboa Island has an artsy-craftsy shopping center with a European flavor crunched into about 3 short blocks. Parking is almost impossible on summer weekends. For exploring, your best bet is to park on one of the side streets lined with small wooden houses, and walk. A bayfront boardwalk circles the island, offering fine views of the harbor.

Just across the bridge separating the upper and lower harbor is the *Reuben E. Lee*, replica of an old-time riverboat, now a three-deck, floating restaurant.

Newport Center

Overlooking the ocean and bay to the south is Newport Center (on Irvine land)—a vast shopping, business, professional, and financial complex. Fashion Island, one of the largest and most tastefully designed shopping centers in the West, features interrelated malls and plazas, one equipped especially for children.

But the big thing is the stores. Designers are deserting Beverly Hills and Pasadena in favor of high fashion for the Newport-Irvine-Laguna crowd. First Bullock's Wilshire swept onto Fashion Island with higher price tags than those normally seen in these beach towns.

The newest addition is California's first Neiman-Marcus. The store's design, a modernistic tri-level, is supposed to fill the shoppers with "a sense of euphoria and well-being," according to the founder's son.

In addition to stores, there are fine restaurants and the Newport Harbor Art Museum (open Tuesday through Sunday; patio lunch served weekdays only).

Upper Newport Bay

Just south of the bridge crossing, the upper bay arm on the east side of the coast highway has a park within a bay. A commercial enterprise called Newport Dunes Aquatic Park, it offers numerous ways of getting out on the quiet, warm waters of the 15-acre lagoon. For a small entry fee, you can use the beach, dressing rooms, playground, wading pool, fire rings, and launching ramp.

You can also rent paddleboards, kayaks, sea cycles, and sailboats. The park is an attractive overnight camping spot for trailers and campers.

For a real surprise in the midst of all the resort hubbub, take Backbay Drive, off Jamboree Boulevard. It leads you along the east shore of Upper Newport Bay—a vast estuary scarcely touched by man and nearly invisible except from here because it is surrounded by bluffs. It is islands and channel at low tide, a minisea at high tide. There are always birds in action, but in fall it swarms with ducks, geese, and other users of the Pacific Flyway. The area is a wildlife preserve. Guided tours take place on Saturday during the winter.

Water sports enthusiasts have to do their water-skiing on the ocean; speedboats are not allowed on Upper Newport Bay.

Corona del Mar State Beach

Corona's state beach, just south of the breakwater, is operated by the city of Newport Beach. Wide and sandy with palm trees, its ½-mile total frontage is divided into two parts. Big Corona is at the east jetty; Little Corona is around the point to the east. The beach is very popular all year; there's a charge for parking. To get there, turn west off the coast highway on any of the streets named for flowers in Corona del Mar between Orchid and Iris.

Look for attractive shops and restaurants along the coast highway in Corona del Mar. Sherman Garden and Library, at 2647 E. Coast Highway, makes an interesting stop for horticultural enthusiasts and for photo buffs. The gardens are open daily; there's an admission charge. Plant lovers will also enjoy nearby Roger's Gardens, which contain 7½ acres of plants.

Development is taking place on the hills to the east of the highway, and your view to the sea is often blocked by exclusive residential development. The topography changes from low, lagoon-backed seashores to a continuing rank of steep bluffs. Irvine Ranch properties account for a considerable stretch of empty shore between Corona del Mar and Laguna Beach, the next town south.

Laguna Beach offers more than sand

Long known as an art colony, Laguna Beach is now a city aware of its French Riviera setting, as well as its problems. Not the least of these is traffic. To follow the coast highway through town on a summer weekend is to experience an interminable series of starts and stops. There are a number of stores where you'll want to pause and take a look.

Painters' galleries are numerous throughout the town. An art lover's first stop might be at the Laguna Beach Museum of Art, 307 Cliff Drive. Open Tuesday through Sunday from 11:30 A.M. to 4:30 P.M., it features an ever-changing variety of media.

The ceramics industry was pioneered here, and many other types of crafts now compete for space with galleries. Often you can watch artisans creating handcrafted pottery, jewelry, clothing, leather goods, rugs, or other articles.

Remote and inaccessible, Laguna Beach was discovered in the 1890s. First-comers built summer homes on the hills, which were followed by more pretentious residences. The colony's boutiques, galleries, little theaters, and coffee houses that sprang up were popular long before Greenwich Village began attracting attention.

Unlike many beach resorts which hibernate during the winter, Laguna holds a Winter Festival in February and March, a May Faire, as well as its famous Festival of Arts and Pageant of the Masters in the summer (see page 57). Since 1932, thousands have gathered annually to see the local residents don costumes and become living pictures. So professional is the performance that it's hard for visitors to believe these "paintings" are really alive.

Laguna has increased its stretch of public beach. Use was formerly limited by the scarcity of street parking. The main beach is along the coast highway in the center of town; it has become a beguiling "window to the sea" park, now that a number of buildings that blocked it have been torn down. To the north are Crescent Bay; Divers Cove, and Heisler Park (with bluff-top fire rings and picnic tables); to the south are pocket beaches such as Woods Cove and Victoria Beach. Surfers and scuba divers are active early in the morning.

In South Laguna is Aliso Beach Park, a ¾-mile frontage with lifeguards, a few fire rings, and a handsome fishing pier. Adjacent Camel Point and West Street pocket beaches have similar small frontages.

Dana Point

Once a cliff over which cowhides were thrown to waiting traders (see references to Point San Juan in Richard Henry Dana's *Two Years Before the Mast*), Dana Point subsequently became a lonely cove frequented by abalone hunters, a park, and now the site of a luxurious marina with accommodations for over 2,000 boats. You can rent one for the day to explore the harbor area.

A manmade harbor created a vast marina, divided into east and west basins, with some 2,500 slips. Encircling the marina are three yacht clubs, a great variety of boating services, docks for sportfishing excursions, several dozen specialty shops at Mariners Village and Dana Wharf, numerous restaurants, and a motel.

At the end of Del Obispo Street, the Orange County Marine Institute offers excursions, sailing lessons, and overnight adventures for children aboard a replica of Dana's ship. You'll find aquariums, marine exhibits, art work with a nautical theme, and a pond where you can touch tidepool creatures. The free museum is open daily except Sunday.

Several miles of paved pathways are popular among roller skaters (rentals are available), and grassy picnic spots dot the areas off Del Obispo Street and Dana Drive. But one of the most popular amusements is simply boat watching. Many Newport-based boats sail down the coast for lunch; you'll see some fancy deck picnics as you walk along the piers.

A trio of beaches

These last three Orange County beaches are good for swimming, and camping is also allowed.

Doheny State Beach is next door to Dana Point. Popular and crowded, Doheny offers camping combined with a safe beach and good surfing. The lagoon on San Juan Creek at the north end of the park is a wild bird habitat. Surf fishing (once better than it is now) and a fair grunion run are attractions.

The park is near the junction of State Highway 1 and I-5 at Capistrano Beach in Dana Point.

San Clemente State Beach is really a dual-purpose park, similar to Doheny. Campsites perch on the edge of a bluff, shaded and separated with mature trees and shrubs. Because the beach is extremely popular, camping reservations are important. For information, write to Pendleton Coast Area Office, 3030 Avenida del Presidente, San Clemente, CA 92672.

Well-established footpaths lead from the cliffs to the beaches below; don't stray off the trails, for the bluffs are crumbly. Swimming is good (lifeguards are on duty), but watch for occasional riptides.

San Onofre State Beach (formerly part of the Camp Pendleton Marine Corps base) was opened for public use in 1971. The beach is not visible from I-5. Take the Basilone Road exit off the highway and follow signs past the nuclear power plant. Campers and trailers occupy the by-passed old coast highway, and three trails lead about ¼ mile down to a usually broad beach.

From Orange County to San Diego

Three routes lead through Orange County to San Diego. All have their advantages. Your choice is determined by your time.

The coast highway. Driving the Pacific Coast Highway takes you by all the beaches and shoreside cities mentioned in the South Coast section. It's a pleasant drive, but if you are in a hurry to get through Orange County to San Diego, or if you wish to avoid the summertime beach crowds, it would be easier to take Interstate 5 (Santa Ana Freeway) or Interstate 405 (San Diego Freeway) to its junction with I-5.

The freeways. These routes take you through Orange County's largest cities, but you won't see many attractions unless you get off. To reach most of the county's main diversions, the freeways are the easiest approach. Most directions to attractions are given in terms of freeway offramps.

The Santa Ana Freeway divides the county in two, with most of the inland points of interest located on nearby main streets. The San Diego Freeway more closely parallels the coast highway, joining I-5 before it heads south to San Juan Capistrano.

The back roads. Still another way to head south through Orange County toward San Diego is on the back country roads. Much of the southeastern part of Orange County is still undeveloped, and meandering roads lead through canyons, over hills, and beside lakes. At times the only companions you'll meet along the route are some uninterested cows.

Eventually to head south you will have to join one of the canyon roads leading toward the freeway. Many of the back country routes end abruptly. Unless you are out for a jaunt, not caring too much about where or when you'll end up, be sure you have a good map of the county with you. Automobile clubs, the Anaheim Area Visitors and Convention Bureau, and Thomas Bros. have the best maps.

San Diego

An illustrious past, a scene-stealing setting, and historic and aquatic parks lure visitors to San Diego. Up the coast lie beach cities, an oceanside racetrack, a rare pine preserve; inland roads lead to Palomar Observatory, an unusual wild animal park, Indian camping grounds, and century-old mining villages. To the south, sample Old Mexico, right across the border.

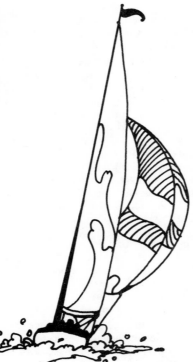

San Diego is constantly changing and consistently charming. At first glance, the city's modern facade belies its old age. But California's oldest town is ever mindful of her rich Spanish-Mexican heritage. Monuments report it and buildings preserve it. A legacy of Spanish place names, graceful architecture, and a relaxed life style reflect San Diego's pride in her past.

California's history began here when Juan Rodriguez Cabrillo landed at Point Loma in 1542. Sixty years later, Sebastian Vizcaino also reached the bay he named San Diego. But the West Coast's first settlement was not established until 1769, when Father Junipero Serra, a member of Portola's expedition, founded Mission San Diego de Alcala on Presidio Hill. The village that grew up around the mission became the anchor point for Spanish domain in California and a terminal point of the famous El Camino Real (the King's Highway), now U.S. Highway 101.

Thanks to a splendid natural setting, an equable climate, and early city planning, this once sleepy little seaside community is now the third largest city on the Pacific Coast. Constant sea breezes keep the air clear and fresh. An average temperature of 70°F. and a low humidity level make San Diego an all-year vacation city.

Water-oriented San Diego also owes her growth to a great harbor. Vast, natural, and almost landlocked, San Diego Harbor is one of the world's best deepwater anchorages. Host to ships from all ports, it is also home of the 11th Fleet, the U.S. Navy's largest.

Up the coast are gems of seaside villages, colorful flower fields, and wide, sandy beaches. The interior, or back country, holds a wealth of surprises, ranging from San Diego's impressive Wild Animal Park to the old-fashioned mountain mining village of Julian.

Across the border lies the fascination of another country—Mexico. This chapter takes a look at several Mexican towns, only a convenient drive from San Diego.

Entertainment. San Diego offers plenty to see and do. Many inexpensive recreational activities are easily accessible; some of the finest attractions are free. San Diego County claims more good public bathing beaches (70 miles) than the rest of California. Boating centers around the harbor and Mission Bay to the north. In the heart of the city are Old Town (the original village) and Balboa Park, location of the San Diego Zoo—one of the largest collections of wild animals in the world.

A sports center, San Diego has major league football, baseball, and soccer, as well as a stadium and a sports arena. You can play tennis, soar, skin dive, deep-sea fish, or sail any time of the year. Golfers will find that one of the 66 courses will suit them to a tee.

Biking enthusiasts and joggers have a choice of several scenic routes marked by signs along the ocean and through the Presidio and Balboa Park. A new bike trail is under development south along San Diego Bay from the Naval Training Center estuary.

Moving around is easy in San Diego. The International Airport (Lindbergh Field) is near downtown; a network of freeways, ringing the city, can take you anywhere within minutes. In about 20 minutes, you've crossed the Southern California border into Mexico or driven up the coast to Del Mar. For the most part, hotels and motels are clustered around the San Diego harbor, Mission Bay,

SAN DIEGO SKYLINE *and bay boating provide exceptional views for landlubbers on manmade Harbor Island.*

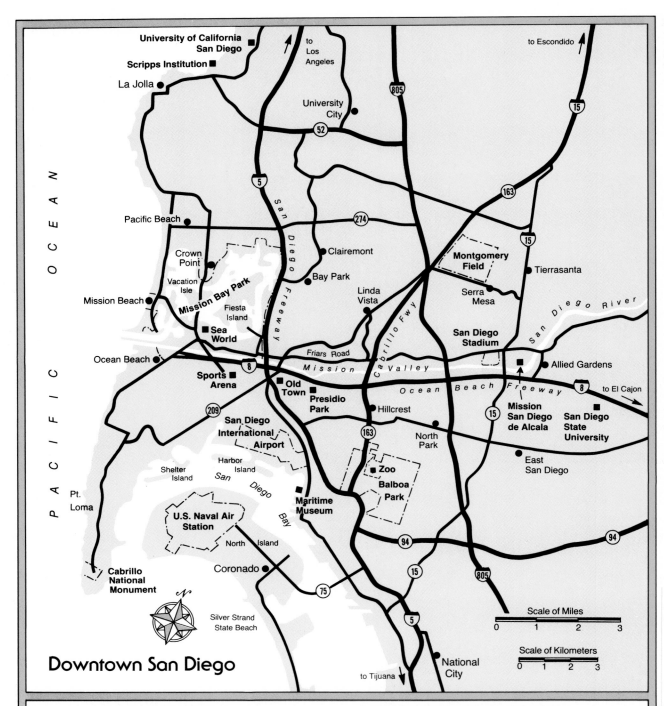

University of California San Diego ■

Scripps Institution ■

La Jolla ●

to Los Angeles →

to Escondido →

805

University City ●

52

5

163

15

PACIFIC OCEAN

Pacific Beach ●

Crown Point ●

Vacation Isle

Mission Bay Park

Fiesta Island

■ Sea World

Ocean Beach ●

Mission Beach ●

San Diego Freeway

274

Clairemont ●

Bay Park ●

Linda Vista ●

Montgomery Field

Tierrasanta ●

Serra Mesa ●

San Diego River

San Diego Stadium

Allied Gardens ●

Friars Road

Mission   Valley

Ocean   Beach   Freeway

8

to El Cajon →

Cabrillo Fwy

Sports Arena ■

8

■ Old Town

Presidio Park

Hillcrest ●

15

Mission San Diego de Alcala ■

San Diego State University ■

209

San Diego International Airport

163

North Park

East San Diego ●

Harbor Island

Shelter Island

San   Diego   Bay

■ Maritime Museum

■ Zoo

Balboa Park

Pt. Loma

U.S. Naval Air Station

North Island

94

94

Cabrillo National Monument

Coronado ●

75

15

805

N

5

Silver Strand State Beach

National City ●

to Tijuana ↓

Scale of Miles
0   1   2   3

Scale of Kilometers
0   1   2   3

Downtown San Diego

Major Points of Interest

Mission Bay Park — aquatic playground with vacation hotels, campgrounds, water sports

Sea World — aquatic shows, exhibits, rides, pearl divers, performing killer whales, shark exhibit

Old Town — State Historic Park offers views of yesteryear San Diego; restored adobes, shops

Harbor Island — manmade isle with hotels and restaurants; excellent harbor view

Shelter Island — glamorous restaurants in a pleasure boat harbor setting

Cabrillo National Monument — commemorates California's discovery; lighthouses, museum, major whale-watching point

Coronado — island setting for West's Victorian-style architectural wonder, Hotel del Coronado

Balboa Park — home for museums, galleries, theaters, San Diego Zoo

Mission San Diego de Alcala — oldest California mission

Mission Valley, and downtown. Close to major freeways, they are easy to locate. Campers will find a wide selection of sites; one campground will rent whatever you forget to bring—including the camper.

Visitors can receive specific information by writing to the San Diego Convention and Visitors Bureau, 1200 Third Avenue, Suite 824, San Diego, CA 92101.

Motorists can follow a 52-mile scenic drive all around town and the surrounding area. Just start anywhere and follow the road signs bearing a white sea gull.

The Tijuana Trolley connects downtown San Diego with the border town of Tijuana, Mexico. Trolleys depart several times an hour all day long from the Santa Fe Depot (Broadway and Kettner streets). The run to the border takes 35 minutes, including frequent stops (seven in downtown San Diego) for loading passengers. You'll need exact change: $1 for adults ($2 round trip), 40 cents for elderly and handicapped. Children under 6 years of age ride free. For information, call (619) 233-3004.

The Water World

San Diego should be viewed from the water. The beautiful harbor is a notable exception to the rule that waterfronts are necessarily ugly and conceal the fascination of great ships. San Diego's provides both visual and recreational amenities for people against a colorful backdrop of commercial and naval vessels. It offers parks where you may stroll and play, a pier and embankments for fishing, boat launching, a small beach, and places to watch the big ships go by or to take a closer look at yachts, tuna clippers, oceanographic crafts, and an antique sailing ship. And it offers thriving complexes of marinas, hotels, shops, and restaurants oriented to a water view.

Shops and restaurants built in Victorian and Spanish styles re-create the past in Seaport Village, a shopping complex at Pacific Highway and Harbor Drive. A turn-of-the-century carousel from Coney Island is a highlight amid the 14 acres of bayside browsing.

Harbor tours

The best way to get your bearings is on a harbor excursion. Both 1 and 2-hour cruises loop close along the shoreline, exposing a full range of air, surface, and undersea craft and harbor activity otherwise hidden from sight.

Boats leave from the well-marked dock on Harbor Drive at the foot of Broadway. In summer, short cruises leave at 45-minute intervals; 2-hour cruises leave twice daily weekdays, more often on weekends and holidays. For winter schedules and exact times of sailings, call (619) 233-6872. The brigantine *Rendezvous* also offers bay tours from Harbor Island; call (619) 223-4105 for information.

Embarcadero

North of the excursion boat dock is the former square-rigger *Star of India*, probably the oldest (1863) iron-hulled merchantman still afloat. Go aboard for a hint of sea life over a century ago. Now painstakingly restored, the ship is moored as part of a Maritime Museum Fleet. You can also visit two other ships in the fleet, the 1800s San Francisco ferryboat *Berkeley* and the vintage steam yacht *Medea*. The museum is open daily; admission is nominal.

Walk north to see some picturesque action on weekdays at the net yard on the seawall dock for long-range tuna clippers. You must stay outside the fence to watch the fishermen mending huge nets.

Don't miss Broadway Pier—San Diego's unique park-on-a-pier—where a lot of net handling takes place and sleek cruise ships are often berthed.

Sport fishers can board a deep-sea fishing charter from several points around the harbor and from Mission Bay. Many excursions fish the Mexican-owned Coronado Islands, 18 miles off the coast. You'll need a license and permit.

Waterfront dining is good along the Embarcadero. A new Mediterranean-style seafood complex offers visitors a choice of buying fresh fish to take home or dining on seafood delicacies.

Shelter Island and Harbor Island

Two manmade vacation "islands" in San Diego Bay accommodate boaters, sailors, sportsmen, and atmosphere-seekers. Though they once were mud and sandpiles built up by dredging operations in the bay, Shelter and Harbor islands are now attractive resort areas studded with forests of boat masts.

Shelter Island offers a fishing pier, attractive marinas, boat launching ramps, restaurants, and hotels. Tropical blooms, torches, and "Polynesian" architecture give the island a South Seas flavor. Winding paths provide good strolling, biking, and bay-watching sports. Friendship Bell is here, the gift of Yokohama, San Diego's sister city in Japan. Really a peninsula, Shelter Island is connected to Point Loma by a salty causeway.

Harbor Island, located opposite the San Diego International Airport, can be viewed from a peaceful vantage point in Spanish Landing Park on Harbor Drive. The island features high-rise hotels, restaurants (one a floating riverboat replica with a grand view), and marinas. On the western tip of the island, a Spanish-style building houses a combination lighthouse and restaurant.

The Navy

San Diego is home to the large 11th Naval District, as well as to many other military installations. Though no longer known primarily as a Navy town, San Diego is still influenced by the activities that the Navy brings.

Naval vessels moored at the Broadway Pier on Harbor Drive hold open house from 1 to 4 P.M. on weekends.

Both the Naval and Marine centers in San Diego present colorful, full-fledged military reviews every Friday. Parades begin at about 2:15 P.M. at the Naval Training Center and at 10 A.M. at the Marine Corps Recruiting Depot. Both centers are located off Pacific Highway; to reach them, drive southwest on Barnett Avenue and enter Gate 4.

Coronado

Coronado's relative isolation gives it the flavor of an island. Actually it's connected to the mainland by a long, scenic sand spit and a graceful bay bridge. Low guard rails on the sweeping span open up a panoramic view reaching from the San Diego skyline south into Mexico.

Hotel del Coronado. Coronado was a sterile, wind-blown peninsula, populated with jackrabbits, coyotes, and occasional wildcats, when Elisha Babcock and H. L. Story bought the 4,100 acres (including North Island) in 1885. Babcock's dream—to build a hotel that "would be the talk of the Western world"—came true in the form of the striking, red-roofed Hotel del Coronado, still operating as the focal point of this area and now a State and National Historic Landmark. Distinguished guests over the years have included United States presidents, Thomas A. Edison, Henry Ford, and Robert Todd Lincoln.

You can rent cassettes from the lobby shop and take a self-guiding tour of this Victorian-style wooden wonder, exploring the intricate corridors and cavernous rooms at the completely self-contained hotel.

Around the peninsula. Across from the hotel, a picturesque boathouse (now a restaurant, designed to match the Victorian architectural style of the hotel) sits at the edge of Glorietta Bay, a small boat harbor that contains a public launching ramp. Adjoining it are a municipal golf course and a public bathing beach (caution: watch for sting rays early in the season). Facing the bay, John D. Spreckels' former home, now the elegant Glorietta Bay Inn, hosts visitors. At the north end of the peninsula is the Naval Air Station, one of the oldest in existence. For a map of the island, stop by the Coronado Chamber of Commerce, 720 Orange Avenue.

Silver Strand State Beach. Millions of glittering seashells gave their name to this 5-mile-long ocean beach, one of America's finest day-use beaches. It stretches almost the full length of the sand spit connecting the tip of the peninsula to the mainland.

The sand is dotted with nearly 400 fire rings and picnic units; the parking lot has space for almost 2,000 cars, and the climate is almost always very good.

Pedestrian underpasses cross beneath State Highway 75 to the bay side, where there is quieter water, good for swimmers and water-skiers.

Point Loma

The high promontory that shelters San Diego Bay from the Pacific Ocean offers a great view of the harbor. On a clear day you can see from the mountains of Mexico to beyond the La Jolla mesa and from the sprawling city of San Diego to the Coronado Islands and out to sea.

Cabrillo National Monument. At the tip of Point Loma is Cabrillo National Monument, one of the smallest, most historic, and most visited monuments in this country (outdoing even the Statue of Liberty).

Cabrillo's statue, a gift from Portugal (homeland of the great navigator), faces his actual landing spot at Ballast Point. The nearby visitor center explains Cabrillo's discovery of San Diego Bay and the events following

it. A glassed-in observatory at the monument gives fine views of the whale migration that occurs each year from mid-December through mid-February. On the high bluff stands a well-preserved lighthouse; it was used from 1855 until 1891, when the waterside lighthouse (still in use) was built.

The monument has a nature trail, a surprisingly unique plant community, and some of the best tidepools left in Southern California (marine biologists invite you to look but not touch). The monument is open daily from 9 A.M. to 5:15 P.M. To reach it from San Diego, go southwest on Rosecrans Street and follow the signs; from Mission Bay, take Sunset Cliffs Boulevard to Catalina Boulevard.

To the tip. A drive through residential Point Loma takes you past the U.S. Navy reservation and through Fort Rosecrans.

A Look at the Past

In 1769, Father Serra chose a hill site overlooking the bay for a mission that would begin the settlement of California. A presidio was also built to protect the mission; this site is now called Presidio Hill. Soon a town began to sprout at the foot of the hill, with a plaza, a church, and the attractive tile-roofed, adobe homes of California's first families.

Spanish, Mexican, and American settlements thrived here; buildings and relics of these periods survive. Some have been restored or reconstructed with adobe bricks shaped at the same site which furnished the original bricks. Much of the restoration is within Old Town San Diego State Historic Park, an area of 6½ blocks bounded by Wallace, Congress, Twiggs, and Juan streets. Old Town is bordered by old residential areas and two modern freeways, Interstate Highways 5 and 8. Its streets are for strolling only.

Old Town

Old Town is no sterile museum display; many shops and restaurants are housed in the district's original buildings and patios. The shopping area, once confined mainly to Squibob Square on San Diego Avenue, has been extended by the addition of Old San Diego Square, at Juan and Harney streets, and Bazaar del Mundo (located in the famous Casa de Pico hacienda). At Bazaar del Mundo you can dine (the Mexican restaurant overlooks the garden), browse in high-quality shops, and mingle with shopping San Diegans. The multilevel Old San Diego Square complex offers much-needed underground parking. Squibob Square's wares are displayed in false-front stores.

Highlights. Walking is the best way to savor the historical flavor. Do it on your own—or take the free walking tour that departs at 2 P.M. every day from the Machado y Silvas Adobe across from the plaza.

Visitors will find the flavor of Old Town one of its fascinations: you can observe bread baking in the outdoor oven behind the Machado house on Saturday, as well as brick making, candle dipping, and wool spinning. You can also take a horse-and-buggy ride (for a

DAYS OF FATHER SERRA are recalled in museum (above) on Presidio Hill, site of first mission. You can take a buggy ride (left) among Old Town Historic Park's restored and reconstructed adobes.

slight fee). These are some of the Old Town sights you'll see.

• *El Campo Santo*, at San Diego and Linwood, is the easternmost landmark in Old Town. This adobe-walled, Mexican Catholic cemetery (1850-1880) was the final resting place for many founding fathers, as well as for a few bandits. It's hard to tell how many people are buried here because so many headstones are missing.

• *The Whaley House*, at the corner of San Diego and Harney, is the oldest brick structure in Southern California. The American-style mansion, the only one of its kind in San Diego, has served as a dairy, funeral parlor, theater, saloon, courthouse, and as the city's first Sunday school. It is reputed to be haunted. The restored house and premises, including such historical relics as a yellow streetcar, are open Wednesday through Sunday from 10 A.M. to 4:30 P.M.

• *The Derby-Pendleton House* (entered through the Whaley House) is perhaps the first prefabricated building in California. The New England-style home was shipped around Cape Horn and put together with wooden pegs. It is now a museum. Your admission fee to Whaley House includes this visit.

• *Chapel of Immaculate Conception*, at San Diego and Conde, was Old Town's first church, converted from an old adobe house and dedicated in 1858. Father Ubach was reputedly the inspiration for "Father Gaspara" of Helen Hunt Jackson's novel *Ramona*—he claimed to have known the characters in the story and their families.

• *Casa de Altamirano*, at San Diego and Twiggs, site of the first printing of the San Diego Union in 1868, is restored as an early day printing office. Originally a home, the building was used as a store before the newspaper was located there.

• *Casa de Pedrorena*, at San Diego between Twiggs and Mason, is a large, restored adobe that is now a popular Mexican restaurant with courtyard dining.

• *Casa de Estudillo*, east of San Diego on Mason, built of logs and rawhide on a lot granted by the governor, was the home of Captain Jose Estudillo, commandante of Monterey and San Diego. The first Spanish *casa* to be constructed on the plaza, it was robbed of roof tiles and reduced to ruin after the family abandoned it in 1881. Extensively restored, the house and garden afford a glimpse of how a comparatively wealthy rancher once lived.

• *Casa de Bandini*, at Mason and Calhoun, originally a one-story adobe, gained a second story when it became a stagecoach station in the 1860s. Built by wealthy Don Juan Bandini (known for his lavish fandangos and dinners), the house was Commodore Stockton's headquarters during the American occupation of California in 1846. Kit Carson also visited here. The adobe now houses a popular Mexican restaurant.

• *Plaza Vieja*, or San Diego Plaza, was the center of town. A comfortable and verdant stop for walkers today, it was once the noisy scene of bullfights and other entertainments. Among the lacy pepper, eucalyptus, and graceful palm trees stands the flagpole that has flown Spanish and Mexican flags for two centuries; the American flag was added in 1846.

• *Casa de Machado*, at San Diego between Wallace and Mason, was built in 1832 for a Spanish Army soldier and his wife. Scarcity of wood required use of adobe in most of the early homes, and here you can see some of the original adobe bricks, formed and placed by the good soldier Machado.

• *The Mason Street School*, west of San Diego on Mason, was the city's first public school building. When replaced, the quaint one-room schoolhouse became a tamale factory. Now restored, it displays mementos of the early San Diego school system.

• *The Machado-Stewart House*, on Congress between Wallace and Mason, was built by Jose Manuel Machado for his daughter, who married John C. Stewart, a shipmate of Richard Henry Dana. Dana described his 1859 visit to the house in *Two Years Before the Mast*. In contrast to the most elaborate Estudillo residence, this small clapboard adobe displays how a man of moderate means may have lived.

• *The Seeley Stable* and barns, at the corner of Juan and Twiggs, is another Old Town attraction. It's a replica of the stables of Albert Seeley, who operated a stagecoach line around 1869. The stable houses the Roscoe Hazard Museum; here, you can see a collection of horse-drawn vehicles and Western artifacts.

• *Casa de Lopez*, a longtime local favorite sometimes called Flynn's House of 10,000 Candles, is a State Historic Landmark at the deadend of Twiggs Street. Walk-through tours are conducted daily.

Heritage Park

In this historic park on the outskirts of Old Town (at Juan and Harney streets), a haven is being established for some of San Diego's oldest Victorians. Currently seven restored structures house shops, offices, and a restaurant.

Presidio Hill

Just five years after Father Junipero Serra and the Spanish soldiers set the Royal Standard, raised the cross, and dedicated the first mission in California, the site was already too small for the mission's growing members. Out of a need for fresh water and in order to be closer to Indian settlements, Mission San Diego was moved in 1774 from Presidio Hill 6 miles east up Mission Valley. The presidio and the old American garrison (Fort Stockton) have long been covered over. Their foundations are outlined in the grassy mounds on the hill. Diggings in the area are archeological excavations.

The birthplace of California is now the home of handsome Serra Museum, a Spanish Colonial structure; of lush Presidio Park; and of the Serra Cross. Made of bricks from Spanish ruins, the cross marks the site of the original mission chapel.

Standing prominently at the heart of the hill and gleaming white in the sun, the Serra Museum exhibits the area's history from mission days through pioneer times. The museum is open daily from 9 A.M. to 4:45 P.M. Monday through Saturday, noon to 4:45 P.M. Sunday.

Mission San Diego de Alcala

The San Diego Mission was the first in the long line of 21 missions built in Alta (upper) California.

The restoration of the "Mother of the Missions" retains the simple facade of the original mission and is characterized by a strikingly graceful campanile. Here you'll discover a museum containing original mission records in Father Serra's handwriting, a reconstructed Indian village, and olive trees from the mission's original grove. Recent restoration includes a visitor center with a mural depicting San Diego's history.

Sunday services are still held in the original chapel. The mission is open daily to the public. Tote-a-tapes for self-guided tours are available.

San Diego Mission is best reached by taking I-8 to Murphy Canyon Road; watch for mission exit signs.

Downtown San Diego

Once a collection of tattoo parlors, saloons, and pawn shops, downtown San Diego is gradually being restored and rebuilt. As the city's skyline grows upwards, restaurants are being opened atop skyscrapers to take advantage of the view.

Although many large stores have been moved to Mission Valley, the stores, streets, and parks of the central part of the city are being cleaned up, and new pedestrian malls are being created.

Walking in downtown San Diego is the best way to get the feeling of this changing city. Central City Association, at 631 Home Tower Building (Broadway at 7th) offers a free pictorial map.

Horton Plaza (bounded by 3rd, 4th, Broadway, and E streets) is a good place to begin your tour. A green oasis, it is home for open-air art shows, soapbox orators, and people-watchers. A visitor information booth, open during the day, provides information about the area.

The Gaslamp Quarter, a 16-block restoration (bounded by Fourth and Sixth and Broadway and the harbor), is worth a look. You can join free walking tours Fridays at noon and Saturdays at 10 A.M. and 1 P.M. Tours depart from the Gaslamp Quarter Council, 625 Fifth Avenue. Shops, galleries, restaurants, and a theater have moved into the aptly named renovated area, but you'll still find traces of its sleazy past. Four "beat cops," costumed in 1890s dress, patrol the area as goodwill ambassadors.

The Charles C. Dail Concourse (formerly Community Concourse) is the center of downtown. Covering more than a full city block (bounded by A and C and First and Third streets), it includes a Convention and Performing Arts Center, as well as the City Administration Building. The 3,000-seat Civic Theatre is home for the San Diego Symphony, San Diego Opera Company, and city and state ballet companies. A huge parking facility tops the concourse.

Little America Westgate Hotel, at 2nd and C streets, is one of the world's leading hotels and one of the very few new ones to be built in the heart of a city. A true luxury hotel, it's full of "wasted" space and such "wasteful" appurtenances as Aubusson tapestries, Baccarat crystal chandeliers, and famous paintings. The lobby is a re-creation of an anteroom at Versailles.

The San Diego Public Library, at the corner of 8th and E streets, is one of the most modern and well-stocked

THE SPA SITUATION

You don't have to worry about gaining weight on at least one kind of San Diego vacation. Because of its mild climate, this area has more than its share of health spas, often referred to as "fat farms."

Spas come in all sizes and shapes—from glamorous resorts to more modest settings. Those listed below are only a sampling of what's available in the area. But don't expect to just drop in for a week or a weekend—you need advance reservations.

According to the dictionary, a spa means "any locality frequented for its mineral springs," and at the modest Hotel Jacumba, in San Diego's back country, people still come to "take the waters." Carlsbad, up the coast, built its early reputation around the similarity of its mineral spring to the waters in Karlsbad, Germany.

Couples frequent Fallbrook's Pala Mesa Spa, an attractive secluded oasis about a mile from a lodge and 18-hole championship golf course. Women check in for a full spa program (exercise, water workouts, and salon service) from 8 A.M. to 5 P.M. daily while men enjoy golf and tennis at the clubhouse. They overnight at the lodge, with separate menus for spa guests and spouses.

The Golden Door in Escondido is frankly for the wealthy and not *too* lumpy. This women-only retreat is decorated in Japanese chic. According to patrons, the mini-meals are worth the very high price of the visit.

Rancho La Puerta, across the border in Tecate, is an earlier, earthier version of the Golden Door. Largest health resort in North America, it exudes a homey atmosphere among 600 acres of unspoiled Mexican countryside. This is one place for the entire family. Hiking, pool activities, yoga, and a vegetarian cuisine highlight the stay.

At elegant Rancho La Costa, up the coast, you'll find a complete spa plus plush extras. Men make up much of the clientele. People not on the spa program also come here to enjoy the 25 tennis courts, dancing, and nightly entertainment. Not too private, it has an atmosphere that at times resembles a large convention. It's a frequent stop for sightseeing buses.

LAGOON REFLECTS arcade and towers of 1915 exposition building in Balboa Park.

libraries in the country. It's open daily except Sunday. Its collection goes back 4,000 years to Sumerian cuneiform tablets (though you can't withdraw them on your library card).

The Firehouse Museum, at 1572 Columbia Street, reveals a glittering array of major pieces of firefighting equipment. You'll even find such oddities as a notorious New York false-alarm box. You can visit the museum on Saturdays from 10 A.M. to 4 P.M. Admission is free.

Villa Montezuma, considered one of the city's finest Victorian mansions, has been partially renovated and refurbished; it's open for public tours from 1 to 4:30 P.M. daily except Monday and Saturday. Located at 1925 K Street, the restored Victorian displays collections of photographs and clothes of the era.

Two Great Parks

Two of the city's most outstanding attractions are examples of careful planning and foresight. Balboa Park, conceived in the 1880s, and Mission Bay Aquatic Park, developed a century later, are destinations for millions of tourists yearly.

Balboa Park

The park came first. Then the city was built around it. Transformed from rattlesnake-infested, hilly chaparral to a public garden with sky-high eucalyptus trees, lush tropical plants, and Mexican Churrigueresque buildings—this is century-old Balboa Park, one of the nation's greatest. Avenues curving through verdant foliage and grassy fields take you to almost any recreational or cultural activity you might seek: art galleries, science and natural history museums, an innovative space theater, the world's largest zoo, a merry-go-round, a picnic grove, and a golf course.

How it began. Optimism and foresight helped shape Balboa Park. In 1868, the city fathers set aside 1,400 acres (nine large lots at a time when the city had only 915 houses) "to be forever a public park." For 20 years the unimproved land supported a dog pound, a trash dump, and a gravel pit until horticulturist Kate Sessions set up a nursery on a few acres in exchange for doing a considerable planting in other areas of the park. By 1910, community planning and action had formed a park.

Two world's fairs added the massive and ornate structures for which the park is known. The 1915 Panama-California International Exposition, commemorating the completion of the Panama Canal, attracted 3 million visitors and is survived by the attractive Cabrillo Bridge (through which most out-of-town visitors enter the park) and much of the cultural center along the Prado area, still the park's center of activity. The Spreckels Pavilion contains the world's largest outdoor organ. Donated in 1915, it has provided Sunday recitals ever since. Built as the only permanent structure of this fair, the unique California Building (home of the Museum of Man), with its familiar Spanish-Renaissance tower rising above the treetops and its ornamental facade depicting California history, has become the symbol of the city of San Diego. Its openwork tiers contain a carillon that proclaims the hour and enlivens the area with a daily noontime concert.

In 1935, the California-Pacific International Exposition contributed a series of structures representative of Southwest history. Added then were the building complex south of the Prado known as the Palisades area, the Old Globe Theatre, and the Spanish Village.

Getting in and around. Four million visitors a year sample the attractions at Balboa Park, and countless more stroll the beautiful paths and picnic in special groves or on the lawns. You can spend an active or a leisurely day here. Walking is the best way to enjoy the lovely park, since the latest phase of development has now closed half of the Prado to cars during the day, creating a pedestrian promenade. The Prado is located east of the central plaza in front of the Fine Arts Gallery.

Scattered through the broad mesa tops and canyons are plenty of recreation spots for golf and tennis, field and target archery, baseball, roque, lawn bowling, shuffleboard, horseshoes, and badminton.

You enter Balboa Park from either 6th Avenue and Laurel Street or Park Boulevard and El Prado. There are big parking lots in the Palisades area, at the zoo, and along Park Boulevard.

Highlights. On the plaza along El Prado, the House of Hospitality has free maps and information on the park. These are some of the major attractions:
• *The Museum of Man,* a must for anthropology buffs, is known for its research on the Indian cultures of the Americas. It includes an exhibit of mummies and offers demonstrations of historical crafts. The museum is open daily from 10 A.M. to 4:30 P.M.; there's a small admission charge.
• *The Old Globe Theatre,* in a grove behind the California Building, was built for Shakespearean productions. Destroyed by fire in 1978, it was rebuilt in 1982 and is now part of a complex of three interconnected stages known as the Simon Edison Centre for Performing Arts. The complex also includes the outdoor Festival Stage, home for the annual summer Shakespeare Festival (mid-June to September), and the intimate Cassius Carter Centre Stage.
• *The San Diego Museum of Art* collection spans the ages—from early Asian art to 20th century pieces (on display in the west wing). There's also a small sculpture court and garden. You'll discover a fine collection of old masters and a special gallery for American artists. Located on the north side of the plaza, the museum is open Tuesday through Sunday from 10 A.M. to 5 P.M. You'll pay an admission charge.

The adjacent Timken Art Gallery houses a collection of American and European art, including a large number of Russian icons. It's open from 10 A.M. to 4:30 P.M. Tuesday through Saturday, and on Sunday from 1:30 P.M. to 4:30 P.M. Admission is free.
• *The Aerospace Museum* greets visitors with a replica of "The Spirit of St. Louis," Lindbergh's famous plane. Its exhibits cover the whole history of flight, from gliders to space capsules. The Hall of Fame salutes aviation pioneers. Open daily from 10 A.M. to 4:30 P.M., the museum charges admission.

• *Casa del Prado* (next to the Botanical Building), a complex of buildings, arcades, and courtyards, in 1971 replaced the decrepit Food and Beverage Building from the 1915 exposition. Casts of existing plaster ornamentation on the building were made for reproduction in permanent materials.

• *The Natural History Museum* has something for all kinds of explorers. Extensive exhibits and a large research library fascinate visitors, and bimonthly nature walks attract adventurers. Ask at the museum for a self-guided horticultural walk around the Prado. This museum on the Southern California environment is open from 10 A.M. to 4:30 P.M. daily.

• *The Reuben H. Fleet Space Theater and Science Center* is a new addition. In the theater, the screen is a tilted hemisphere; image and sound surround you. Not confined to showing the sky as seen from earth, the theater's microprocessor-controlled system of more than 80 projectors takes you into space, past planets, in view of stars changing configuration as you move. In the adjoining science center, you operate ingenious gadgets demonstrating principles of sensory perception. Listen to your heartbeat; look at the inside of your eye; create pop art with a harmonograph; or match wits with a computerized teaching machine. The center is open daily from 9:45 A.M. to 5 P.M. and 7 to 9:30 P.M. daily during the winter; 9:45 A.M. to 10 P.M. in summer. Showtimes vary; call (619) 238-1168 for a schedule.

• *San Diego Zoo* is extraordinary. Here one of the world's largest collections of wild animals lives in surroundings as natural as man can provide. Lions roam freely behind good-sized moats, and exotic birds fly free in a tropical rain forest. You may even see a guinea fowl strutting independently on the walk, helping to hold down the insect population. This manmade jungle holds some of the rarest animals in the world.

High above the zoo canyons, an aerial tramway called Skyfari whisks you on an exciting ride over the grottos and mesas that are home for the animals in this cageless zoo. The Skyfari leaves near the zoo entrance over a lagoon colored by Chilean flamingos and black swans, rises over the nearby seal show (free performances are held in the afternoon), and travels above the active and popular residents of the Great Ape Grottos in Monkey Mesa. When you're not looking closely at animal activity beneath you, you can enjoy a spectacular overview of Balboa Park.

The orange gondolas reach their highest point of 170 feet over Stock and Crane Canyon and terminate at Horn and Hoof Mesa, where inhabitants include antelope, bison, kangaroos, and wallabies. If you do not choose to make the return trip immediately, you can disembark here and tour the western end of the zoo before returning by tramway or walking back.

On the ground, you can see the 128-acre zoo on a guided tour bus that takes in 3½ miles in 40 minutes, including areas not easily reached by walking. You can save steps and time this way, planning where you'd like to revisit and also catching a performance by stage-struck bears or other animals that are cued by your guide.

The zoo is open all year, from 9 A.M. to dusk. Deluxe admission packages include entrance to the zoo, guided bus tour, round-trip Skyfari ride, and admission to the Children's Zoo.

• *The Children's Zoo,* a wonderful zoo within a zoo, puts the four-year-old nose to nose with the animal kingdom's younger members. Benches and drinking fountains are also appropriately scaled down. Garden paths wind through an aviary in which tiny, colorful finches fly overhead and perch in nearby branches and birdhouses, past swimming turtles, to the baby elephants begging peanuts. A cuddly but lazy koala sleeps in the V of a tree, a tolerant Galapagos tortoise offers a ride on his great hulking shell, and friendly little deer and barnyard animals come to be petted and fed by their equally friendly little visitors. One of the most delightful attractions is the small hatchery where you can watch baby chicks peck out of their shells. If you wish, you may hold some of the fluffy yellow newborns in your hands. Another treat is the nursery for baby animals unable to be cared for by their mothers. Here you're likely to see diapered infant chimps and orangutans romping in playpens with their toys, anticipating the bottle of milk administered by nurse attendants. Signs identify the "babies" by name and give their birth dates, weights, and feeding schedules.

Mission Bay Aquatic Park

Mission Bay, now a beautiful aquatic playground right on the edge of downtown San Diego, was once a vast and productive estuary, home for resident waterfowl, resting place for migratory birds, and nursery for fish and other sea creatures. Originally named "False Bay" when Cabrillo mistook it for San Diego Bay, it degenerated into a silt and trash collector, popular as a fishing hole for those who could brave the mosquitoes, until community action finally transformed it into one of the most beautiful resort areas on the coast.

Twenty years of dredging and development have created a maze of islands and lagoons, 27 miles of beaches, free public boat-launching ramps, picnic areas, campgrounds and trailer park, children's playgrounds, golf courses, a marine park, and miles of beautifully landscaped, grass-covered coves.

Hotels and campgrounds. The hotels of Mission Bay are worth seeing for their unusual architectural qualities, as well as for their location. Many have now gone high-rise to take advantage of the view. Vacation Village makes extensive use of streams and lagoons for landscaping. Mission Bay Visitor Information Center, just off I-5 at East Mission Bay Drive, provides information on hotels and maps of the park. Reservations are a "must" during peak summer months and three-day holiday weekends.

Vacationers who like to "rough it" can easily settle in at Campland, on the north shore of the bay by way of Olney Street. Here resort-equipped campsites rent for $20 and up a night (prices are highest in summer). Nearby are a parking area for boats, a swimming beach, and complete rental facilities—for everything from campers and bedding to boats and skis. To reserve a site, write Campland on the Bay, 2211 Pacific Beach Drive, San Diego, CA 92109; or call (619) 274-6260.

Water sports are Mission Bay's reason for being. At the many marinas, visitors can rent paddle boats or ocean-going sloops—any type of boat they desire. Traffic on the bay is organized so that one water activity is separated

from another. Water-skiers use a 1½-mile course with several beaches reserved as pick-up and landing areas; power boats roar over the same 3-mile course used by hydroplanes and competition speedboats during organized races; sailboats reign in the western cove of the bay. Small racing sloops, tiny dinghies, exotic outriggers, and swift catamarans dart across the cove all year long.

Fishing is enjoyed from a comfortable lawn chair on the beach, from a small skiff, or from the deck of a sportfishing boat. Within the bay, fishermen land halibut, flounder, bass, croaker, and perch.

Sea World makes a big splash. San Diego's 80-acre aquatic park within a park is one of the world's largest oceanariums, featuring some popular added attractions as well. Besides outstanding aquarium exhibits and a variety of water shows, you'll find a Japanese Village, an innovative children's playground, a sky tower, an aerial tram, and hydrofoil boats.

Water show stars include Shamu, a remarkably agile black and white killer whale; Google, a trained elephant seal weighing 1½ tons; a water-skiing chimpanzee; a penguin on skates; and a live shark exhibit. At the Water Fantasy Show, colorful lights and explosive dancing fountains perform like fireworks set to music. All shows are free. Presented on the hour and half-hour, they average 20 minutes in length; to see them all, consult your time schedule and the map distributed at the gate.

One of the park's newest exhibits is the Penguin Encounter. Inside the building, an Antarctic ecosystem has been created for some 300 birds. Thankful that you're on the room-temperature side of the glass, you glide on a conveyor belt past penguins flapping in an "ocean," waddling on snowy banks, and screeching in rookeries. The catchy exhibit includes six 6-minute films on the birds and their habitat.

The Sky Tower ride, highest of its kind in the United States, makes slow turns up and down its 320 feet, giving you an unobstructed 360° view of Mission Bay and surrounding territory. The Skyride tram takes you up 70 feet over the waters of Mission Bay to the Atlantis Restaurant for lunch or sightseeing. Hydrofoil boats zoom over the bay's famous speed course.

An exotic feature of Sea World is the Japanese Village, which flies the giant Koinobori fish kite. Here Japanese pearl divers will retrieve a pearl-bearing oyster for you from the bottom of the pool. You can have the pearl extracted on the spot and mounted into jewelry.

Walking through mature gardens between the arenas and exhibits, visiting the manmade tidepool, and shooting pictures at pre-picked spots will be a pleasant part of your visit. Sea World's horticultural exhibitions are outstanding. If you need to, rent a whale stroller for the small ones and check out the diaper changing facilities on your map before you begin your stroll.

It takes about 5 hours to see all the park, open daily from 10 A.M. until dusk. To get a behind-the-scenes peek at marine mammals, waterfowl, and other sea life, take a 1½-hour guided tour. The cost is about $2 for adults, $1 for children; one-price park admission is around $7 for adults, $4 for children over three. Sea World is on Perez Cove at the southern edge of Mission Bay Park; to get there, follow Sea World Drive.

North of San Diego

Many of the area's attractions are located north of San Diego—off Interstate Highway 5 and along the coast on State Highway 21; inland on Interstate Highway 15 and State Highway 78. You could make a fast loop trip in one day, but you may want to take more time to visit quaint seaside communities, flower fields, a famous biological institution, an oceanographic museum, rare Torrey Pines, and the large San Diego Wild Animal Park.

Captivating La Jolla

Fronting the sparkling Pacific and its broad beaches and built over beautiful coves, caves, and cliffs, La Jolla is aptly named. It means "hole" or "caves," according to Indian legend, but the more common interpretation today is from the Spanish word meaning "jewel" or "gem." La Jolla is not a touristy place. It is the quiet edge of the big city of San Diego, a 5-mile section of Mediterranean California at its most beguiling.

If you come north from the main part of San Diego—as most visitors are likely to do—the quick route is by I-5, taking the Ardath Road exit. You can also drive the older, longer route up La Jolla Boulevard from Pacific Beach. Neither route reveals much of the La Jolla experience, which begins when you get out of your car.

The sea beauty of La Jolla is the reason for everything else here. You'll find all the beach pleasures: swimming, diving, surfing, rock fishing, tidepool exploring, beach walking.

The beaches are a magnet here, and every beach has a character of its own. Some vary considerably with the tides, as well as with the seasons. Below Prospect Street, which curves through the heart of the old village, the beaches nuzzle under sandstone bluffs in a series of small crescents and coves. If you stand on the sidewalk on Coast Boulevard and look over the railing above La Jolla Cove (the northernmost of the beaches below the city proper), you'll see why it has been a favorite for years of sunbathers, swimmers, and skin and scuba divers. Intimate and protected, it has a gentle surf. The clear water and undersea gardens hold such prizes as spiny lobster and abalone. On the bluff above the cove is Ellen Browning Scripps Park, where you can stroll green lawns or sit and enjoy the sea air, watching the beach below.

South of Boomer Beach (ideal for the expert body surfer) and connected to the park and the cove by a promenade is the Children's Pool. This small beach has a curving breakwater that keeps the surf gentle enough for small children.

At the foot of Bonair Street is Windansea Beach, celebrated as one of the best places on the coast for surfing. Swimming here can be dangerous.

To visit one of the La Jolla caves, go to the end of Coast Boulevard and enter through a curio shop, descending 133 wooden stairs (not recommended for the infirm). You pay a small admission charge. Just seaward of the cave entrance, a bluff-top trail (part of an ecological reserve) runs easterly through about a half-mile of semiwild city park past a rocky gorge called Devil's Slide. The view of

La Jolla Bay is spectacular from this sometimes dizzying overlook. Close by, on the sheer face of the cliffs, you'll see birds—cormorants, pelicans, sea gulls—watching the waters for fish.

There's no beach at the foot of these cliffs. You have to get well north of the village before you see the second kind of La Jolla beach—wide, hard-packed sand with shallow water some distance out. Kellogg Park and the La Jolla Shores Beach are public and equipped with fire rings, play equipment, rest rooms, showers, and a lifeguard all year. The southern part of the beach is reserved for swimming, the northern for surfing. The private La Jolla Beach and Tennis Club, with its 1930s Spanish architecture and striped beach tents reminiscent of F. Scott Fitzgerald's Riviera-based novel, *Tender Is the Night*, marks the south end of this stretch of beach.

Exploring the village should please you. The charm of La Jolla today owes much to its isolated setting on a natural peninsula bounded by Mount Soledad and the ocean, and to the efforts of its tradition-minded citizens. Residential-scale buildings, mature trees, brilliant tropical flowers, and the La Valencia Hotel tower give La Jolla the flavor of a classic resort town.

La Jolla is for strolling. Parking places are almost impossible to find; the layout of the streets is confusing; pedestrian traffic is erratic. Although the main street (Girard Avenue) has as wide a selection of shopping as you'll find anywhere in San Diego, the best walking is along the mile or so of Prospect Street from the cottage shops and plazas on the north to the museum on the south. Shops range in character from one specializing in understated tweedery to a Scandinavian import shop. The varied restaurants here often occupy old houses; several have a sea view. The popular old La Valencia Hotel offers meals indoors or out, along with a view from the tower. The La Jolla Museum of Contemporary Arts fits well into this community of many artists. It's open from 11 A.M. to 5 P.M. Tuesday through Friday, from 12:30 to 5 on weekends, and on Wednesday evenings. Tours are offered during the week; schedule yours in advance.

Sherwood Hall, adjacent to the museum, is active year-round with productions by the La Jolla Civic University Orchestra, lectures, films, stage plays, ballets, and other cultural events.

Scripps Institution

La Jolla is world-famed as the center for research on the secrets of the sea. Located on the pier north of La Jolla Shores Beach is Scripps Institution of Oceanography, well known for its ocean study and now a part of the University of California at San Diego. The aquarium museum offers studies of tide motion, archeology, and beach lore. Its hours are from 9 A.M. to 5 P.M. daily. Admission is free; there's a small fee for parking. The pier is not open to the public.

The beach around Scripps Pier is a favorite for swimming, and you'll probably see considerable surfing action north of it.

The San Diego-La Jolla Underwater Park was established near Scripps to preserve the shoreline and underwater life of La Jolla Canyon. Buoys and shore markers define the limits of the reserve.

Torrey Pines Mesa

The expanding edge of La Jolla is a former wilderness thick with groves of eucalyptus and unique stands of the rare Torrey Pines. Torrey Pines Road takes you from La Jolla up onto the mesa to join the old coast highway. Set in the thickest of the eucalyptus forests is the University of California at San Diego. Drive through the campus and visit the art museum at Revelle College.

The Salk Institute for Biological Studies, a surrealistic city of concrete, rises above the trees at the top of North Torrey Pines Road. Named for Dr. Jonas Salk, it was founded in the hope that scholars from different disciplines—including the arts—could move toward an understanding of life. The Institute's exterior has been called the most powerful architectural statement on the West Coast. Guaranteed to make you react, it creates a proper setting for the energetic study that takes place inside. Tours are offered Monday through Friday from 11 A.M. to 2 P.M.

Next to the Institute is an active sail plane area where, on weekends, you can watch the pleasant sport of soaring—and often hang gliding—over the waves. A little farther north are two municipal golf courses. Even if you don't golf, you can have lunch at the restaurant (the only one on the mesa), with its grand view of the ocean. The complex also includes a comfortable motel.

Torrey Pines State Reserve protects some rare trees. The only natural grove of Torrey Pines in the world grows along the ocean here and on Santa Rosa Island 195 miles away. The rare pines in this beautiful, wind-shaped area are gnarled relics of a past age. The slanting trees were clinging to the eroded yellow sandstone cliffs when Cabrillo's ships first sighted California.

Occupying the whole northern tip of the mesa, the park is reached by North Torrey Pines Road. It is a good place for family hiking, having well-marked trails and picnic facilities. To hike along the ocean, use the north entrance to the park off U.S. 101. For beach hiking, consult a tide table to avoid being caught by rising waters.

Torrey Pines Reserve opens at 8 A.M. and closes at 10 P.M. from April to October; it closes at 5 during the winter. Admission to the reserve is free, but there is a parking charge. Most people find that merely driving through doesn't seem enough. The refreshing and fascinating change of scenery invites close-up exploration.

Coastal towns

Between Torrey Pines and Oceanside along the coast is strung a chain of small beach communities, interspersed with state and county beaches. These are some of the more interesting attractions:

Del Mar, a quiet, picturesque village, is best known for its horse-racing track (open from late July to mid-September).

Rancho Santa Fe (turn off I-5 at Via de la Valle) was originally a Spanish land grant. Douglas Fairbanks, Sr. founded Rancho Zorro in the 1920s, and Bing Crosby later owned the original ranch house. In and near the town are more eucalyptus trees than anywhere else in

DOLPHIN SPLASHES *front-row visitors to Sea World (left), an aquatic playground on Mission Bay. Elegant Hotel del Coronado (below), a Victorian landmark, presents more formal face.*

California—the result of an unsuccessful try by the Santa Fe Railway to use the wood for railway ties. The Rancho village has a small shopping area reminiscent of old-time La Jolla and a restaurant.

Encinitas, with its acres of flower fields, is a colorful sight when the flowers are in bloom. The largest poinsettia fields in the state turn nearby hills red in December. The "safest beach in California" is the city's claim.

Carlsbad built its reputation around the similarity of its mineral water to that of the original Karlsbad, Czechoslovakia, in what was then Bohemia. The Alt Karlsbad Hanse House (now a gift shop) is built over the spring. Nearby Twin Inns is a Victorian memento, having served country-fried chicken to happy diners since 1919 on the same blue willow pattern plates.

Oceanside, gateway to Camp Pendleton Marine base, has been a beach resort since the 1800s. The original fishing pier was operating in 1910; jutting into the sea for 1,900 feet, it attracts throngs of fisherfolk. At one end of the 4-mile beach are a boat harbor and a replica of a Cape Cod village.

Visitors are welcome to drive through Camp Pendleton. On the grounds you'll discover the former ranch house of Pio Pico, the last of California's Mexican governors.

Escondido, avocado capital of the world, is reached by following State Highway 78 inland from I-5 or by heading north on I-15 from San Diego.

The city's most famous attraction, the San Diego Wild Animal Park, is east of the city on San Pasqual Valley Road (State 78). Also along this road is the site of one of the least-known battles in U.S. history, and almost the only one fought in the conquest of California. A marker commemorates the 1846 battle between General Pico's native California troops and General Kearney's U.S. Army. The U.S. troops lost in what historians call the bloodiest battle of the Mexican War.

From Escondido, you can pick up State Highway 6, one approach to Palomar Observatory. It can also take you to pretty little Lake Wohlford for fishing, to the Bates Brothers Nut Farm (15954 Woods Valley Road) for a tour, and to groves where, in season, tree-ripened tangerines and Valencia oranges are sold from roadside stands at cut-rate prices.

Seven miles northwest of Escondido (off I-15—exit north on Mountain Meadow Road) is Lawrence Welk's theater-museum in the Village Center shopping arcade. At the nearby motel/restaurant, you might catch a band performance.

Temecula, 55 miles north of San Diego on I-15, is Southern California's newest wine-growing center.

(Continued on page 78)

WELCOME TO MEXICO

Although it's easy to visit Mexico, your trip will be even more enjoyable if you familiarize yourself with some information before you cross the border.

Tourist cards. You don't need a passport to visit Mexico, but if you go more than 75 miles into the interior (Ensenada and Mexicali are within this limit) or stay longer than 72 hours, you will need a tourist card. The cards are free from the Mexican Consulate and the Mexican Government Tourist Office in San Diego, but you must supply proof of your United States citizenship.

Car insurance. It is advisable to obtain auto insurance from a Mexican insurance company before you cross the border. American agents are not licensed to do business in Mexico, where an automobile accident is a criminal offense for which you can be detained until claims are adjusted. The Convention and Visitors Bureau in San Diego will provide a list of reputable Mexican insurance firms; some are located on your way to the border crossing. Short-term Mexican insurance is not expensive.

Driving. Traffic regulations similar to those in the United States are enforced. Speed limits are posted in kilometers (1 km=.62 miles), so be sure to make the reckoning. Road signs are generally in Spanish, but shapes and symbols are universally understood. Baja California has some new highways (including the road to its tip), but they are unfenced, so watch for livestock on the road. Major highways (1, 2, and 5) are well patrolled by Mexico's green emergency repair jeeps. Service is free, except for cost of parts. Gas stations are generally far apart; be sure to fill your gas tank at every opportunity.

Currency. Most Mexican stores will accept either pesos or dollars. You can exchange currency at banks, your hotel, or at currency exchange booths. The exchange fluctuates. Both Mexican and U.S. prices are indicated by dollar signs.

Customs. United States Customs permits each person to bring back $400 worth of goods without duty. Beyond that amount, you must itemize each purchase. Check the *Customs Hints* booklet, free from customs offices, for detailed information on declaring purchases over $400. California visitors may now bring back alcoholic beverages whether returning by commercial carrier or private car. The limit is one quart.

Rooms and meals. Good accommodations at reasonable prices and restaurants where you can eat with confidence are found in the Mexican towns discussed in this chapter. Besides Mexican restaurants, there are many North American, European, and Oriental establishments.

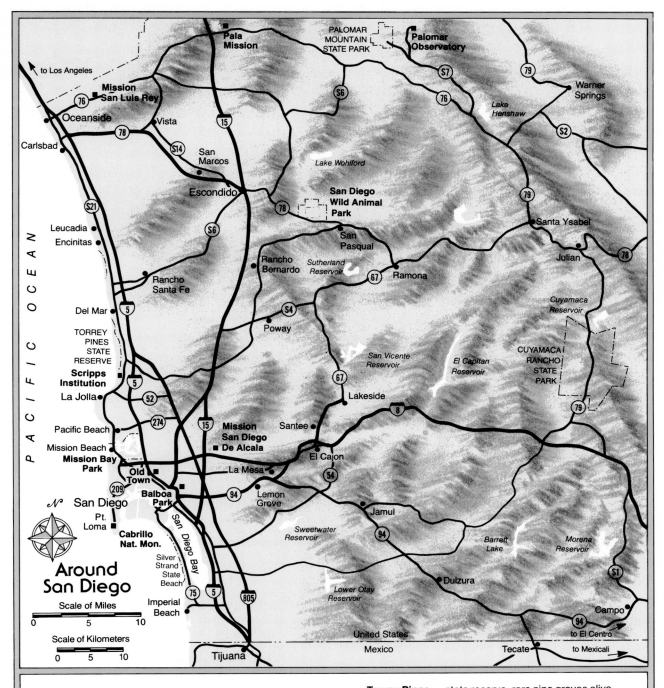

Pala Mission

Palomar Observatory

PALOMAR MOUNTAIN STATE PARK

to Los Angeles

Mission San Luis Rey

S7

79

Warner Springs

76

Oceanside

Vista

S6

76

Lake Henshaw

Carlsbad

78

S2

S14

San Marcos

Lake Wohlford

79

Escondido

San Diego Wild Animal Park

Santa Ysabel

15

78

S21

Leucadia

S6

San Pasqual

Julian

Encinitas

Rancho Bernardo

Sutherland Reservoir

78

P A C I F I C   O C E A N

Rancho Santa Fe

67

Ramona

Cuyamaca Reservoir

Del Mar

5

S4

TORREY PINES STATE RESERVE

Poway

San Vicente Reservoir

El Capitan Reservoir

CUYAMACA RANCHO STATE PARK

Scripps Institution

5

67

La Jolla

52

Lakeside

8

79

Pacific Beach

274

Mission San Diego De Alcala

Santee

Mission Beach

15

Mission Bay Park

Old Town

El Cajon

Balboa Park

La Mesa

54

209

94

Lemon Grove

San Diego

Pt. Loma

Jamul

Sweetwater Reservoir

Barrett Lake

Morena Reservoir

N

Cabrillo Nat. Mon.

Silver Strand State Beach

San Diego Bay

94

Dulzura

S1

Around San Diego

75

5

805

Lower Otay Reservoir

Campo

Scale of Miles

0   5   10

Imperial Beach

94

to El Centro

Scale of Kilometers

0   5   10

United States

Mexico

Tecate

to Mexicali

Tijuana

Major Points of Interest

Palomar Observatory — 12-story observatory and museum-exhibit hall; camping, picnicking

Pala Mission — Indian chapel in back country

Mission San Luis Rey — impressive "King of Missions"; picnic grounds, museum, public tours

Wild Animal Park — animals roam freely in spacious habitat; visitors view from monorail

Del Mar — "beside-the-sea" horse racing track

Torrey Pines — state reserve, rare pine groves alive when Cabrillo discovered California; active sail planing

Scripps Institution — public tours offered at museum for sea study; nearby underwater park

La Jolla — pearl of beach towns with intriguing shops, restaurants, caves

Tijuana — gateway to Mexico; shopping, jai alai, bullfights

Cuyamaca Rancho State Park — former Spanish ranch; Indian relics; hiking, riding

Julian — historic gold mining town; tours, festivals

AFRICAN ELEPHANTS take a morning walk. Moat separates their enclosure from San Diego Wild Animal Park's open space.

. . . Continued from page 76

Most of the wineries that allow visitors line the Ranch California Road exit. Temecula is also home for the Frontier Historical Center (27999 Front Street), a museum focusing on the days of Buffalo Bill Cody and Wyatt Earp. Billed as "the world's largest Western history collection," it includes wax figures of some of the era's heroes and villains, a re-creation of Tombstone, and a display of more than 1,000 of the "firearms that won the West." The museum is open daily from June through November, closed Mondays the rest of the year.

San Diego Wild Animal Park

An innovation in American public zoos, the San Diego Wild Animal Park is also on State 78 near San Pasqual. The first zoo to give its breeding herd animals so much roaming room that it resembles their native habitat, it's already had some births, rare for animals in captivity. Developed in 1972 in chaparral terrain evocative of the dry upland plains of Africa, the park is home to some 2,200 animals—many of them rare and endangered species—who roam the park's 1,800 acres. This compares with 5,500 animals on the parent San Diego Zoo's 128 acres.

Visitors are kept mostly at a distance so as not to disrupt the animals. A monorail train takes you through the park on a 5-mile drive that lasts a little less than an hour. One tip: Bring a pair of binoculars. The animals are most active and visible in late after-noon and early morning when the sun is mildest, the crowds thinnest.

The 1½-mile Kilimanjaro Hiking Trail offers spectacular vistas for animal observation and photography, plus picnicking sites. Nairobi Village, just inside the park entry, presents animals in a closer setting. You walk through a giant, free-flight, free-form aviary. You will also see babies in the animal nursery, lemurs on an island, flamingos in a lagoon, newborn animals, green iguanas, and lowland gorillas. And you can pet less exotic animals in a *kraal* (corral).

In addition, you'll find shops, outdoor eating facilities, and, in summer, live musical entertainment.

The park is open daily from 9 A.M.; closing hours vary from 9 P.M. in summer and on fall weekends to as early as 4 P.M. in winter. Summer visitors may stay until 11 P.M. Admission includes animal shows, monorail, and entrance to Nairobi Village.

To reach the park from San Diego, take Via Rancho Parkway exit from I-15 east onto San Pasqual Road, and follow the signs.

Rancho Bernardo

Red tile roofs are all you see of the town of Rancho Bernardo from I-15, south of Escondido, but it's worth turning onto the Rancho Bernardo exit just to visit the Mercado. Of all the enclaves of art and craft shops that have sprouted up in Southern California recently, this is one of the most handsome and lively.

Bold graphics and bright banners stand out against the two-story, tile-roofed buildings, faintly Mediterranean in inspiration. Grouped around courtyards at plaza level and on balconies are 40 shops, studios, and eating places. Artisans concentrate on creating pottery, jewelry, candles, and many other wares.

Visit daily, 10 A.M. to 6 P.M. Some craftsmen are always there; you'll see most on weekends.

The Back Country

Oceanside is a good jumping-off spot for a loop trip of the back country of San Diego County. A land of rural charm and historical intrigue, it offers rambling hills, meadows, rocky mountain peaks, and desert. Two or three days will go fast in the back country—it is full of Indian lore, past and present; California mission and gold mine history; pleasant ranches and farms; spectacular views; good hiking, riding, and camping. Not the least of its charms is that it offers the rare treat of unhurried country driving. Camp overnight in a forested state park, stop at a dude ranch in Warner Springs, or stay in the old Julian Hotel. For a circle trip of the area, follow State Highways 76 and 79 and U.S. Highway 80 between Oceanside and San Diego.

Mission San Luis Rey

Off State 76 just 5 miles east of Oceanside is one of the most impressive restorations in the mission chain, Mission San Luis Rey. Crowning a hill that dominates a beautiful valley, the "King of the Missions," founded in 1789, was the largest and most populous Indian mission of the Americas. Known for its artistic facade, the gracious and dignified mission (which at one time covered 6 acres) was built by a padre and Indians who had never before worked with tools.

The first pepper tree in California, which provided the padres with peppercorns to grind for seasoning, was brought from Peru in 1830 and still stands here. The trees were so widely planted that they are now called "California pepper."

On the always colorful grounds, you'll find picnic tables in a shady grove, an old cemetery, a small museum, and a gift shop. Now a seminary, Mission San Luis Rey is open to the public from 9 A.M. to 4 P.M. Monday through Saturday, and from 1:30 to 4:30 on Sunday.

Pala Mission

Located in the tranquil river valley a little farther east on State 76, San Antonio de Pala Mission, actually an *asistencia* (or branch) of Mission San Luis Rey, is the only chapel in the mission chain still used by a predominantly Indian congregation. This is the original building, built in 1815, with Indian frescoes still on the walls and an attractive separate campanile.

Behind Pala, the Tourmaline Queen Mountain echoes

days of lucrative gem mining that rivaled the activity in the gold rush town of Julian.

Palomar Observatory

Southeast of Pala, State 76 winds through Pauma Valley, site of the Palomar Observatory. The turn-off to Palomar is 5 miles beyond Rincon Springs, where the road rises abruptly through chaparral and rock-covered countryside and offers a winding but scenic ride.

High on Palomar Mountain are the great silver dome of the 12-story observatory, operated by the California Institute of Technology, and a museum-exhibit hall, where a tour will brief you on the workings of the large telescopes. The Hale, a 200-inch telescope weighing 500 tons, is viewed from a gallery. You may want to wear a sweater; the working interior of the dome must be kept at night-time temperatures, since even a few degrees of variation can cause distortions. The observatory is open daily from 9 A.M. to 5 P.M.

From the road up Palomar Mountain, you can turn west to Palomar Mountain State Park. This Sierralike country has many camp and picnic sites, good views, and trails to explore. You'll probably see the wild pigeons for which this area was named. As you drive in, ask the ranger for directions.

If your vehicle is heavily loaded, you should approach Palomar from Lake Henshaw, where the road is more gradual and less rough. The lake has boating and fishing. No matter which way you go up, you may want to descend this way to continue your loop trip.

You can spend some time at Warner Springs, a few miles off the loop on State 79. A ranch and golf resort, Warner Springs accommodates you in simple or luxurious adobes.

Santa Ysabel

The white-stuccoed chapel of Mission Santa Ysabel is on the site of the *asistencia* of the San Diego Mission, built in 1818. Rebuilt in the mission style about 1920, the church is still used. Surrounded by pleasant trees, a wishing well, a windmill, and picnic tables, the mission welcomes visitors

In the little town of Santa Ysabel, the old general store is claimed to date back to 1870. A good reason for stopping in this town is the Dudly Pratt Bakery, where nearly 50 varieties of bread are made. A little beyond here, on State 78, you can take a trip into the Anza-Borrego Desert State Park, headquartered in Borrego Springs. (This desert country is discussed on page 95.) A few miles farther along State 79 is the old gold rush town of Julian.

Julian

High in the pine and oak-covered hills, you'll find the mountain settlement of Julian, where a town started over a century ago and time stopped before the false-front buildings could go out of style.

A gold strike in 1869 turned Julian into a boom town, making it the second largest town in San Diego County. The end of the boom halted progress and settled the town

into a comfortable little agricultural community allowing supermarkets, super highways, and subdivisions to pass it by. Even today, you reach Julian on meandering, tree-lined country roads nearly empty of traffic and uncluttered by commercial development. Appaloosa ranches; cattle-speckled hillsides; apple, pear, and peach orchards; and fruit and homemade jam stands compose the scene.

Main Street in Julian retains its original false-front stores, wooden sidewalks, and the Julian Hotel (built in 1887). Here you'll also find homey restaurants, stores selling homemade pies from locally grown wares, and real sarsaparilla. You'll even find an adaptable parking lot offering space to "horseless carriages, stuttering bicycles, and mothers-in-law." Hardly changed, old homes still cling to the hillsides around town, and the old George Washington Mine, the first operated in the area, can still be reached from the end of Washington Street on a footpath. The mine entrance has been shored up, but you can still see ore cars on tracks running into the mine. You can also look into an assay office and a blacksmith shop nearby—both reconstructed.

Another mine in the area, the Eagle, is open for tours. To reach it, take C Street in the middle of town and follow the signs to the mine. It is open daily from 9 A.M. to 5 P.M. The short guided tour includes an explanation of gold mining.

The Julian Museum, located where State 79 turns west for Santa Ysabel, is in an old masonry building once used as a brewery and a blacksmith shop. It is open from 11 A.M. to 5 P.M. on weekends. A more recent article of memorabilia is a mail pouch with parachute, dropped by the Coast Guard in 1938 to inaugurate Julian's first air mail delivery.

Cuyamaca Rancho State Park

An area of rugged mountain terrain and intermittent streams, Cuyamaca Rancho State Park lies about 40 miles from urban San Diego with views of the ocean to the west and the desert to the east. Its wilderness is graced by much bird and wildlife and wildflowers in all seasons. The name "Cuyamaca" is a Spanish version of the old Indian word for "the place where it rains."

Formerly a Spanish rancho in what had been isolated Indian country, the state park now features Caballos Campground, accommodating horseback riders; a nature trail at Wooded Hill; and an Indian exhibit containing relics of early Indian life. Some of the things depicted here, such as acorn gathering, are still practiced.

For those who like to ride and hike, there are over 75 miles of trails to explore. From the Paso Picacho Campground, you can climb to three peaks. On a clear day on top of Mount Cuyamaca, you can see from the Pacific Ocean to the Salton Sea and from Mexico to San Bernardino. Allow about 3 hours for the round trip.

For a leg-stretching return

For the return trip to San Diego you can follow either I-8 or take pokier, two-lane State Highway 94.

Off Interstate 8: Visit Santee Recreation Lakes in the small community of Santee. Here are six small reservoirs with islands reached by raft-ferry. The recreation area features small-boat channels, fishing, swimming, and picnicking.

Bird lovers will enjoy Silverwood Wildlife Sanctuary near Lakeside (a 167-acre reserve with trails, displays, and picnic spots). It's open Wednesdays and Sundays. From Lakeside, turn right on Maplewood and left on Ashwood, becoming Wildcat Canyon Road, for 5 miles.

Off State 94: Slow down at Boulevard or you'll miss the Wisteria Candy Cottage with homemade confections including 17 kinds of divinity, hand-dipped chocolates, nut brittles, fudge, and other temptations. The hours are 7 A.M. to 7 P.M. daily.

At both Lake Morena County Park (3 miles north of Cameron Corners) and Potrero County Park you can picnic or camp overnight.

Turn south at State Highway 188 for 2 miles to take a look at slow-paced Tecate just over the Mexican border.

Across the Border

Mexico is right next door when you're in San Diego—and most visitors find it an irresistible lure. Though Tijuana receives most of the traffic, there are two other border crossings—Tecate nearby and Mexicali beyond the mountains. It's only 2 hours from San Diego to Ensenada, south of Tijuana, on scenic Bahia Todos Santos; and San Felipe, on the Sea of Cortez, is only 127 miles south of Mexicali. For details on these and other Mexican cities, see the *Sunset Travel Guide to Mexico*.

After passing through the sleepy village of San Ysidro on I-5, you come to the dry Tijuana River bed and the gateway arch sweeping over 25 lanes of traffic that marks the end of California and the beginning of Baja California, Mexico. At the border (just 15 minutes from downtown San Diego), the bustling city of Tijuana brings you instantly to Mexico.

Tijuana

Tijuana (te-*wah*-nah) lays claim to the title of most visited city in the world—with some 30 million border crossings yearly. It's easy to see why the attraction is so strong. Many who come are weekenders attracted by horse and dog racing, the summer Sunday bullfights, or camping on the beach seaward of Tijuana. Many are active and curious shoppers seeking out the fine handicrafts, import stores, and colorful arcades of the shopping areas. And yet others come to experience a foreign culture, so accessible from the U.S. Realize that, as a border town, Tijuana is not typically Mexican.

To enjoy your visit more, it is best to know what to expect of this very diverse and busy city. The Tijuana Convention and Visitors Bureau has visitor information booths both at the border and on the main street (Avenida Revolucion).

Getting there. To get to Tijuana from San Diego, you can take the Greyhound bus (120 W. Broadway), the Mexicoach (Santa Fe Depot), or the popular Tijuana Trolley (see page 65) to the border.

You can also park a car on the U.S. side of the border and walk across, then take a Mexican taxi downtown or to the Cultural Center for a nominal fee. If you decide to drive across the border, be sure to stop at one of the Mexican insurance offices; American insurance is usually no good once you cross the border.

The new Tijuana. With a population of over a million, the city is growing in new directions. Paseo de los Heroes is the grand boulevard of the redevelopment zone, where the old bed of the Rio Tijuana has been transformed from a flood plain with squatters' huts into a channeled river bordered by landscaped avenues. Crown jewel of the new zone is the $35-million Tijuana Cultural Center, with an Omnitheater, performing arts center, and anthropological museum. At the center, you can shop, dine, or see a film on Mexico's sights and sounds splashed across a 75-foot screen (there's an admission charge). The center is open from 11 A.M. to 7 P.M. daily (until 8 P.M. weekends). The entrance fee is small.

Across from the cultural center lies Plaza Rio Tijuana, a modern, sprawling shopping center.

The old Tijuana. It's still there and still fun—and you'll notice change. Revolucion, the main street, was the first face-lift patient. Now there are more places to sit and watch the passing scene, plus fountains to sit beside and trees to sit under. A juxtaposition of old and new greets you at each block. Narrow old paseos and arcades bulge with goods from all over Mexico. A steady buzz of invitations to browse may turn up pleasant surprises.

Shopping. Tijuana's finds range from the richest Mexican folk art to the gaudiest of tourist gimcracks. Some of the best goods can be found at government-sponsored stores on Revolucion: Fonart (east side between calles 6 and 7) and State of Puebla (west side between calles 2 and 3). Also try Galeria Lucias (upstairs off an arcade between calles 5 and 6) and Bazar Las Palomas (rear of the same arcade). For your convenience, most prices are marked in dollars.

Sports are varied and different south of the border. The biggest crowd-attractor to Tijuana is Caliente Race Track, a couple of miles from downtown on Agua Caliente Boulevard. Its beautiful modern facilities include good restaurants and shops. Thoroughbreds race weekend afternoons the year around. In the evenings (except Tuesdays), the course is converted for greyhound racing.

Jai alai (hi-li), a colorful and often dangerous sport that is billed as the world's fastest ball game, is four centuries old. Traditionally played by the Basques in a show of grace, skill, and strength, jai alai offers thrills and pari-mutuel betting nightly except Thursday most of the year in the imposing Fronton Palacio on Revolucion at 7th Street.

Tijuana has two bullrings, both named and patterned after the famous ones in Mexico City. The downtown ring, El Toreo de Tijuana, is easily reached by way of Agua Caliente Boulevard. Plaza Monumental, 5 miles out of town near the ocean, is the second largest bullring in the world (the largest is in Mexico City). Whether or not you see a bullfight, it's a wonderful place to visit— enjoy beautiful landscaping, patios, toreros' chapel, and views of the Pacific Ocean. The classical art of bullfighting is celebrated Sunday afternoons from May through September.

Occasionally on Sundays, the local *charros* (cowboys) stage rodeos (or *charreadas*). There are several rodeo arenas; ask at the information booths in town when a rodeo is scheduled and where you can find it.

Tijuana to Ensenada

Outside Tijuana you find the ramshackle hillside huts of the Mexican poor. You'll also find industry, part of the new diversification of Tijuana, particularly eastward from Caliente Race Track on the Tecate Road, also known as Mexican Highway 2.

By following the Second Street extension to the ocean (or taking the direct route from the border), you encounter a change of scenery at Playas de Tijuana. Here you can pick up the scenic freeway, which takes you 65 miles south from Tijuana to the seacoast town of Ensenada. This four-lane, divided toll road in many places parallels the old Ensenada Libre (free) route, which takes you through rural Mexico but also slows you down. The 90-minute freeway drive takes you past spectacular cliffs and sea views.

Ensenada

With a pace much more relaxed than Tijuana's, Ensenada also has a much more inviting setting, curving gracefully around the bay of Todos Santos. Shoppers delight in the fact that Ensenada is a duty-free port. You'll also find several good restaurants; Hussong's Cantina is Baja California's famous watering hole.

Fishing is so excellent that Ensenada is known as the "Yellowtail Capital of the World." Pleasure boats abound in the protected harbor; cruise ships stop for a short stay. The world-famous Ensenada-Newport International Yacht Race, held during Mexico's Cinco de Mayo (May 5 independence celebration), attracts more than 500 participants.

Tecate

For a Mexican border town, Tecate is relatively quiet and uncommercial, but you will find it busy for a town its size, especially during festivals. It is about 30 miles east of Tijuana and 72 miles from Ensenada on good roads.

A famous beer that bears the town's name makes Tecate a popular refreshment stop. The brewery and Hidalgo Park are the town's main attractions. The city has a good restaurant (Los Candiles) and a small hotel (El Dorado). A few miles west of town along Highway 2 is Rancho La Puerta, a widely known health spa that attracts many Southern Californians.

Mexicali

Mexicali, the capital of Baja California, has a population of about 500,000, compared to Tijuana's million. Located in the center of a vast cotton-producing valley, it does not cater to tourism, nor is the U.S. dollar the chief currency. English is spoken at the main hotel (Lucerna), at the few tourist shops, and at some restaurants.

Palm Springs

Most glittering of desert oases, Palm Springs introduces a land for sun worshippers. Beyond the pools, tennis courts, and golf courses lie rugged mountains (accessible by tram), palm-studded canyons, Coachella Valley's acres of dates, and inland Salton Sea. Great desert parks (Joshua Tree and Anza-Borrego) preserve terrain, and, along the Colorado River, Lake Havasu preserves reconstructed London Bridge.

Perhaps nowhere else do mountains and desert meet more abruptly than at Palm Springs, famed desert playground about 100 miles east of Los Angeles. To the west, the San Jacinto Mountains—often snow-draped in winter—drop sharply to the valley floor thousands of feet below. To the east, the sun—most important resource of the Southern California desert country—rises and shines all year, and the air is warm and dry.

Palm Springs, center of an expanding community of resorts, stands in desert that is mostly tamed. But close by is land rugged and open enough to urge your investigation of its tenacious plants, its shy animals, its rocks and sands, and its silent canyons. And the mountains, pine-covered and verdant in their upper reaches, offer spectacular views from the heights and some surprises in the easily accessible side canyons.

Nearby is Salton Sea, once a dry desert wasteland and now a recreation area popular for motor boating and water-skiing. Undeveloped desert canyons and unusual rock formations around the sea invite exploring.

Not far from the highly civilized resort areas surrounding Palm Springs and the activity of the Salton Sea are preserves of desert lands whose "stars" are the spiny ocotillos, sculptured Joshua trees, time-carved canyons, and wind-blown sands, all in the earth and sun colors of the desert.

Two great desert parks—Joshua Tree National Monument and Anza-Borrego Desert State Park—reveal the differences between the high and low desert.

The Colorado River, boundary between California and Arizona, is a boating mecca. Lake Havasu, formed by a dam on a once-wild river, is a water-world playground. On the Arizona side, in Lake Havasu City, is the London Bridge, reassembled from its original site on England's Thames River.

One of the great virtues of this vast land is that it seems far removed from California's more populous regions. Here, understated resorts provide bases for exploring, and campgrounds abound on empty stretches of sand, along the water's edge, or among pine-forested mountains.

Overview of "The Springs"

Palmiest desert resort in California or almost anywhere else, Palm Springs is known—perhaps too well—for the celebrities it attracts in winter. This oasis with one swimming pool for every 2½ registered voters is well equipped for those who like to live lavishly, but it offers more than that.

Palm Springs offers California's low desert climate at its best. Here, the steepest high mountain escarpment in the West (the 10,000-foot rise of the San Jacinto range) acts as a natural climate conditioner, throwing the whole town into shadow every afternoon, while the Coachella Valley to the east continues to shimmer in the sun. The mountains also give Palm Springs one more weather bonus: they act as a barrier against the ever-encroaching smog from the west.

Seen from the air, Palm Springs appears to be developed in a kind of checkerboard fashion—residences and commercial establishments in one giant square area, open desert in another. There's a good reason.

SAN JACINTO PEAKS *provide backdrop for desert golf course near Palm Springs. Winter oasis is dubbed "Golf Capital of the World."*

The city is divided into mile squares, every other one belonging to the Agua Caliente Indians, original settlers of the land. The land on which the Palm Springs Spa Hotel is located, as well as much other local real estate, is owned by the Agua Calientes.

If you drive up into verdant Palm Canyon, south of town, you'll enter the Indian reservation and pay a toll to proceed farther into Palm and other tributary canyons along the east side of the mountains.

Palm Springs is a wealthy community—but in a sense, its real wealth perhaps still belongs to its original owners.

Old-timers still think of Palm Springs as "the village." Some movie folk call it "The Springs." But more than just a resort, it is also a jumping-off point for desert adventure.

Something for Everyone

Visitors find in this desert city a wide range of activities. For those who like to swim, golf, play tennis, hike, picnic, ride horses, bicycle, bump through the sand on dune buggies, fly planes, watch polo or baseball, shop, bathe in hot-water spas, or relax in the sun, Palm Springs offers excellent facilities.

Golf

Known as the "Golf Capital of the World" (see below), Palm Springs has golf courses that stay green all year.

The entire community boasts almost three dozen courses. The Palm Springs Municipal Golf Course, one of the few public courses, is located at 1885 Golf Club Drive. Clarkston's Golf and Recreation Center (1001 S. El Cielo Road) features a nine-hole course, putting green, and night-lighted driving range and miniature golf course.

To play at private clubs, you usually must be a guest of a member, though a number of clubs offer reciprocal privileges to members of other private clubs. Some hotels provide guests with temporary cards; two major hotels have their own courses. You will also find public courses in surrounding desert cities.

Tennis

If you are interested in tennis, you'll be pleased to find 27 public courts. The Palm Springs Tennis Center (1300 East Baristo Road), with the feeling of a private club, allows you to make reservations before arriving. This municipal complex offers nine night-lighted courts, 11 automatic ball return practice lanes, a pro shop, and professional instruction. During the off-season (summer), courts are free.

Other public courts include those at Palm Springs High School (2248 E. Ramon Road), De Muth Park (4375 Mesquite Avenue), and Ruth Hardy Park (700 Tamarisk Road).

Several of the major hotels provide courts for guests; the well-known Palm Springs Tennis Club allows hotel and cottage guests to use its courts, but the Palm Springs Racquet Club is strictly private.

PALM SPRINGS — A GOLF CAPITAL

Golf is one of the main reasons people flock to the Palm Springs area. In 1951, the area's first championship course—the Thunderbird Country Club—was built in what is now the town of Rancho Mirage. It inaugurated a new era and made golf the prime influence on the character of Palm Springs.

Actually, the pilgrimage to Palm Springs began 30 years earlier. As visitor numbers increased, first class facilities became a major necessity. Those hotel facilities were built, but some people preferred to have their own homes in the desert. Thomas O'Donnell was one of them, and his love of golf resulted in the construction of a nine-hole course in his front yard. This golf course was really the first of its kind in the area.

Later promoters, realtors, and land developers saw the advantage of building and selling homes within range of a golf course. At that time courses were built around private homes, but soon they spread to hotels and then to country clubs with names like Eldorado, Marrakesh, Tamarisk, La Quinta, and others, as well as Thunderbird—all built to accommodate golf's popularity and to serve residents already living in the desert.

Palm Springs itself has everything from championship layouts to tricky three-pars and miniature golf. The desert communities as a whole have a greater concentration of golf courses in fewer square miles than anywhere else in the world—thus the nickname "golf capital of the world."

Many charity events—the Nabisco-Dinah Shore Invitational Golf Tournament, the Bob Hope Desert Classic, and others—take place on courses in Rancho Mirage.

You get a list of the courses, public and private, from the Palm Springs Convention and Visitors Bureau at the airport. One of the best public courses is lovely Palm Springs Municipal Golf Course, among the finest in the country. Palm Desert Country Club and Desert Crest Country Club (Desert Hot Springs) are two more courses that welcome visitors. Indio has three public courses, and you'll even find one at Salton Sea.

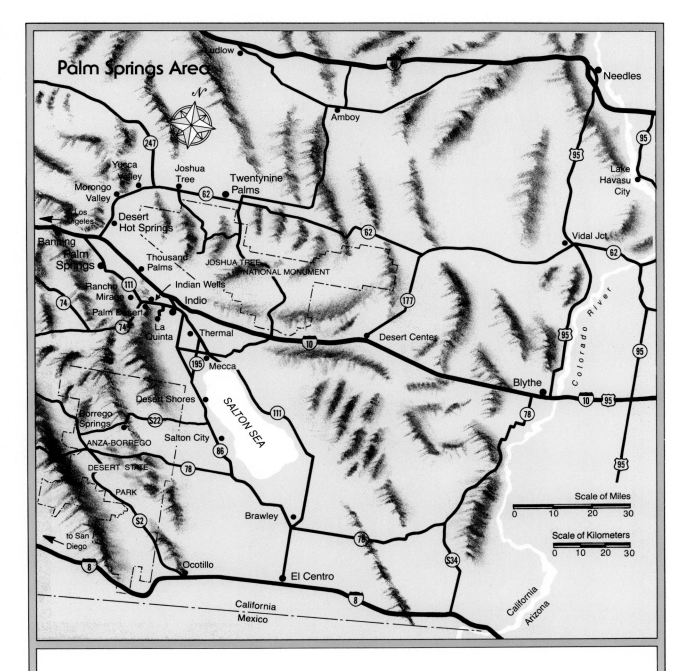

Palm Springs Area

Major Points of Interest

Twentynine Palms (Joshua Tree National Monument) — Visitor Center nature trail leads to palm forest

Anza-Borrego Desert State Park (Borrego Springs)—over ½ million acres of Colorado Desert wilderness; contains badlands and oases, wildlife and wildflowers, resort accommodations, and campsites

Date Gardens (Indio)—the "Date Capital of the U.S." Wander through date groves, watch a movie on the date palm's love life, have a date shake

Salton Sea — boating, fishing, camping. Float in below-sea-level salt-water lake, once inland sea

Lake Havasu (Colorado River)—beautiful lake offers water sports, camping, trailer park. See London Bridge, surrounding English village setting

Palm Springs—climb from desert floor to top of Mt. San Jacinto in 18 minutes on Aerial Tramway; tour celebrities' homes; view art exhibits in Desert Museum's striking setting; explore scenic Palm Canyon; swim, hike, play tennis or golf in one of country's top resorts

BRIEF BUT BREATHTAKING
*is ride that lifts visitors from
desert heat of Palm Springs
area to cool 8,500-foot
mountain level.*

Other sports

If you enjoy two-wheeled sightseeing and exercise, you can explore the city and foothills on any one of five separate bike trails. Local cycling shops rent bikes and carry trail maps. Riders will want to tour the nearby scenic canyons on horseback; contact Smoke Tree Stables at (619) 327-1372.

The California Angels, an American League baseball team, maintain spring training headquarters here. Visitors may attend spring practices and exhibition games, mostly in March, at the baseball stadium at East Ramon Road and South Sunrise Way, near the airport.

Shopping and browsing

Shopping in Palm Springs is a popular diversion. In addition to several shopping centers, intriguing shops line Palm Canyon Drive. Many top national and California retail stores have branches here, providing opportunities for both window gazing and serious shopping. In this pace-setting community, new spring fashions are introduced in October before being put on the general market.

Palm Springs is also becoming known as an art center, with galleries and exhibits attracting many visitors each year. Most of the galleries are along the main downtown streets; the town also has an excellent new art museum (see page 88).

Your season in the sun

Palm Springs' magnet is its climate, especially from mid-October to mid-May. The days are generally sunny, warm, and cloudless, with dry air. Winter temperatures are comfortably warm—70° to 90°F. during the day; desert winter nights can dip to 25°, though 40° is a more usual minimum. In summer, daytime temperatures average in the 100°s, but the very low humidity keeps you relatively comfortable. Rainfall is scant. Most of the under-3-inch annual average falls in brief storms from November through April.

The Palm Springs "season" is from mid-December through April. During these months, particularly in January, February, and March, advance reservations are advisable. You'll find equally good weather (and fewer people) during the fall and spring seasons.

What to wear in Palm Springs? It's almost always "shirt sleeve" weather, with an accent on casual sports clothes. Men and women wear shorts downtown, but bathing suits are restricted to pool lounging. Women's sun dresses and pants outfits are popular, as are men's sport shirts and jackets.

Accommodations are many and varied. Hotels, motor inns, condominiums, and trailer parks (a number with landscaping, pools, and recreational facilities) are located in and around the city; room rates are competitive with those in other popular resort communities. Rates vary with the season (prices are lowest in summer). For specific information on accommodations and reservations, write to the Palm Springs Convention and Visitors Bureau, 255 N. El Cielo, Suite 315, Palm Springs, CA 92262; or call (619) 327-8411.

Exploring the City

As you approach Palm Springs from the northwest, the shadowy blue and dusty pink bulk of the layered San Jacinto Mountains provides an imposing backdrop of constantly changing colors and shadow patterns. Both contrasting and harmonizing with its surroundings, the city has assimilated the colors and textures of the desert.

Getting your bearings

Your introduction to Palm Springs is Palm Canyon Drive, lined with more than 1,800 palm trees along its 5-mile length. These trees aren't imports—they're native to the area. Illuminated at night, the beautiful palms are the only "street lamps" on this major thoroughfare.

From the moment you enter the city limits on State Highway 111, you notice the absence of billboards. In addition, you'll find few above-ground power lines or telephone poles, no large signs, no prices displayed, no neon or moving signs, and no high buildings. The uncluttered and unobtrusive character of the city is closely regulated.

Automotive navigation. The street grid makes it easy to find your way around Palm Springs. Palm Canyon Drive (a one-way route going south) is both the main arterial and the main shopping street. Indian Avenue, the secondary arterial a block east, runs one-way to the north through the central part of the city. At Tahquitz-McCallum Way, the street numbering divides between north and south.

The older portions of Palm Springs are worth visiting for their lush garden plantings and handsome old trees. West Arenas Road leads you to one interesting district near the Palm Springs Tennis Club. In the north part of town, Via Las Palmas takes you west into a neighborhood of elegantly landscaped homes. Numerous movie stars and entertainers have homes in these areas of Palm Springs.

Tour opportunities. Gray Line, Celebrity Tours, and Palm Springs Safari all offer you the chance to see celebrity homes and other popular sights; balloon, helicopter, and plane rides are available for those who prefer a bird's-eye view of the city. You can explore the area on your own, of course: Palm Springs offers taxi, bus, and limousine service, as well as nine car rental agencies. Walking the flat area is easy.

Palm Springs at night

Downtown Palm Springs is relatively tranquil in the evening. There are numerous good restaurants, though many of the most popular eating places are southeast of Palm Springs toward Rancho Mirage.

With an emphasis on sports and sun activities, this is an early-to-bed community. During the season, several hotels and restaurants offer entertainment and dancing. If you search, you'll even find a disco. But unless you know some of the residents, you're not likely to get a peek at the social life of the city's glamourites.

A historical corner

A good place to begin your exploration of Palm Springs is at the corner of Tahquitz-McCallum Way and Indian Avenue. Here is the Palm Springs Spa Hotel & Mineral Springs, an elaborate structure that houses the bubbling hot springs sacred to the Agua Caliente Indians. If you're not a guest at the spa, you can still enjoy these hot springs for a reasonable admission charge. You can take your pick of mineral baths, individual Roman "swirlpools," rock steam and infrared inhalation, needlepoint showers, massage, immersion in a 104°F. outdoor mineral pool, and an exercise gymnasium.

An 1853 government survey party noted that the Indians attributed special healing powers to the springs and considered them sacred. Today, the only reminder of this sacred shrine is a memorial plaque on the building—and, of course, the same "healing" waters.

Palm Springs Desert Museum

This fascinating museum and cultural center moved to handsome new quarters in 1976. It is now located directly behind the Desert Inn Fashion Plaza on Museum Drive, a block west of Palm Canyon Drive.

Two sunken sculpture gardens enhance its impressive exterior, and the 20-acre grounds include a sculpture court financed by Frank Sinatra. Inside you'll find a permanent fine arts collection, exhibits explaining the desert's natural history, and a 450-seat theater for the performing arts.

In the natural history galleries, two 50-foot dioramas of the desert by day and by night feature the common plant and animal inhabitants. Another diorama, 80 feet long, shows the desert at about 10 A.M. on a typical spring morning. In addition there are close to 1,300 Indian artifacts, including fine examples of basketry and rug making.

The museum is open Tuesday through Friday from 10 A.M. to 4 P.M., and weekends from 10 A.M. to 5 P.M.; it's closed in summer and on major holidays. You'll pay a moderate fee to view the building and grounds. Museum shops offer interesting gift items.

Living Desert Reserve

This 1200-acre park is just 15 miles southeast of Palm Springs, in the Colorado Desert town of Palm Desert. The park's focus is on local flora and fauna: plantings at the James Irvine Garden, one section of the reserve, include Joshua trees and 18 other species of high-desert succulent plants.

An ethnobotanical garden contains plants the Indians used for food, fiber, soap, and other purposes. Both gardens are described in a printed trail guide.

New to the reserve are the Pearl McManus Hall, an exhibit building featuring an "after sundown" room housing a variety of desert dwellers; the animal hospital; an aviary; and a bighorn sheep enclosure.

The Living Desert Reserve is at 47-900 S. Portola Avenue, about 1½ miles south of State 111. It's open daily, 9 A.M. to 5 P.M., from September through May. Adults pay a nominal admission fee; there's no charge for visitors under 17 with an adult.

Moorten Botanical Garden

A stroll through this garden/wildlife sanctuary lets you take a look at many of the world's deserts. Founded in 1938, the private preserve has since collected 2,000 kinds of plants—flora typical of the arid regions of Africa, Central America, and North America. The collection is a diverse one; you'll see rare and unusual specimens, blossoming cacti, and some aptly named plant "personalities" (the "bearded grandfather" cactus, for example). The "cactusarium," a garden just for cacti, hosts botanical courses and research.

The 4-acre garden holds some surprisingly verdant spots; benches here provide a place for you to rest and watch the birds. At the garden's entrance, you can buy plants, rocks and minerals, and books on identifying and growing desert plants.

Located at 1701 S. Palm Canyon Drive, the garden is open daily from 9 A.M. to 5 P.M. Expect a small admission charge.

Miss Cornelia White's house

Built in 1894 from railroad ties, the small house near the corner of Indian Avenue and Tahquitz-McCallum Way contains memorabilia of early Palm Springs, including the town's first telephone. Former home of a pioneer woman, the house is maintained by the Palm Springs Historical Society and is open Tuesday through Saturday, as well as Sunday afternoon. Admission is free; donations are accepted.

Cabot's Old Indian Pueblo Museum

The desert has long attracted its share of eccentrics, and Cabot Yerxa was one. His unconventional home near Palm Springs stands testimony. Now a museum, the house with its unusual memorabilia is open to visitors.

In 1913, Yerxa homesteaded his land, but he didn't start the four-story house until 30 years later. Most of it was built within 5 years, but Yerxa added to it until his death in 1965. Working with recycled lumber, railroad ties, and handmade adobe bricks, he styled the house after the cliff dwellings of his Pueblo Indian friends. Odd-shaped pieces of glass he liked became parts of the 150 windows in 35 rooms.

Though he discovered hot and cold springs on his land, Yerxa was sparing with water. A bucketful was used first for cooking, then to wash dishes and clothes, later in a foot bath, and finally to water the flowers.

Scattered throughout the house are his odd mementos: an 8-foot stuffed brown bear; pictures of prospector Yerxa in Alaska with his friend Theodore Roosevelt; and an Indian medicine man's vestments, made of elk skin and human hair, given to him in 1929.

The museum at 67–616 E. Desert View Avenue in Desert Hot Springs (north of Palm Springs) is open daily except Tuesday. There's a slight admission charge, but the operator throws in a free guided tour.

Aerial tramway

When days get hot on the desert floor, Palm Springs residents and visitors have an instant escape route to

the high country of Mount San Jacinto, where the air is pine-scented and temperatures are 40 degrees cooler.

The tram trip up the mountain—beginning in the rugged Chino Canyon on the north edge of town—is refreshing, exciting, and beautiful any time of the year. You get an excellent view of the valley desert carpet, dotted with green palms and 7,000 blue swimming pools. Because of the awesome engineering challenges presented in its construction, the tramway, built in the early 1960s, has been called "the eighth engineering wonder of the world."

In a period of 2 years, 20,000 helicopter missions hauled men and materials to narrow ledges for construction of the towers. Today, the two 80-passenger trams move up and down one of the sheerest mountains in North America, over granite recesses deeper than the Grand Canyon.

The climb to the Mountain Station (8,516 feet) from the valley floor takes 18 minutes. This station is situated at the threshold of San Jacinto Wilderness State Park, where chattering jays and chipmunks attest that you are indeed in a different world. The top of Mount San Jacinto is a 6-mile hike from the tram station. Below sprawls the great desert expanse of the Coachella Valley, including the Salton Sea. On a very clear day the mountain ranges of Las Vegas are visible. At Mountain Station you can eat in the restaurant (open for lunch and dinner), shop in the gift store, and watch a free movie on the dramatic construction of the tram.

Behind Mountain Station a heated boardwalk leads down to Long Valley, where you can picnic in summer and rent sleds and sliding saucers in winter. During the summer, mules carry you from the top of the tram into the valley. Cross-country skiing is good from this point; ski equipment can be rented.

To reach the tramway base, turn off State 111 north of town and follow the signs. Public transportation is also available from Palm Springs. The Valley Station has a gift shop, snack bar, and cocktail lounge. Be sure to save your tramway trip for a clear day; a desert haze will play havoc with the view.

The tram operates from 10 A.M. to 7:30 P.M. (from 8 A.M. on weekends) October through April; from May through Labor Day, it remains open until 8:30 P.M. After Labor Day, the tram is closed for annual maintenance for 4 to 6 weeks.

Into the Mountains

Though the tram is the most dramatic way to reach the upper level of the San Jacintos, you can enter this mountain recreation area by way of Banning (Interstate Highway 10) or the Riverside-Hemet route (U.S. Highway 395 and State Highway 74). The latter is the Pines-to-Palms Highway, part of an enjoyable loop drive to Palm Desert or Palm Springs.

Small in area but high on the horizon, the craggy ramparts of the San Jacintos support a cool, green, much-sought-after summer retreat between the hot wheat and orchard country of the San Jacinto Valley on the west and the hotter desert of the Coachella Valley on the east. The forested backbone slants up gradually from south to north until it breaks away suddenly at the tremendous north face of San Jacinto Peak—one of the world's most abrupt escarpments, rising from near sea level to 10,804 feet, face to face with Mount San Gorgonio (this area's highest mountain) across the San Gorgonio Pass.

Jumping-off place for exploring the upper San Jacintos by road or trail is the forest community of Idyllwild—a logical place to headquarter while you become acquainted with the region and decide where most of your interests lie. Available are hotels and motels, restaurants, camping supplies, and pack and saddle stock.

Mount San Jacinto Wilderness State Park

This mountain park offers more than 50 miles of hiking trails. Only two campgrounds—Idyllwild and Stone Creek—are accessible by automobile, but many primitive areas stretch along the riding and hiking trails. Whether you enter the wilderness area on horseback or on foot, you'll need a permit. Apply in person at the Long Valley Ranger Station at the top of the tramway or write the park headquarters (P.O. Box 308, Idyllwild, CA 92349).

San Gorgonio Pass

If you take Interstate 10 east to Palm Springs, you pass Beaumont and Banning, lying in the divide between the San Bernardino and San Jacinto mountains. Side trips off the freeway in early spring reveal billowy colors of cherry and peach blossoms in nearby orchards and of apples up in Oak Glen. Later in the summer, you can pick your own fruit or get it from a roadside stand. Some apple stands around Oak Glen also offer homemade pies and cider.

Canyons east of the mountains

The scenic and historical canyons close to Palm Springs, for centuries the home of the Agua Caliente Indians, offer beauty and exploration for hikers, horse riders, bird watchers, botanists, and camera enthusiasts.

Tahquitz Canyon, containing a 60-foot waterfall, is the closest to town but is closed to the public at present. Its beauty was recorded for posterity in the original film version of *Lost Horizon*.

Palm Canyon cuts south from Palm Springs up into the mountains for more than 14 miles, dividing the San Jacinto from the Santa Rosa mountains. This valley was the traditional summer retreat of the Agua Caliente Indians, who still own this land of shady palm groves and cool streams. There are traces of old Indian campsites in remote sections.

To reach the canyon, drive south on Palm Canyon Drive (past the Canyon Hotel). Shortly after the road enters the Indian reservation, you'll come to a toll gate, open from 9 A.M. to 4 P.M. daily except during the period from May 15 to October 15, when the canyon is closed to the public because of extreme fire hazard.

During a "wet" year, the canyon may be closed for a slightly shorter time (June to September). Contact the Bureau of Indian Affairs, (619) 325-2086, for information. A small fee includes admission to Andreas Canyon. The last half-mile requires cautious driving.

You pass a number of interesting tributary canyons along the way, all containing fine stands of palms, many more than 1,000 years old. Proceeding south, the valley narrows, and you cut through the slot of Split Rock. Then the road climbs steeply to a level parking area called Hermit's Bench, where you'll find a souvenir shop, cold drinks, and rest rooms.

The steep but well-improved trail starts here, first dropping down into the canyon. Picnic tables are available, but there is no drinking water. The palms here reach an impressive height; for a short, pleasant outing, walk a mile or two along the trail winding beneath them. This is a popular trail for horseback riding.

Andreas Canyon's parking area is just over a half-mile off the main road in a grove of sycamores and cottonwoods. A clear stream runs the year around. You'll find picnic tables, rest rooms, and a wading pool (2 feet deep after a rain). The grounds are well cleared, shady, and pleasant, often crowded on weekends. Look for mortar holes gouged in large rocks near the parking lot; the Indians once used them for grinding meal. A trail follows the stream for about 4 miles along a climbing, winding route up to the head of the canyon.

Near the parking area stands a particularly impressive grove of native California fan palms (*Washingtonia filifera*), their skirts trimmed well above the ground to reduce fire hazard. These are survivors of ancient groves once widespread throughout the valley.

Murray Canyon, hidden between Andreas and Palm, has a stream flowing most of the year. From the Andreas parking area, you walk south to the canyon on a well-marked trail. Another trail leads up to a stand of fine palms. This large canyon is popular with the horsy set.

The Coachella Valley

Southeast of Palm Springs and the nearby resort areas is Coachella Valley, part of the Colorado Desert, which extends east to the Colorado River and south to the shores of the Gulf of California. The valley is endowed with a great variety of plant and animal life. There's a special fascination here in the transformation to rich farmland that has been wrought by 20th century irrigation. Average rainfall is under 2 inches a year, but artesian wells discovered around 1855 played an important role in the area's agricultural development. Many of the valley's 60,000 cultivated acres are below sea level.

From Palm Springs through Indio ("Date Capital of the United States") and south to the Salton Sea, 200,000 date palms annually yield 40 million pounds of dates of numerous varieties. You pass thick gardens of date palms along the highways. Dates and various date concoctions are sold at roadside stands on State 111 and 86; here's your chance to try a date milkshake. At Shields Date Gardens, 3½ miles west of Indio, watch a 25-minute film on how dates are grown. There is also a rose garden well worth viewing. The popular Indio National Date Festival (held in connection with the Riverside County Fair in mid-February) features an Arabian theme, with camel races (see page 93).

The most productive general farming in the valley is in the southeastern section, where the two largest cities, Indio and Coachella, are processing and shipping centers for a wide variety of agriculture. Not until you approach the Salton Sea does the desert take over again. Even here, development is underway, increasing the recreational facilities at this lake that is saltier than the oceans (see page 93).

South of the Salton Sea lies the Imperial Valley, greater in area than the Coachella Valley and acre-for-acre the most productive agricultural region in the world.

Lake Cahuilla, one of Riverside County's newest parks, makes a stopping spot for a picnic. If you bring a boat, you can also go fishing (license required). Swimming is a good way to cool off on a hot day. The park is open daily from 7 A.M. to sunset. There's a day-use fee plus an extra charge for fishing.

Joshua Tree National Monument

Though civilization is changing the character of the desert surrounding Joshua Tree, this area remains a rare desert sanctuary. The monument (lying at the edge of two great deserts—the low Colorado and the high Mojave) is a transition land of beautiful desert studded with dramatic trees and plants and covered with wildflowers in spring. It is less a playground than an area dedicated to the preservation of a characteristic desert scene and the wildlife it supports. In Joshua Tree you can drive, hike, climb, picnic, and camp.

The monument covers more than 850 square miles and is located east of Palm Springs, less than an hour's drive away. The Cottonwood Springs (or south) entrance is 25 miles east of Indio on Interstate 10; the north entrance on State Highway 62 can be reached through the towns of Joshua Tree and Twentynine Palms (the park headquarters).

The living desert

The distinctive plants and animals of this region are notable for their adaptation to the heat and aridity of the desert habitat.

The Joshua tree (*Yucca brevifolia*), most famous of the native plants, is actually a giant member of the lily family and one of the most spectacular plants of the southwestern deserts. Clusters of white blossoms, sometimes 14 inches long, appear at the ends of its angular branches; the plants have been known to attain a height of 40 feet.

Growing at 3,000 to 5,000-foot elevations in the central and western parts of the monument, the Joshua tree will bloom in March and April, except during unusually dry years. Legend has it the Mormons named the plant "Joshua tree" or "praying plant" because of its upstretched arms. At first, the newcomer might confuse it with the Mojave yucca (*Yucca schidigera*), more common at lower elevations and distinguished by much longer leaves and a shorter stature.

(Continued on page 92)

90 AROUND PALM SPRINGS

*ALGERIAN DATE PALMS
(above) rise against distant
Santa Rosa Mountains in
Coachella Valley. Sunset
heightens drama of Joshua trees
(left) in national monument.*

... Continued from page 90

In addition to extensive stands of Joshua trees, the monument has the distinctive ocotillo, the feathery nolina, and many colorful kinds of cactus with large, showy blossoms. Stately California fan palms are found in several of the shady oases. One grove in Lost Palm Canyon contains more than 100 of these trees.

The spring wildflower show at Joshua Tree is dependent upon winter rains. Average annual rainfall here is 5 inches. In a normal year, the color show begins in lower elevations as early as March.

Wildlife in the monument resembles that of other desert regions, but it is more abundant here because of the higher altitudes and a cooler, more varied climate. As with plant life, adaptation is necessary to the animals' survival. The kangaroo rat with long tufted tail is often seen around campgrounds at night. This creature and other native rodents manufacture water in their own bodies and can survive a normal lifetime without a drink. The largest animal, the desert bighorn sheep, is impressive but rarely seen. You're most likely to spot a coyote or the lively, side-blotched lizard (little brown uta). Thirty-eight species of reptiles and amphibians and 249 kinds of birds have been reported in the monument.

History unfolds in the monument

Joshua Tree National Monument has a long history of human habitation. Artifacts discovered along an ancient river terrace in the Pinto Basin indicate the presence of primitive man in days when there was enough water to support a culture. Much later, Indians who mastered the art of desert survival settled at springs and waterholes and left traces of their campsites. Old mine shafts and mills on the hillsides attest to settlement around 1865 by gold prospectors—the first white men to arrive. The cattlemen who followed left small dams or "tanks" at natural rock basins to catch rainwater for their herds.

Visiting the Desert Queen Ranch (also called Keys Ranch) is like taking a time-capsule trip back almost a century. This little-known landmark in the monument is better preserved than many desert ghost towns.

Trips are scheduled from mid-February through Memorial Day and mid-October through mid-December. A schedule for the hour-long guided tour is available at the visitor center in Joshua Tree.

At the ranch you'll see bedrock mortars, signs of Indian habitation; an adobe barn dating from the 1880s, when the area was reputedly a cattle rustler's hangout; and a stamp mill from the Desert Queen Mine of the 1890s.

But the dominant presence is that of William Keys, a colorful character who homesteaded here just after World War I, raised a family, and died here in 1969. You'll visit his now-derelict ranch house, guest cabins, school teacher's cabin and tiny schoolhouse, dam, and orchard. All of these—even the family tombstones in a touching little burial plot on the premises—are examples of Bill Keys's own handiwork.

Scattered around the landscape is a veritable catalog of old-time appliances—cars, trucks, and farm gear— all reminders of the old days when the nearest town, Banning, was 50 miles away over road so rough it hardly merited the name.

Climate and accommodations

Because much of Joshua Tree is high desert, the weather is pleasant most of the year, particularly on winter days. The altitude ranges from 1,000 to 6,000 feet in the Little San Bernardino Mountains. Since most roads are at the 3,000 to 4,000-foot level and go as high as 5,185 feet at Salton View, the monument seldom gets too hot for comfort even in summer. Most visitors come from October through May. Remember that desert nights get cold.

Joshua Tree offers several good campsites. Be sure to bring your own fuel and water; gathering firewood in the monument is prohibited, and only the Cottonwood and Black Rock Canyon campsites and the headquarters at Twentynine Palms have running water. For information, write to Joshua Tree National Monument, 74485 National Monument Drive, Twentynine Palms, CA 92277; or call (619) 367-7511.

You'll find no lodging or eating facilities within the monument, but accommodations are available in and around the entrance towns.

Exploring Joshua Tree

Your visit can include several interesting stops and adventures on your way to—and within—this diversified monument. If you are traveling State 62 to the north entrance, look for interesting antique and junk shops. Big Morongo Canyon Wildlife Preserve, at Morongo Valley, has a stand of large cottonwoods and springs that create a natural oasis.

Yucca Valley, between the San Bernardino Mountains and Joshua Tree, is built among fantastic rock formations, thick stands of Joshua trees, and spring wildflowers. Shortly after entering town, you can turn off to Pioneertown, site of many Hollywood westerns. The Pioneer Pass Road continues to Big Bear Lake but is accessible only by four-wheel-drive vehicles. On a mountain overlooking the town, Desert Christ Park features large Biblical figures sculptured of white concrete.

Along Old Woman Springs Road in Landers (north of State 62) are trailer parks for recreational vehicles and horse riders. This road also takes you to Giant Rock Airport; here, in three rooms hewn from a mammoth desert boulder, UFO buffs gather to discuss "sightings." Still another Yucca Valley attraction is the Hi-Desert Nature Museum.

Twentynine Palms, the northeastern gateway and headquarters to the monument, was once a watering place for prospectors. Now it is an oasis for health seekers, retired persons, aspiring artists, and tourists.

An early visit to the visitor center and museum here will acquaint you with the fascinating land that you are about to explore. This building contains displays, desert artifacts, and maps and brochures. Ask the rangers for additional information. A self-guided nature trail leads through the nearby palm oasis.

Cottonwood Springs, at the south entrance (just north of I-10), is another visitor center site. A 4-mile trail takes you to Lost Palms, an oasis known for its bird life and wide variety of native palms.

Hidden Valley is a few miles in from the Joshua Tree entrance to the monument. Legend has it that the massive boulders and haphazard rocks here were once hideouts for cattle rustlers. Today, they shelter a campground and provide an intriguing jumble for agile explorers. To reach the valley from the parking lot, you can either climb through a narrow passageway under jumbled granite or take a surface trail. A 1½-mile nature trail winds through the valley.

Salton View, at the end of the paved road that runs south from Hidden Valley, is 5,185 feet high, giving you a panoramic view of the area stretching from Mexico and the Salton Sea (235 feet below sea level) to the San Jacinto and San Gorgonio mountains (over 10,000 feet above sea level). Nearby, the Lost Horse Mine area is rewarding for its display of desert plants and its view to Pleasant Valley.

To reach Lost Horse Mine, you follow a dirt side road to a trail. The walk (about 2 miles each way) is too long for a 1-day visitor to the monument, but the mine remnants are quite complete and interesting.

Squaw Tank, a self-guided motor nature trail, is marked by a sign from the main park road. You'll cover 18 miles of sweeping views, inactive mines, and a fine stand of barrel cactus. Remnants of early Indian habitation are found in this area. Nearby, the climb to the top of Ryan Mountain (5,401 feet) is a steep 1.5 miles but well worth the effort.

Old Dale and New Dale, in the eastern section of the monument, is basin and range country, often overlooked by visitors.

Nature trails are numerous. Other than those already mentioned, there are well-marked walking trails at Cholla Cactus Garden and Cap Rock, each keyed to explanatory booklets.

Arch Rock, about 300 yards east of White Tanks campground, is a remarkable span of granite you can walk under. Descriptive signs mark the way.

Salton Sea

Sandwiched between the rich farmlands and resort centers of the Imperial and Coachella valleys is one of California's most interesting stretches of desert—the below-sea-level depression that contains Salton Sea.

Once a dry desert wasteland, the sea was formed in 1905 when the Colorado River overstepped its bounds; billions of gallons of its flood waters were impounded in the basin. The sea remained at a nearly constant level until about 15 years ago. Then the water began rising steadily, overtaking deserted resort buildings and leaving them half-submerged in ghostly silence.

When and how to go. Salton Sea is a hot place in summer, but winter temperatures stay in the comfortable low 50s to high 80s. Water temperatures drop as low as 50°F. in midwinter and climb to as high as 90°F. in summer. The best months are November and December and February through April.

The sea is circled by good highways—State Highway 86 on the west, State 111 on the east. The highway between Anza-Borrego Desert State Park and Palm Springs passes along its southwest shore. Dusty side roads and rocky trails lead to hot mineral springs, Indian relics and petroglyphs, rock-hunting grounds, ancient shell deposits, colorful canyons, and sand dunes.

Where to stay. The 17,868-acre Salton Sea State Recreation Area, about 26 miles northeast of Indio on State 111, provides both primitive and improved campsites and picnic areas. Brochures describing the recreation area and its facilities are available; write to the Park Supervisor, Salton Sea State Recreation Area, P.O. Box 5002, North Shore, CA 92254 (or call (619) 393-3052).

Almost all campsites are available on a first-come, first-served basis. There's one exception (a 25-site area); call Ticketron to reserve a spot here from October through May. You'll also find privately owned campgrounds near the recreation area.

(Continued on page 95)

CAMELS RACE IN INDIO

A highlight of Riverside County's National Date Festival at Indio in mid-February is the wild camel race. At best, camel racing is a precarious sport for riders and handlers and a hilarious spectacle for watchers.

Members of the International Order of Camel Jockeys (an organization of Nevada and California-based camel riders who promote this ancient sport) insist camels dislike each other, the rider, and handlers who help the rider mount.

Camels stomp, kick, bite, and spit. At the starting line (if the camel ever gets there), he's apt to buck, drag handlers in circles, run away, or lie down and refuse to participate at all. When the camel is on the run, the jockey must hang on and bounce precariously 6 or 7 feet above ground, holding his saddle (no stirrups) by skill, grit, and lots of luck. Betting is risky.

Both camel and elephant racing are listed as "intermission" events during the National Horse Show in the fairgrounds main arena (State Highway 111 and Arabia Street). Admission to the arena is moderate, and spectators attest to the popularity of the entertainment. Get there early for a seat as close as possible to the race route.

BLOOMING OCOTILLOS dot desert after torrential summer rains. Many are preserved in Anza-Borrego Desert State Park.

. . . Continued from page 93

What's happening. Motor boating and water-skiing are the major water attractions, and racers consider the sea one of the fastest bodies of water in the world because it is below sea level, a circumstance that is advantageous for internal combustion engines. If you are interested in seeing one of the larger racing or skiing meets, watch the Los Angeles or San Diego newspapers for times and dates. Strong winds create waves up to 10 feet high at times; the park has a storm alert system.

Varner Harbor is the hub of most boating and fishing activities at the recreation area. The well-equipped marina offers rentals, supplies, and boatwashing facilities. The breakwater is popular with croaker fishermen; corvina and pargo fishing is best from a boat. Fish planted in the 1950s by the Department of Fish and Game have survived, but the gradual leaching of minerals from the land has made the sea more salty, leading to a decline in good fishing.

Salton Sea National Wildlife Refuge

The east shore highway takes you close to the water for several miles before swinging east about halfway down. The sea then drops from sight and you could easily miss one of its most fascinating aspects: the great bird gatherings on the south shore.

A short detour gives you a close look. State 111 turns south at Niland; after about 4 miles, turn west on Sinclair Road. In about 6½ miles (1 mile before the pavement ends), you reach the shore at Salton Sea National Wildlife Refuge. A short trail up a pile of gargantuan twisted rocks (appropriately named Rock Hill) leads you to a panorama point. The setting is serene, but hardly quiet. When the geese are there in force, they bicker in an impressive din. Birds are attracted by the shallows and ponds and by marshes and fields beside the sea. In winter, some 150 species can usually be seen.

The refuge once extended far out into what is now the sea, but rising water reduced 32,000 above-water acres to only about 3,000.

The nearby desert

Because the desert around Salton Sea has not been developed, it is full of fascinating natural features.

Mecca Hills, a choice desert country just north of Salton Sea, has three canyons that are favorites of desert explorers—Painted Canyon, Box Canyon, and Hidden Spring Canyon. All are reached along State Highway 195 a few miles west of Mecca. The smoke tree (*Dalea spinosa*) and desert ironwood plant (*Olneya tesota*) found throughout the hills are full of purple blossoms.

Rocks and formations abound in this desert region. About 7½ miles due west of Mecca, you'll find the Fish Traps, circular pits formed from piles of large travertine-covered boulders. Archeologists aren't certain why these pits were built, but their favorite theory seems to be that the stones were collected by Indians and piled in these circular forms to trap fish in ancient Lake Cahuilla, which covered the Salton Sink from about 900 to 1400 A.D.

Travertine Rock is a mound of enormous boulders located approximately 100 yards off State 86 about 6 miles south of its intersection with State 195. Once partially submerged by Lake Cahuilla, the mound is covered with a scaly, knobby limestone (actually not true travertine but a calcareous rock called tufa). A climb to the top (about 200 feet) reveals a full view of the Coachella Valley and its miles of farms plotted in geometric precision.

The country south of Travertine Rock along State 86 is happy hunting ground for amateur geologists and rock collectors. Each year desert rains sweep clean the broad shallow washes of the Santa Rosa Mountains and carry down brightly colored and oddly formed quartzites, flints, granites, schists, and sandstone. Look for them in washes around the south end of the sea—the farther from the highway the better.

Anza-Borrego Desert State Park

Anza-Borrego is a large desert. The area preserved within state park boundaries extends almost the entire length of San Diego County's eastern edge from Riverside County to the Mexican border. It ranges from 100 feet below sea level near the Salton Sea to 6,000 feet above on San Ysidro Mountain. You can't see it all in one visit. Covering over half a million acres, the desert comprises more than two-thirds of all the land in California's system of preserves.

The southern part of the present state park was originally a separate desert park named for Captain Juan Bautista de Anza, the Spanish explorer who pioneered this route to Alta California in 1774. Borrego State Park, taking its name from the Spanish word for "sheep," adjoined it on the north. In 1957 the two parks were combined.

Anza-Borrego is often pictured as a wrinkled wasteland of harshly eroded, nearly barren clay and gravel, possibly because its gullied badlands are its most extraordinary phenomenon. There is more to it than that: cool piny heights, springs and oozing *cienagas*, spectacular though brief waves of wildflowers in spring, and native fragrances of pervasive sage, subtle cottonwood, and even more subtle earth. Today's visitor can traverse a terrain nearly as wild and untouched as that found by early Spanish visitors. Many travelers consider November through May the best time of year to explore this desert—then it has a clean-washed, fresh look.

This state park is one of California's last untamed desert areas. The privately owned enclave of Borrego Valley in the northern part of the park is the only section to have been developed, and with development isolated to that region, Anza-Borrego can remain one of California's last frontiers. Like Palm Springs and Salton Sea, the valley taps underground sources for water. Nearby, 6,000 acres of former wasteland are cultivated for grapes, gladioli, citrus fruits, and grains. Along with its farms, subdivisions, shopping centers, golf courses, and airports, the area offers tourist accommodations.

Wildlife is worth watching for. Some desert bighorn sheep still live in remote areas of the north end of the park and in the Santa Rosa Mountains beyond. At points

farthest away from human activity, the natural desert is often a noisy place, with the humming of winged insects, the buzz of the cicada, the croaking of frogs in the springs and marshes, and the sounds of many birds.

About 600 species of plants are native to the park. Depending on altitude and exposure, desert flowers bloom profusely in March and April. Wildflowers range from tiny, pin-size blooms to clusters of red on the ocotillo, which punctuate the landscape after a rainstorm. The California fan palm groves and the stands of smoke trees are among the finest anywhere, but Anza-Borrego is most renowned for its low, fat-boled elephant trees (*Bursera microphylla*), fairly common in parts of Baja California but north of the border practically confined to the Anza-Borrego region.

Driving is not difficult. More than 600 miles of roads follow the scenic, weathered hills and flatland. Though a deftly handled automobile can do surprisingly well in the desert, there are many roads that require high clearance or even four-wheel-drive vehicles. Pickup campers can get to some remote places; jeeps are advisable for the really tough routes.

Rangers conduct family cars in caravans to many scenic destinations and can point out roadside geological features, sea fossils, wildlife, and some unusual plants.

Camping has a unique feature here. This is the only California state park in which you may camp anywhere you wish. The only regulations are that you drive on established roads (horses and hikers are not restricted), that you not light fires on the ground, and that you leave things just as you found them. The nearest ranger will come to your rescue if you've camped off the beaten path and have failed to check in at a prearranged time the next day. Camping areas vary from highly developed (Borrego Springs) to less than the basic (your own site in a remote spot).

Desert camping is most popular from November through May, though there may be high winds or a few very cold nights during these months.

For a short visit to the park, it is best to select a relatively small area and explore it thoughtfully. Check at the visitor center for information. If you can spend several days, establish a preliminary headquarters near one of the ranger stations, where you can attend campfire programs, get latest information on backcountry driving conditions, and check out and back in for your own safety. Based on locations of active ranger stations, the most logical divisions of the park and some of their features are listed here:

Borrego Springs, a small resort community at the foot of San Ysandro Mountain a few miles north of State Highway 78, is the center of park activity. Park headquarters is Borrego Palm Canyon, 3 miles northwest of Borrego Springs. For a list of lodgings, write to the Chamber of Commerce, Borrego Springs, CA 92004. State 78 and County Road S2 are the major routes leading into the park. The Borrego-Salton Sea Road (County Road S22) parallels State 78 as a short cut from Borrego Springs to Palm Springs, Indio, and the Salton Sea.

Borrego Palm Canyon is the site of park headquarters and the most improved campground in the park. Its many conveniences include gas stoves, ramadas (sun

shelters), showers, and trailer sites with hookups. Nearby are several points of interest: a 1½-mile, self-guided nature trail leading up to a canyon of palms; the most famous view point in the park, overlooking barren, spectacularly eroded Borrego Badlands; date groves; and a jeep road to Pumpkin Patch, a flat area covered with large, round concretions of unexplained origin.

Culp Valley is in high country, up to 4,500 feet. Here you'll find primitive camping on semiwooded land with many huge boulders. From here a dramatic view extends across Borrego Valley to the badlands. Culp Valley is a cool retreat from the summer heat of the lower desert.

Tamarisk Grove has an improved campground that faces the beautiful, flowery slopes of the North Pinyon Mountains and a remarkable natural concentration of cactus. Good auto exploring is possible on a primitive road along San Felipe Creek and Grapevine Canyon. Borrego Valley is a few minutes away by way of Yaqui Pass. Yaqui Well, a historic watering spot above Tamarisk Grove, has magnificent desert ironwood trees and a busy wildlife population.

Blair Valley can be reached on the Overland Stage Route, hacked through historic Box Canyon by the Mormon Battalion and still in use as County S2. A year-round "use" area, Blair Valley has improved campgrounds at Old Vallecito Stage Station and at Agua Caliente Springs.

Fish Creek comes into view along a dramatic motor route up Fish Creek Wash through Split Mountain to Sandstone Canyon, with a jeep trail continuing through Hapaha Flat to the Pinyon Mountains. Eerie mud hills and elephant trees are features of this area. Supplies and meals are available in Ocotillo Wells.

Bow Willow has many palm groves, especially in the Mountain Palm Springs area; about 300 *torotes* (a Spanish word for "elephant trees") in Torote Canyon; a smoke tree forest; the old Carrizo Stage Station site; many inviting roads, jeep trails, and foot trails; the Well of the Eight Echoes (some say only seven); and the Dos Cabezas area, with monumental rocks, lava flow, a mine, Mortero Palms, and the giddy, canyonside tracks of the San Diego and Arizona Eastern Railway.

The Colorado River

With its most renowned handiwork the Grand Canyon, the mighty Colorado carves through rugged terrain on the earth's surface, winding some 1,400 miles before reaching the sea. Once described as "too thick to drink and too thin to plow," the once-raging river (forming a natural boundary between California and Arizona) was used by early American Indians as a thoroughfare for canoe travel. Petroglyphs cut in rocks near Lake Havasu City are believed to be shoreline messages of these ancient river voyagers.

Important today as a major water supplier to the metropolitan areas on the Southern California coast, the Colorado River has been harnessed by dams and developed into a vacation and recreation area. Once traversed by paddle wheel steamers, the river is now dotted along its shoreline with campgrounds and marinas.

Most of the 265 miles of river from Hoover Dam in Nevada to the Mexican border are suitable for public recreation purposes. Along the lower Colorado River, Havasu Lake is the largest recreational development, increasingly popular each year.

This is "low desert" country where the summers are hot, and in July and August, boating, fishing, and water-skiing at the lakes are outstanding.

Around Needles

At the Arizona border, the town of Needles is at the junction of two major highways—Interstate 40 and U.S. 95. Established in 1869 as a steamboat landing and supply station on the Old Emigrant Trail, Needles today has many boating facilities. Good beaches line the river, and diversified fishing is possible in the Havasu National Wildlife Refuge. A marina and golf course add to the attractions. The nearby rock formations known as "The Needles" are visible from the highway crossing at Topock; they are a backdrop for the spectacular boat trip down through Topock Gorge to upper Lake Havasu.

Park Moabi is 11 miles southeast of Needles on I-40. The park surrounds a lagoon opening into the river, directly across from the wildlife refuge. Launching facilities, boat docking, and boat rentals (including houseboats) are available. Secluded, sun-bleached, sandy inlets invite camping, and fishing is good.

Topock Gorge to Lake Havasu is an easy weekend trip on a houseboat through spectacular multicolored canyons. Fishing is varied: deep trolling may produce striped bass or trout; catfish are plentiful for bait fishermen plumbing holes in warmer bays.

Though onshore camping is prohibited in many areas, houseboaters may anchor overnight in sheltered bays and backwaters. Park Moabi is the best place to rent a boat.

For information on other recreation activities and facilities along this section of the Colorado River, write to the Economic Development Department, County Civic Bldg.—West, 175 W. Fifth Street, San Bernardino, CA 92415; or call (714) 383-2913.

Lake Havasu

Construction of Parker Dam in 1938 not only tamed the lower Colorado River but also created a 45-mile-long fresh-water lake that, contrasting with the raging red river, was quiet and very blue. Named Havasu (an Indian word for "blue water"), this lake is lined with deep bays and picturesque coves. Set between the Chemehuevi, Mohave, and Whipple mountains, the beautiful lake has become a favorite destination for sports enthusiasts and the setting for an extensive recreational development—Lake Havasu City.

Three national championship water sports contests annually take place on Lake Havasu: the Desert Regatta for sailing craft in May, the National Invitational Ski Championships in midsummer, and the Outboard World Championships.

The London Bridge is the most conspicuous addition to the desert landscape around Lake Havasu. This historic span, moved block by block from its site on the Thames River, was reassembled across dry land. Then the mile-long channel now separating the airport island from the shore was excavated beneath it. After the bridge was sold by the city of London for almost $2½ million, it took an additional $5½ million to dismantle the 130,000 tons of granite, ship them 10,000 miles to Lake Havasu City, and reassemble them. The bridge looks at home in an English village setting, with pub, restaurant, and shops built around it. A London double-decker red bus is parked on the waterfront. In early October an annual week-long event celebrates the London Bridge Anniversary.

Lake Havasu City, 19 miles south of Interstate 40, is served daily by scheduled airlines from Phoenix and Las Vegas. Private planes dot the parking strips, and amphibians take off and land on the water. Hotels are located in the middle of the shopping center, overlooking the lake, and near the golf course. Facilities for campers and trailers are at Havasu Cove on the lakefront.

Lake Havasu State Park

A 13,000-acre preserve, this park has headquarters at Pittsburgh Point on the airport island. Check with rangers for information on camping around the lake. There is no shoreline road, but roads do penetrate to the shore at a few points for boat launching. At some points are resorts, boating facilities (including rentals), trailer parks, and camping spaces.

The park has wide, sandy beaches with picnic tables, fountains, barbecue pits, showers, and rest rooms. The blue green bay offers good water-skiing, limited only by your endurance, and safe swimming in exceptionally clear water.

Anglers usually catch their limit of bass, trout, crappie, bluegill, and channel fish. The clear, cold Colorado River waters connecting Lake Havasu and Lake Mohave to the north are noted for good bass and trout.

For additional information about the park, write to Lake Havasu State Park, 1350 W. McCulloch Boulevard, Lake Havasu City, AZ 86403.

The lower Colorado

The Imperial Dam, near Yuma, Arizona, mixes work and play. Here water is diverted to irrigate the lands of Southern California and Arizona. But the dam also raises the water level of the Colorado, widening the river for 30 miles upstream and providing good facilities for boaters, anglers, and water-skiers.

A good introduction to the stretch of Colorado between Blythe and Martinez Lake is the annual fall Colorado River Cruise. On this overnight family campout, each small flotilla of motorboats is accompanied by an experienced guide who allows plenty of time for exploring.

The launching begins on a Saturday morning at Blythe for the 6-hour trip to the night's camp at Martinez Lake; the return cruise the next day, going against the current, takes longer. For trip details and entry forms, write to the Blythe Chamber of Commerce, 201 S. Broadway, Blythe, CA 92225.

Santa Barbara

Spanish Santa Barbara offers an entree to surrounding beach communities, pastoral inland valleys, and off-the-road missions. North on El Camino Real, visit Danish Solvang, dig for Pismo clams, and begin a coast-hugging trip from Morro Bay to San Simeon, site of incredible Hearst Castle.

Santa Barbara is a city of obvious beauty and year-round allure. Spreading north from a wide and gently curving beach, the city lies in a sunny sheltered plain. Offshore to the south, the Channel Islands seem a protective barrier against the ocean beyond. And behind the city, the mountains of the Santa Ynez range form a rugged east-to-west backdrop. Yet its stunning setting is not the foremost thing you notice about Santa Barbara. Most likely you will be impressed by the signs of its historical perpetuation: the Spanish and mission architectures; adobes, old and new; tile roofs; bell towers; and the Spanish love of color.

Not all of Santa Barbara's urban charm is manmade—nature contributes a gentle lushness that contrasts with and enhances the traditional buildings. Like living picture frames around large-scale masterpieces, stately palms ring many buildings. Fir trees—decorated at Christmas—are planted along the streets, marking pedestrian crossings. Santa Barbara's cultural calendar is testimony to the city's love for plants and flowers—the International Orchid Show is held here every spring, and the Santa Barbara National Horse and Flower Show occurs annually in mid-July.

Visitors can choose from a varied schedule of events, ranging from popular Old Spanish Days in August, to the earlier Summer Sports Festival, and the Fishermen's Festival in spring.

Some of Santa Barbara's warmest, sunniest days are in autumn. Fishing holds up well into fall, and ocean temperatures remain warm enough for swimming into December. In September you find a significant change in accommodation prices; off-season rates are in effect until June.

Spaniards who settled here called it "La Tierra Adorado" (the beloved land); today's visitors find it hard not to share their enchantment.

This chapter also takes you into the inland hills, where you can drive country roads or camp beside a peaceful lake. Solvang, in the Santa Ynez Valley, is a paradise for those partial to Scandinavian culture and shopping possibilities. The Ojai Valley is lake and mountain country, home of the largest land birds in North America—the condors.

Stretch your trip up the coast to include Pismo Beach (clam capital), inland San Luis Obispo, Morro Bay with its prominent rock formations, and San Simeon, headquarters for touring "Hearst Castle," now a State Historic Monument.

An Architectural Heritage

The big earthquake of 1925 destroyed many of the city's post-Victorian structures, forced early demolition of others, and opened the way for Santa Barbara to express its Mediterranean consciousness in the course of rebuilding. An architectural review board has been approving or rejecting designs for business and public buildings ever since.

Spanish names were given (or restored) to streets in the heart of town, with the one significant exception of State Street, which did not revert to the Spanish tongue twister "Calle del Estado." Most of the reconstructed adobes are within a block or two of De la Guerra Plaza.

TILE ROOFS and palm trees, sprinkled throughout the city, lend Mediterranean touch to coastal Santa Barbara.

Downtown Santa Barbara

The 12-block downtown area (bounded by Victoria, Chapala, Ortega, and Santa Barbara streets) includes Pueblo Viejo (Old Town), a historic preserve and original core of the city that surrounded the Presidio. As you walk around, you'll find plaques and markers identifying early buildings. Only a few are open to visitors.

In downtown Santa Barbara you won't feel dwarfed by a Manhattanlike cluster of high-rises—the area is designed for pedestrians. Buildings, with few exceptions, are four stories or less, tightly controlled by a height ordinance that can't be varied unless approved by the voters. At the Santa Barbara Chamber of Commerce (1301 Santa Barbara Street), you can pick up a copy of the Red Tile Tour, a guide and map for a 24-mile scenic drive in and around the city. Park in any of the nine city lots shown on the downtown tour map; the first 90 minutes parking is free.

State Street is perhaps the best place to begin the tour. Rebuilt as a plaza boulevard in 1969, it is the heart of downtown. In the 1960s, Santa Barbara's downtown was decaying. Competition from the new La Cumbre Plaza shopping center a few miles away was cutting off retail trade. New shops were opened downtown, and convenient parking brought back business. Though State Street is still a main artery, its wide, landscaped sidewalks shield pedestrians from traffic.

Wherever you begin your exploring, you'll find some interesting buildings and shops along your route. Here are some highlights of Old Town:

The Santa Barbara Museum of Art (corner of State and Anapamu streets next to the public library) is small, bright, airy, and—unlike other landmarks on the route—modern. Soft natural light enters the gallery through skylights, falling on Greek, Roman, and Egyptian sculptures and priceless glassware; an encircling gallery and adjacent halls contain impressive collections of Asian and American art from many periods. The museum is privately supported. It's open daily except Monday and holidays, from 11 A.M. to 5 P.M. (Sunday from noon to 5). Guided tours take place at 1:30 P.M. weekdays, 2 P.M. weekends.

The Santa Barbara County Court House buildings and grounds cover a square block bounded by Santa Barbara, Anacapa, Anapamu, and Figueroa streets. Built in 1929, the courthouse, with its great archway, wrought-iron balconies, gay mosaics, murals, red-tiled roof, romantic towers, and hand-carved doors, resembles a Spanish-Moorish castle. It's truly architecture on a grand scale. Above the entrance arch on Anacapa Street is an appropriate Roman motto in Spanish; the nearby English version reads, "God gave us the country. The skill of man hath built this town."

Built on the site of the first encampment in this area of peripatetic Portola and his men (1769), the courthouse and elaborate sunken gardens are the setting for pageants, concerts, and celebrations. Most notable is Old Spanish Days.

In the Assembly Room, huge, two-story murals colorfully depict Santa Barbara history, including the arrival of Juan Rodriguez Cabrillo in 1542, the founding of Mission Santa Barbara in 1786, and Colonel John Fremont's 1846 announcement heralding American rule in California.

The tower, El Mirador, whose only access is the elevator that operates on weekdays, provides an unequalled view of the city and courthouse grounds.

Today, many courthouse functions take place in the new county administration building located nearby, but the courtrooms, law library, and some of the offices are still used. You can visit the courthouse on weekdays from 8 A.M. to 5 P.M. and weekends from 9 to 5. Free guided tours are given Friday at 10:30 A.M.

The Santa Barbara Historical Society Museum, at the corner of De la Guerra and Santa Barbara streets, houses many of the city's historical treasures. Representative of the old and new, the building is made of adobe bricks formed from soil at the site and is reinforced with modern steel.

One wing is devoted to the Mexican and Spanish periods of Santa Barbara's history and displays a carved statue of Saint Barbara from the Royal Presidio, fascinating old letters, early costumes, and relics of Richard Henry Dana's famous visits to the city, including a model of his brig, *Pilgrim*, and a portrait of its captain.

The museum, home of the Santa Barbara Historical Society, offers free admission. It is open afternoons except Monday; you can take a guided tour Wednesday and Sunday at 1:30 P.M.

Casa de Covarrubias and Historic Fremont Adobe are around the corner, at 715 Santa Barbara Street. The casa, built in 1817, hosted the last meeting of Congress under Mexican rule. Colonel Fremont made the adobe his headquarters after the American takeover in 1846.

The Rochin Adobe, at 820 Santa Barbara Street, is sheathed in clapboard as protection from the weather. Built of adobe salvaged from the Presidio ruins, it is a double house with two street entrances. Privately owned, it is not open to the public.

Lobero Theatre, at the corner of Anacapa and Canon Perdido, stands on the site of the city's first theater.

El Presidio de Santa Barbara State Historic Park (122 and 123 E. Canon Perdido) includes some of the city's oldest structures: the recently restored Padre's quarters, the Presidio chapel, El Cuartel, and La Caneda Adobe.

Founded in 1782, the Presidio was the fourth and last Spanish army post in California. El Cuartel—then soldiers' quarters—was built soon after the Presidio in the original quadrangle. Across the street from El Cuartel is La Caneda Adobe. This lovingly restored house contains both a private residence and the office for the Santa Barbara Trust for Historic Preservation.

The park, including exhibits and a museum shop in El Cuartel, is open weekdays from 9 A.M. to noon, and from 1 to 4 P.M.; weekend hours are noon to 4 P.M. The park is closed on major holidays.

The Hill-Carrillo Adobe (11 E. Carrillo Street) was built by Massachusetts-born Daniel Hill in 1826 for his Spanish bride. The most modern house of its day, it had wooden floors instead of the usual hard-baked clay. Now fully restored, it's open weekdays from 9 A.M. to 4 P.M.

(Continued on page 103)

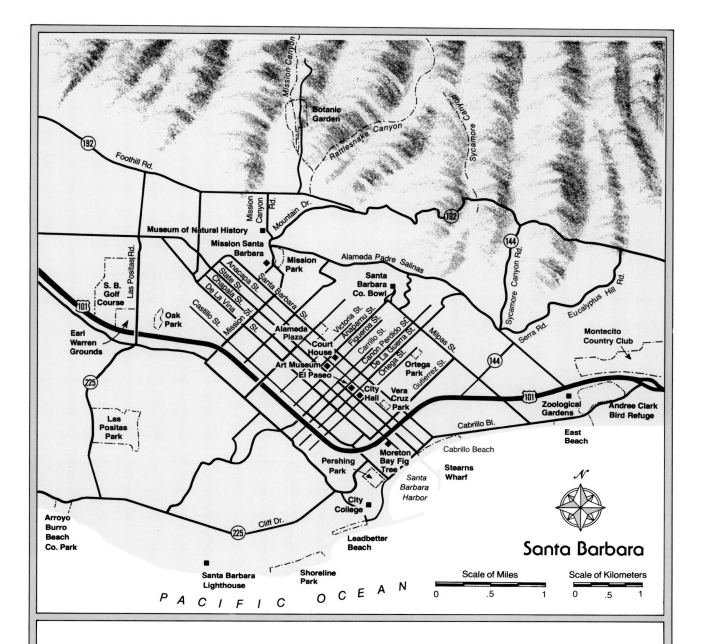

Major Points of Interest

Santa Barbara Court House (downtown) — Spanish-Moorish castle facade; historical murals; good city view from tower

El Paseo (downtown) — Mediterranean shopping arcade built in and around historic adobes; indoor and outdoor cafes

Mission Santa Barbara (Mission Canyon) — picturesque "Queen of Missions" still in continuous use by Franciscans

Museum of Natural History (just north of mission) — fascinating exhibits focusing on natural phenomena of the West

Santa Barbara Botanic Garden (1½ miles above mission) — indigenous California plants displayed in their natural settings

Moreton Bay Fig Tree (corner Chapala and Montecito streets)—one of the nation's largest trees, planted in 1877; branch spread of over 160 feet

Santa Barbara Zoological Gardens (overlooking waterfront) — children's park features zoo, playground, picnic area among landscaped grounds

Andree Clark Bird Refuge (waterfront) — preserve for geese, swans, migrant fowl; trails permit biking, hiking

SAVORING THE OUTDOORS
ranks as year-round activity in
Santa Barbara. Pedestrians stroll
downtown streets (left), eat at side-
walk restaurants (below), enjoy
splashes of color in El Paseo's
entryway (bottom).

. . . Continued from page 100

El Paseo (15 E. De la Guerra Street), a picturesque shopping arcade reminiscent of Old Spain, was built in and around the adobe home of the De la Guerra family. It was begun in 1819 by mission Indians, and a brick in the wall of the passageway bears the date of completion — 1826. Casa de la Guerra, noted for its hospitality, was made famous in Dana's *Two Years Before the Mast* as the setting for a colorful Spanish wedding fiesta.

Some of the shops spill over into the Orena adobes next door. Here the antiques you see are for sale. Elsewhere in El Paseo you can find stores specializing in leather goods, candles, books, local pottery, and Mexican, Scandinavian, and Oriental imports. Art stores and galleries are particularly at home here. The El Paseo restaurant is a popular spot for full-scale lunch or dinner. For simpler daytime fare, the El Paseo Cafe offers an outdoor dining area.

Across the street is the plaza where the first City Council met in 1850 and where the first City Hall was located. During Fiesta Week, it becomes a colorful *mercado* (marketplace).

Mission Canyon

You can take many drives into the hills behind Santa Barbara, but one of the prettiest is Mission Canyon Road. It begins at the old mission and takes you north into the hills to the Museum of Natural History and Santa Barbara Botanic Garden. This "back country," a beautiful, semirural area on the slopes of the Santa Ynez Mountains, is separated from the city by 500-foot-high foothills known as "The Riviera."

The scenic drive along The Riviera on Alameda Padre Serra winds through a pleasant residential area (with a rambling hotel), giving you a beautiful view of the city and the ocean. You can turn into some of the little canyons, but they are somewhat difficult to navigate. To return to town easily, take Gutierrez Street.

Mission Santa Barbara

Overlooking the city from a knoll at the end of Laguna Street sits the tenth in a long line of missions. Founded in 1786 by Father Fermin Lasuen, it is the only mission that has been continuously in the hands of the Franciscans.

Having a unique stone facade—the only California mission to display two similar towers—"the Queen of the Missions" is a popular subject for photographers. Design for the facade was copied from a Roman book on architecture written by Vitruvius in 27 B.C. (The book is still in the mission archives.) The strange mixture of classical and mission style was later retained when the face was rebuilt because of earthquake damage and wear.

The water system developed by the mission padres was so complete that part of it is still used by Santa Barbara's water company. You can see an Indian-built dam in the Botanic Garden.

Off the arcade corridor (the floor tiles were made in 1811) are three of the original rooms, one a primitive kitchen. The rooms and artifacts suggest some of the quality of mission life when the Franciscans were teaching the Indians not only religion and language but also agriculture and some 50 crafts.

Under huge pepper trees, the Moorish fountain flows into a stone laundry basin where Indian women once washed their clothes.

You can enter the old cemetery through a Roman archway with two real skulls and crossbones hanging above it, a common sight in Mexican churches.

The mission altar light has burned constantly since the mission was built. Still used daily as a parish church, the mission is open to the public from 9 A.M. to 5 P.M. Monday through Saturday, 1 to 5 P.M. on Sunday. The chapel, curio room, and library contain relics of the mission days. Self-guided tours cost 50 cents for adults and are free to children under 16.

Museum of Natural History

You'll find this museum just 2 blocks north of Mission Santa Barbara, at 2559 Puesta del Sol Road; it's set amid 2 acres of wooded ground. Displays cover a range of topics, but the focus is on natural phenomena of the West, including regional plant and animal life, geology, and prehistoric Indian culture. There are well-conceived exhibits, comprehensible even to young children; some perform mechanically at the push of a button.

Museum hours are 9 A.M. to 5 P.M. Monday through Saturday, 10 A.M. to 5 P.M. Sunday and holidays. Tours are offered on Sunday at 2 P.M. The museum is closed on major holidays. Call (805) 682-4711 for further information.

Nearby Gladwin Planetarium has closed circuit television, enabling several people to view the skies together through the large telescope. Call (805) 682-4334 for admission rates and program information.

Santa Barbara Botanic Garden

Indigenous California plants, from wildflowers to giant redwoods, grow in their natural settings on 65 acres in Mission Canyon, just 1½ miles above the mission.

Over 5 miles of trails wind through canyon, desert, channel island, arroyo, and redwood sections along historic Mission Creek, and past the old dam and aqueduct built in 1806 to supply water for the mission. The History Trail takes you back to the days when the local Indians had to support themselves from the land, using plants for food, drink, soap, medicine, and household needs. Self-guided, the trail begins and ends near the Information Office. Plan about an hour for a leisurely walk.

Spring and summer offer the most colorful tours of the garden. Flowering shrubs, poolside plants, and brilliant wildflowers blaze in the meadow section; the ceanothus (mountain lilac) flowers white and blue; and the desert section comes alive with blooming cacti, yuccas, and wildflowers.

The Botanic Garden, at 1212 Mission Canyon Road, is open all year from 8 A.M. to dusk. You can take a guided tour on Thursday at 10:30 A.M. Admission is free.

Another Santa Barbara park of interest to gardeners is Franceschi Park on Mission Ridge Road, high on the crest of The Riviera.

Attractions around Town

As you drive the scenic route around Santa Barbara you'll pass through the Montecito and Hope Ranch areas. These rank high among the country's most luxurious residential communities. Both areas have private country clubs and golf courses. North of the Hope Ranch section, campers will find an RV park, and near the beach, in the Montecito area, is another camping facility with complete camper hookups.

Earl Warren Showgrounds

Horses and horse shows are very popular in Santa Barbara. Hardly a month goes by without an amateur local or regional horse show. The Earl Warren Showgrounds, Las Positas Road at U.S. 101, is home for Santa Barbara's National Horse and Flower Show, held annually in mid-July. This top-rated event combines equestrian excellence with entertainment and 22,000 feet of garden displays. Another popular event is the annual San Fernando Arabian Horse Association Show held Memorial Day weekend. This colorful activity is free for spectators.

Moreton Bay fig tree

The Moreton Bay fig, at the corner of Chapala and Montecito streets, is the largest tree of its kind in the nation. Native to Australia, it was planted by a little girl in 1877. Today, it's believed that 10,000 people could stand in its shade at noon. Measurements made in 1970 indicated a branch spread of 160 feet.

Fernald House and Trussel-Winchester Adobe

Multigabled, 14-room Fernald House (414 W. Montecito Street) is a Victorian mansion handsomely furnished and accessorized in fitting style. The lovely stairway and carvings throughout the house attest to yesteryear's craftsmanship. The adobe next door was built in 1854 with timbers from a wrecked ship and bricks. Both houses are owned and maintained by the Santa Barbara Historical Society. They're open on Sunday only, from 2 to 4 P.M.; there's a small admission fee.

Carriage house

The vintage surreys, hansoms, and buggies of the Carriage Museum look their best for the Old Spanish Days parade in August—their annual chance to show they're still street-worthy. Decorated to a turn, carriages carry dignitaries along the line of march.

The rest of the year the venerable vehicles are on display in the museum at 128 Castillo Street, a block inland from Cabrillo Boulevard. Look sharp for the building; it sits back from the street next to a field. You can visit the old-timers without charge any Sunday from 2 to 4 P.M., except the Sunday before the parade. The Sunday after the parade, the museum holds an open house from 1 to 4 P.M.

At the Waterfront

It is a surprise to many people that Santa Barbara has a southern exposure to the sea. In fact, the California coastline runs almost due west from Ventura to Point Conception, the magic dividing point for California's coast. South of Conception, the climate is Mediterranean; north of it, waters grow progressively cooler. Santa Barbara is as Mediterranean in her waters as in her architecture.

In spite of Navy missiles to port (Point Mugu) and Air Force missiles to starboard (Vandenberg Air Force Base on Point Conception), Santa Barbara boasts one of the most alluring stretches of developed coastline that you will find. Miles of wide, gently curving beaches are lined with palms. Swimmers, surfers, picnickers, scuba divers, fishermen, and grunion-hunters enjoy it all, except in a few places where oil rigs take over.

The main pier, Stearns Wharf, could be called an extension of State Street, the city's main thoroughfare. Rebuilt after a fire several years ago, it offers shops, restaurants, and good ocean views.

Cabrillo Boulevard, a palm-lined drive along the ocean, is especially popular with strollers and cyclists. To the west of the wharf, West Cabrillo Boulevard is lined with attractive motels, nearly all with swimming pools and many with balconies facing the yacht harbor. Nearby are a municipal swimming pool, a lovely shaded park, and—west of the yacht harbor and breakwater—another stretch of beach. The municipal pool, Los Banos del Mar, is open all year; there's also a wading pool.

The picturesque 92-acre yacht harbor, protected by a long breakwater, shelters the local fishing fleet, as well as hundreds of pleasure craft.

East of the wharf, the curving beach extends to the Andree Clark Bird Refuge at the end of East Cabrillo Boulevard.

Weekend art activity on the Santa Barbara waterfront is so lively that rows of canvases and sculpture stretch as far as a mile along East Cabrillo Boulevard. At this "Arts and Crafts Show" you'll find pottery, leather craft, metalwork, handmade clothing, and jewelry, in addition to paintings. Open only to local artists, the nonrestrictive, unjuried show is extremely popular.

Andree Clark Bird Refuge

A landscaped preserve along the beach protects geese, swans, and other fowl. There are trails for biking and benches where one can sit and photograph, or just observe tame birds. Bird feeding is discouraged.

Just east of the refuge, turn right on Channel Drive to see the lovely gardens of the Santa Barbara Biltmore Hotel and the exclusive Montecito district.

Zoological Gardens

Situated on a hilltop on East Cabrillo Boulevard is a garden of play and adventure formerly known as Child's Estate. Overlooking the ocean and the refuge, this park has a charming garden zoo, playground, and picnic area.

It is being developed by the community of Santa Barbara, which also oversees the displays.

Most animals at the zoo meet youngsters at eye level. From lacy white strutting peacocks to ruffled little ducklings swimming with their mothers in pathside ponds, the animals seem at once natural and friendly. Their names are often presented in a childlike scrawl on signposts. From the zoo entrance, a 24-gauge miniature train takes you on a tour past the adjoining Andree Clark Bird Refuge and fresh-water lagoon.

Athletic and popular seals show off in a sealarium with viewing portholes for visitors of any height. At the Rancher's Pet Park, children delight in mingling with tame animals—small deer, domestic and African pygmy goats, cows, and pigs.

Besides Susi the Chimp, Herman the Llama, the alligator, owls, bobcats, and the rest of the community, the park also contains a wild west playground of rocky hideouts, a covered wagon and tepee, and a rest area for parents. The fountain, pergola, and picnic area are peaceful stops.

The zoo is open daily except Monday from 10 A.M. to 5 P.M. Admission is moderate; the train ride and parking are extra.

The beaches

Along the 70-mile stretch of coastline running due east between Point Conception and Ventura are a number of state and county parks centered around beaches characterized by a lack of strong winds and predominantly warm waters.

Jalama Beach, just north of Point Conception, is the most isolated and uninhabited of the area's beaches; no supplies are available. It is the only point of public access to the Point Conception fishing grounds. Rough surf prevents swimming or boating; however, the beach is reached by a very scenic road. Rock hunting is good here, and Jalama is probably the southernmost driftwood beach along the Pacific Coast.

Between Point Conception and Santa Barbara are five beach parks: Gaviota State Park (public fishing pier, boat rentals, swimming, campgrounds, trailer sites, picnic and camp fees); Refugio Beach (swimming, surf fishing, camping, picnic tables, picnic and camp fees); El Capitan Beach (campgrounds, trailer sites, boat rentals, boat launching ramp, picnic and camp fees); popular Goleta Beach (sheltered cove for boats, electric boat hoist, fishing pier, swimming, picnicking); and Arroyo Burro Beach (surf fishing, swimming, picnicking) at the outskirts of Santa Barbara.

The long beach area in Santa Barbara proper is open to the public, except for a few spots that are reserved for occupants of some oceanfront hotels.

Carpinteria State Beach, just off U.S. 101 at Carpinteria (campgrounds, fishing pier, boat launching ramp, food concession, picnic and camp fees), calls itself "the world's safest beach." A long, sandy slope extends into deep water with no riptides.

Emma Wood State Beach is about 3 miles north of Ventura (campgrounds, surf fishing, swimming). The last beach in this area is San Buenaventura State Beach, facing the city of Ventura. Ventura's beaches are wide, sandy, and inviting. Walkways line the main section of the city beach, offering fine ocean views.

Water sports

For many visitors, the activities centered around the ocean are the main attraction of Santa Barbara.

Surfing and snorkeling are good a few miles north or south along the shore from Santa Barbara. You will find clear water for snorkeling and reefs that push the mild, incoming swells up into respectable, long-lasting, diagonal waves that are good for surfing. Some of the best water is at Arroyo Burro and Leadbetter beaches, both west of the breakwater; they're rough but inviting.

Boating centers around the yacht harbor. A concrete launching ramp (fee required, $1 in quarters) and a large parking area for boat trailers at the foot of Bath Street are provided. You can rent motor boats or sailboats in any of several classes.

Water-skiing takeoff area is the beach immediately to the east (lee side) of Stearns Wharf. After launching your boat at the yacht harbor ramp, you usually do your skiing between the wharf and East Beach. You can stay inside the natural breakwater formed by offshore kelp beds if the water is too choppy outside.

Offshore fishing is about as productive here as anywhere else along the California coast. Party boats usually head for Santa Cruz, largest of the Channel Islands, and anchor in a relatively sheltered zone. At a day's end, with ordinary luck, you should have more than enough rockfish.

Some charter boats are available at the yacht harbor for pursuit of albacore, big-game tuna, marlin, and sailfish. But for a day or a half-day of less ambitious deep-sea angling at minimum cost, you can go to Sea Landing at the foot of Bath Street and Cabrillo Boulevard. Here you will find a harbor and an offshore excursion boat. All equipment you will need and a temporary California fishing license are available.

No license is necessary for pier fishing. Still-fishing with shrimp for bait may produce a nice haul of tasty perch.

The Channel Islands

Lying south of Santa Barbara across the Santa Barbara Channel are the Channel Islands. A clear day will reward you with a glimpse of them from the mainland; otherwise, only their mountainous outlines are hazily prominent in the mist.

The islands are in fact the tops of submerged mountains—possibly the continuation of the Santa Monica range. To ensure the preservation of rare indigenous wildlife, five of the Channel Islands were designated a national park (the nation's 40th) in 1980. The waters surrounding the park were subsequently declared a national marine sanctuary.

The residents of "America's Galapagos" include cormorants, sea lions, and California brown pelicans; trail systems and boat tours give you the chance to observe these and other fauna and flora. Plant enthusiasts won't be disappointed with the island's unique trees, shrubs, and wildflowers. The vivid blooms of the giant coreopsis steal the show in late winter, visible from the mainland and far out to sea as splashes of brilliant yellow.

Park headquarters and the visitor center are at 1901 Spinnaker Drive in Ventura harbor; hours are 8 A.M. to 5 P.M. daily except major holidays. Call (805) 644-8262 for information, including specifics on transportation and primitive camping. Reservations for transportation arrangements are strongly encouraged. Prepare for the islands' variable weather by dressing in layers; rubber-soled shoes improve boat footing.

Around Santa Barbara

The leisurely atmosphere and relatively slow pace you find in Santa Barbara also extend into much of the surrounding countryside. Even when U.S. 101 and the ocean beaches are crowded with vacationers, just a few minutes away you can enjoy peaceful back-country driving or lakeside camping. In this inland area, rolling hills and soft meadows dominate the landscape, and quiet little communities fit the slow tempo.

Goleta Valley

One quick and easy trip is to the beautiful modern campus of the University of California at Santa Barbara, located 10 miles west of town near Goleta. Follow U.S. 101 west; signs direct you to the seaside campus. Biking is a popular activity in Goleta, and you can easily find a bicycle to rent. Bike trails are marked; an easy ride will take you past many historic landmarks, the Santa Barbara airport, the marshland of Goleta Slough, along the beach, and through the college, despite signs to the contrary; ask at the gate for instructions.

Stow House, heart of a once vast ranch, was built in 1872. This gracious country home, outbuildings, and gardens are now maintained by the Goleta Valley Historical Society. Wide verandas and gingerbread detailing adorn the outside; inside, the rooms are furnished with period antiques, including a square grand piano, a portable piano that folds up to trunk-size, and (in a child's room) an old-fashioned doll house. You can wander through the parklike gardens, a carriage house, and a bunkhouse containing a collection of Chumash Indian artifacts. From U.S. 101, take the Los Carneros Road exit and drive north toward the mountains for 3 blocks. The house is open most weekends from 2 to 4 P.M.

Stow Grove Park, on La Patera Road, was formerly a part of the Stow Ranch. Now the 13-acre park has picnic tables and a barbecue area in a grove of redwood trees, unusual for Southern California.

Dos Pueblos Orchid Company is one of the world's largest growers of cymbidium orchids. It is located off U.S. 101 at Ranchos Dos Pueblos (15 miles north of the airport). Visitors are welcome from 8:30 A.M. to 4 P.M. Sunday through Thursday.

Hope Ranch Park, just northwest of Santa Barbara (take La Cumbre exit from U.S. 101), is reached by another pleasant drive through a luxury residential development that was formerly a great ranch.

Ojai Valley

For a pleasant lake and mountain loop trip from Santa Barbara to Ventura, or as a byway en route to Los Angeles, the Ojai Valley has much to offer. The moon-shaped valley is well insulated by its altitude and by the Topa and Sulphur mountains against the fog, wind, and smog that sometimes bother the nearby coast. Some say that Ojai (pronounced O-high) is the Indian word for "The Nest," a name given the valley because of its protected location. Coming from Santa Barbara, leave U.S. 101 at Casitas Pass Road (which joins State Highway 150 to the valley) for a drive through land dotted with orchards, streams, and ranches. Among California valleys, Ojai ranks high as a year-round resort.

Lake Casitas, west of Ojai, is a favorite spot for camping, boating, and fishing (swimming and water-skiing are prohibited). These activities are located at the upper end of the reservoir where boat rentals are available at the landing. You can fish or explore the many inlets and coves while you enjoy the shelter and scenery of the surrounding mountains. Campsites are numerous and spacious, though few are tree shaded; trailers are permitted. Day-use and overnight camping fees are small.

An observation point at Lake Casitas Dam on the southeast end of the lake is reached from State Highway 33 or Santa Ana Road on Casitas Vista Road.

Ojai has changed very little over the years. It manages to preserve a pleasant atmosphere of the early Spanish days in some of its buildings and maintains a certain easy manner in its way of life. A shopping arcade with a facade of arches and the post office bell tower distinguish the main street. Civic Center Park in the heart of town is the hub of the community's active life. Cultural activities, arts and crafts, and special events are nurtured in Ojai. The Ojai Musical Festival in May is the highlight of the year. A colorful Folk Dance Festival is staged every other year. Ojai Artists' Art Sunday is an extremely popular outdoor event. The inns, motels, and fine restaurants of this quiet town are inviting. Resort facilities of the Ojai Valley Inn include an 18-hole golf course. Ojai is also a leading tennis center.

Many miles of wild and rugged mountain terrain stretch beyond this serene little valley, noted for its air of contagious leisureliness. For automobile explorers, there are creeks, campsites, and places to picnic. North on State 33, Wheeler Gorge at 1,000 feet is the largest and most popular of public camping parks. You'll pass scenic Matilija Dam. Farther north is a back road to Piedra Blanca, a spectacular outcrop of large, white sandstone rocks. On State 150 going east, several pretty little canyons—Bear, Sisar, Wilsie, and Horn—nip into the mountains, and side roads follow their streams for only a few miles. At Dennison Park, barbecue pits and tables are shaded by tall oaks. Here is perhaps as nice a place as you can find for a picnic with a view.

Ventura & the Santa Clara Valley

Bypassed by the freeway, Ventura is well worth a stop. It offers miles of beaches and a great pier for fishing, and it is the cast-off spot for sightseeing trips to the Channel Islands. From October to March, the Monarch butterflies winter around Ventura, coloring the sky orange.

(Continued on page 108)

SOLVANG'S Danish architecture (left) and Lompoc's colorful flower fields (below) invite motorists to drive back roads around Santa Barbara.

. . . Continued from page 106

Ventura also provides a base for exploring the Ojai Valley and the Santa Clara Valley. It's an easy day's drive to wander through the back country.

Ventura. The Visitors and Convention Bureau (785 S. Seward Avenue) publishes "mini-tours" of the area with good maps and points of interest. Plazas, plantings, and a new downtown museum make this a good place to start a walking tour. The handsome Ventura County Historical Museum at 100 E. Main Street houses Chumash Indian and Spanish relics, plus displays on the surrounding oil wells and agriculture. Hours are 10 A.M. to 5 P.M., Tuesday through Sunday.

City Hall is also part of the tour. Built in 1912, it's a Roman-Doric wedding cake of a building, waiting for the reception to begin. You can explore its cavernous interior weekdays from 8 A.M. to 5 P.M. Visible from the freeway, the courthouse is 1 block off Main Street at the end of California Street.

The 2-hour walking tour also includes Mission San Buenaventura, which appears a modest, graceful lady-in-waiting to the Queen of Missions in Santa Barbara. Next door, archeologists are digging for mission artifacts, and a pleasant little park centers around the restored mission aqueduct and filtration house.

Two historic adobes are the Ortega Adobe downtown and the Olivas Adobe on Olivas Park Drive (en route to the harbor).

Picnickers head for tree-shaded Plaza Park at Santa Clara and Chestnut streets, or the beach promenade at the south end of California Street. (The promenade and Surfer's Point Park at its west end are good places for vicarious surfing.)

Down at the harbor you'll find sportfishing boats, restaurants, and the Channel Islands National Park headquarters. From here you can take the regularly scheduled excursions to Anacapa Island.

Oxnard. South of Ventura on State Highway 1, Oxnard began life around the turn of the century as a sugar beet processing center. Little trace of the farming community remains. Today, Oxnard has a strong U.S. Naval stamp because of the installations that dominate so much of the shore south of Ventura at Port Hueneme and Point Mugu. Though inland from the sea, Oxnard has easy access to beaches. Closest is McGrath State Beach, 7 miles south on Channel Islands Boulevard. At Port Hueneme, in Building 99 at the Naval Construction Battalion Center, you can visit the Seabee Museum, which houses numerous cultural artifacts from the countries where Seabees serve.

Santa Paula. In the Santa Clara Valley, at the junction of State Highways 150 and 126, this little town is the shipping center for the valley. Here, lemons and oil compete for space. The valley had one of California's earliest oil booms, a fact memorialized in the California Oil Museum (Tenth and Main streets).

Condor country. Fillmore, east on State 126, is the entrance point into the Sespe Wildlife Area of Los Padres National Forest, home for North America's largest land bird, the condor. Called "Thunderbird" by the Indians, this endangered species sometimes can be seen soaring effortlessly over the valley in search of food. Since these birds lay only one egg every 2 years and may abandon their young at the approach of man, much of this

---

TOURING A NEW WINE COUNTRY

Pack a picnic and meander through the state's newest major premium wine district, just off U.S. Highway 101 within Santa Barbara and San Luis Obispo counties. The district extends about 100 miles south from San Miguel (site of a mission and some of the earliest vineyards) to the Santa Ynez Valley (location of Solvang and two more missions, Santa Ines and La Purisima Concepcion). Some 50 vineyards stretch across almost 10,000 acres. Use the list below to get started; you're sure to make your own discoveries along the way. For further details, see the *Sunset* book *Guide to California's Wine Country.*

You can start your tour going either north or south. The best towns in which to assemble picnic supplies are Santa Barbara, Solvang, and San Luis Obispo.

• Santa Barbara Winery (202 Anacapa Street, Santa Barbara)—open 10 A.M. to 5 P.M. daily.
• Santa Ynez Valley Winery (365 Refugio Road, Santa Ynez)—weekend tours and tasting, 10 A.M.

to 4 P.M. or by appointment. Telephone (805) 688-8381.
• J. Carey Cellars (1 mile east of Solvang on State 246 at 1711 Alamo Pintado Road)—open for tours and tasting daily except Monday, from 10 A.M. to 4 P.M.
• Firestone Winery (Zaca Station Road north of Los Olivos)—10 A.M. to 4 P.M. daily except Sunday; tours, tasting, sales room.
• Zaca Mesa Winery (9 miles northeast of Buellton, on Zaca Station/Foxen Canyon Roads) —guided tours and tasting daily from 10 A.M. to 4 P.M.
• York Mountain Winery (State Highway 46 from Morro Bay to Paso Robles)—10 A.M. to 5 P.M. daily; restored century-old winery with artifacts.
• Hoffman Mountain Ranch (tasting room at 24th Street exit in Paso Robles); winery visits by appointment; ask at tasting room.
• Estrella River Winery (6.5 miles east of Paso Robles on State 46)—open daily from 9 A.M. to 5 P.M. Gift shop and picnic sites available.

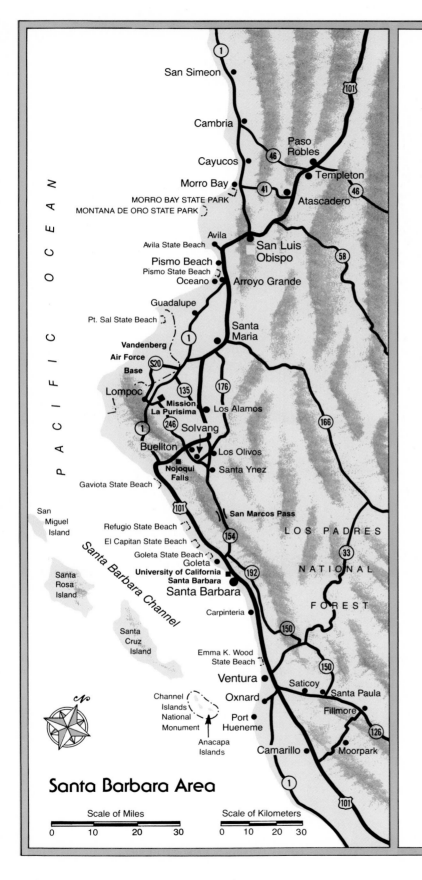

Major Points of Interest

Hearst Castle (San Simeon)—famous mountaintop mansion now historic monument; guided tours of buildings

Paso Robles—gateway town to the wine country of San Luis Obispo-Santa Barbara counties. Take a walk back through time at Mission San Miguel Arcangel

Morro Bay—atmospheric seaside resort-fishing town dominated by Morro Rock; sportfishing and clamming popular here

San Luis Obispo—great place to look at an old California city; Path of History walk past mission, adobes, Ah Louis store

Pismo Beach—California's largest expanse of sand dunes; camping available in nearby Oceano; clamming

Lompoc—site where over half of the world's flower seeds are produced. Tour Vandenberg Air Force Base and the museum of Chumash Indian artifacts

Mission La Purisima (west of Buellton)—restored mission, now historic park; original crafts displays; large gardens

Solvang (Santa Ynez Valley)—Danish village complete with windmills. Don't miss bakeries; visit Mission Santa Ines

Nojoqui Falls (near Solvang)—lovely 164-foot cascade. Enjoy a picnic or hike in the county park named after these graceful falls

University of California at Santa Barbara (Goleta Valley)—seaside campus 10 miles west of Santa Barbara. Visit Storke Tower's magnificent carillon

Ojai Valley—pastoral back country drives through ranches and resorts; Lake Casitas provides fishing, boating, camping; town of Ojai offers music and arts festivals

Ventura—beach city with mission and original adobes; starting point for boat trips to Channel Islands and into Santa Clara Valley; home of condors, citrus, oil wells. Visit California Oil Museum in Santa Paula

Oxnard—access to beaches (closest one is McGrath State Beach). View Seabee Museum in Port Hueneme's Naval Construction Battalion Center

Channel Islands (offshore)—take a boat trip to islands (Anacapa and Santa Barbara) from Ventura; now national park

Santa Barbara Area

Scale of Miles
0 10 20 30

Scale of Kilometers
0 10 20 30

BOATS ROCK at anchor as afternoon fog slowly dissipates over hills around Morro Bay harbor.

country is closed to traffic. Because so many people come to see the famous birds, the Forest Service has set up an observation site about 15 miles north of Fillmore.

Follow A Street (later becoming Goodenough Road) about 3 miles north and then turn right onto an oiled road occasionally marked Squaw Flat (side roads lead to oil rig sites). When you reach a sign reading Dough Flat, park and scan the cliffs to the east. Condors can be seen above these cliffs before they leave the sanctuary to forage. There is also an observation point atop Mount Pinos, accessible by dirt road off the highway in from Gorman. Plan to make a day of it to catch any of the big birds coming home to roost. The best time to visit is winter and early spring.

Santa Ynez Valley

Snuggled between the Santa Ynez and San Rafael mountains in back of Santa Barbara is the Santa Ynez Valley, a land of rich green hills and multicolored flower fields, of cattle and horse ranges, and of stagecoach towns and missions.

Since its discovery by the Portola expedition in 1769, this valley has been known as cattle country. Modern ranchers were preceded by Indians, padres, and Mexican rancheros. Today, large ranchos from Spanish land grants retain their names, if not their original size, and the *Rancheros Visitadores* (by invitation) symbolically perpetuate the old Spanish custom of helping neighboring ranches at roundup time. Each May this dedicated group of horsemen starts off on a 4-day ride.

At the western end of this unspoiled pastoral valley, where its river meets the sea, you can see the rising missiles at Vandenberg Air Force Base. Plan a loop trip through the Santa Ynez Valley from Santa Barbara along State Highways 154 and 246 to U.S. 101 for a pleasant day.

Time really hasn't stood still along State 154, but the

back roads wander among the hills in gentle contrast to the rush and noise of U.S. 101. Climbing through historic San Marcos Pass, once the stagecoach route north, you'll have a panoramic view out over the foothills to the ocean.

Lake Cachuma. About 11 miles beyond the San Marcos Summit, you'll come to the entrance of Lake Cachuma Recreation Area. This 9,000-acre county park centers around Lake Cachuma, a reservoir created when a dam was built across the Santa Ynez River in 1953.

California live oaks and native white oaks shade the grassy camping and trailer spaces. There are fire pits, tables, and shower and laundry facilities. A store, filling station, snack bar, and post office are inside the entry gate.

In winter when the water cools, the lake is stocked with fingerling rainbow trout and Kamloops trout from British Columbia. As on most Southern California lakes, angling slows down during the heat of summer. Cool spring and fall months provide the best fishing. Tackle and boat rentals are available. If you're interested in reserving a boat during fishing season, call Cachuma Boat Rentals at (805) 688-4040 for detailed information.

No swimming or water-skiing is allowed here because the lake supplies drinking water for Santa Barbara. But three swimming pools are open from April through October.

Lake Cachuma Recreation Area is open all year, 24 hours a day, and a ranger is on duty most of the time. There is a daily admission and parking fee, plus an overnight camping fee. Crowded in the summer, the park takes no camping reservations, so plan to arrive early and make a day of it.

The little valley towns. On a short loop trip from Santa Ynez to Los Olivos and Solvang, you'll see a picturesque area affected only slightly by California's growth.

Santa Ynez, formerly the valley's busiest community, has retained its high-front buildings and old west atmosphere. A new Western Town complex has been added. The white-steepled church, built in 1897 at the corner of Tivola and Lincoln streets, is one of the oldest church edifices in the valley. On Sagunto Street you can visit a historical museum (open weekend afternoons) and a park.

Los Olivos was known as a stage stop for the famous Butterfield Stage Lines. Today, the old stagecoach inn, Mattei's Tavern, built in 1886, is a State Historic Landmark.

Ballard, established in 1880, was the first settlement in the valley. You'll still see some of the old homes and the Little Red Schoolhouse founded in 1883. A beautiful drive in the foothills from here is out Alamo Pintado Road.

Solvang. "Sunny valley" is the translation of the Danish name Solvang. In this town that reflects its Scandinavian heritage, windmills are prominent features, and the old-world appearance of homes and businesses comes from thatched, aged copper or steep tile roofs with traditional storks perched on top, stained-glass windows, and high dormers. More recent additions of gas lights and cobblestone walks set the scene for residents walking in *traeskos* (wooden shoes).

At first glance the town suggests a quaint environ-ment manufactured for tourists. Then you discover it possesses the chief element of a true Danish community—real Danes and their descendants. The village was established in 1911 next to Mission Santa Ines as a place to educate immigrants from Denmark. It acquired its Danish facade (over its Spanish architecture) only after visitors began to discover it as a cultural enclave and source of European foods and goods.

For 2 days in mid-September, colorful Danish Days bring out costumes in Solvang; you'll see the Danish flag flying everywhere.

Mission Santa Ines, another of the old missions still in use, is located a short distance east of the main business district. Founded in 1804, it is one of the best restored of all the missions. You can tour the museum, church, and cemetery daily.

Shopping in Solvang leans heavily toward imports from Denmark and other northern European countries, with an emphasis on gourmet and delicatessen foods, traditional and contemporary housewares, toys, apparel (especially shoes), and things that can be classified only as gifts. These days you will also find imports from other parts of the world.

But the shops that really made Solvang famous are the bakeries, many of which serve pastries and coffee. If you visit some of the bakeries in the morning when activity is light, you may be able to watch the preparation and baking processes. Shops open by midmorning but close up tight at 5 P.M.

Atterdag Road is worth seeking out. There you will find Bethania Church, patterned after a typical rural Danish church. Inside you'll see an interesting, hand-carved wooden pulpit. A scale model of a fully rigged ship hangs from the ceiling, facing the altar—a common tradition in Scandinavian churches. Farther along on Atterdag Road near the Solvang Lutheran Home is a famous chiming wind harp.

Buellton. Three miles west of Solvang is Buellton, a hospital town with the curious distinction of being the "home of split pea soup" (a specialty of Andersen's Restaurant). At the crossroads of U.S. 101 and State 246, Buellton is the gateway to the valley for freeway drivers, only minutes from points of interest in all directions.

Look for La Purisima Concepcion Mission nestled in a valley 15 miles west of Buellton. If you can visit just one mission, especially with children, this should be it. Carefully restored in the 1930s, it is state controlled.

Lompoc. Long, rainless summers in the Lompoc Valley help to produce over half of the flower seeds grown in the world. One of spring and summer's most beautiful spectacles occurs here beginning in May when several thousand acres of flowers bloom, turning the landscape into a rainbow of color. Hues of row after row of sweet peas, poppies, calendulas, nasturtiums, and larkspurs compete for your attention into September.

Fields are not open for public browsing because the flowers are grown commercially for seed, but you can see most of them from the road. Maps showing field locations are available from the Chamber of Commerce at 119 E. Cypress Street. The annual Flower Festival in late June includes a parade and guided tour of fields.

In the museum at Cypress and H streets, you can see an extensive exhibit of Chumash Indian artifacts. The museum is open weekend afternoons; admission is free.

Nojoqui Falls. One of the most graceful waterfalls in all California is the highlight of the scenic drive along U.S. 101 between the coast and Solvang. You leave the freeway about 5 miles north of Gaviota Pass on a road marked "To Nojoqui Falls County Park." The 2-mile drive traverses choice countryside of green fields and native oaks. From the north, go to Solvang and then turn south on Alisal Road. It's 6.5 miles.

From the parking lot, a short walk on a woodsy path along a clear creek brings you to the waterfall, which is usually at its best in late winter and early spring—it generally dries up in summer.

Up the Coast

Following El Camino Real (U.S. 101) northward adds even more memorable dimensions to your travel in Southern California. It's easy to see the Spanish and Indian influence on this part of California—between Los Angeles and San Francisco—when the map spells out such musical names as Guadalupe, Santa Maria, Oceano, Nipomo, Arroyo Grande, San Luis Obispo, Morro Bay, Cayucos, and Cambria. You'll drive through valleys, pastures, and (on side trips) along the ocean-front.

Sleepy Nipomo (off U.S. 101) in its heyday was considerably larger than now-bustling Santa Maria. Today most of the original buildings are gone, having fallen victim to fire or removal to the larger town. One exception is the Dana house, once home for the famous Dana family, original settlers in the area.

The freeway by-passes most of the historical and recreational spots. To see these, it's better to take to the back roads. Following State Highway 166 west from Santa Maria to Guadalupe (on State 1), you pass through more large flower seed farms. Countryside tours take place from May to September.

Pismo Beach and nearby coast

State 1 is the back entrance to the home of the Pismo clam. The broad, surf-swept arc of the bay provides an ideal environment for clams. But unfortunately for these creatures, the shore is too accessible to clam-loving humans. As a result, the greater part of the beds has been made a preserve. Only the north end of the state park, north of Oceano, is now open to digging. But that is still the main reason visitors come to these pleasant towns and their wide and level beaches.

Adventure-seeking dune buggy riders also congregate in the area, particularly on the July 4th and Labor Day weekends. Most people bring their own vehicles; you can rent a ride at one of several spots along the beach.

Pismo State Beach, which has some 6 miles of shoreline, runs south from the town of Pismo Beach through Oceano and on into the north end of one of California's best and largest expanses of sand dunes. Shifting sands often overrun the camping area, but the dunes make the park special. Here you can picnic, hike, climb, or slither up and down the slopes.

Public automobile entrances give access to the beach. One is from Oceano, a once-aspiring seaside resort of the Victorian era. A couple of gingerbread houses remain—one set incongruously amidst a mobile home park.

At the north end of the park, in the town of Pismo Beach, is a pier. Fish can be caught from it, and so can party boats for deep sea fishing. You will also find the necessary equipment and information for clam digging; there's good activity in the winter.

Avila Beach nestles within the north arc of San Luis Obispo Bay. Along the beach front is a small park, organized for active recreation. Water along the shore in this cove is warm, always above 60°F. and frequently into the low 70° range, ideal for ocean swimming. Facilities include a fishing pier, picnic tables, fire rings, charter boats, launching ramp, and rental concession for salty gear.

San Luis Bay Inn, with golf course and tennis courts, is set among scenic hill country. It's a lovely drive from U.S. 101 to Avila Beach; a freeway exit leads to the country road that runs to the beach.

San Luis Obispo

Cradled in a small valley with the Santa Lucia Mountains forming a gentle backdrop, San Luis Obispo is the county seat and center of a vast grain, livestock, poultry, and dairy region. The city grew up around Mission San Luis Obispo de Tolosa, established in 1772.

California State Polytechnic University, which has the largest undergraduate agricultural division in the West, is situated on rolling hills overlooking the city. Its Spanish-style and contemporary buildings spread over a 2,850-acre campus, attractively landscaped with tropical and semitropical plants and trees, some of them rare.

State 1 and U.S. 101 separate in San Luis Obispo, and from this point you can explore the Santa Lucia Mountains or follow the coastline north to Morro Bay and fabulous San Simeon.

Exploring the town. From the visitor's point of view, perhaps the best thing to happen to San Luis Obispo was to have a freeway relieve the city of downtown highway traffic. If you're just passing through town, your most lasting impression will be the "pink palace" (Madonna Inn), southwest of the main business district. It's worth a stop just to see the lobby; overnighters have a choice of rooms varying from the Safari Room to the Cave Suite. It's wise to reserve in advance, as the hotel is usually fully booked.

If you detour into the city, though, you'll discover one of the most surprising showcases of California history on the coast. Starting with the Spanish era, nearly every period and contributing culture, including the Chinese, is represented in the architecture. Many of the nostalgic remnants are lived in or nicely adapted to present-day use.

San Luis is livelier than you might expect a museum town to be. Exploring is made more meaningful by a *Path of History*. You walk (or drive) a route marked by a line painted in the street. With no short cuts, the walk is a little more than 2 miles and takes about 1½ hours. A free brochure, available at the County Museum (corner of Broad and Monterey streets) or from the Chamber of Commerce (1039 Chorro Street), describes about 20 stops on the way.

Among the high points are Mission San Luis Obispo, the San Luis Obispo County Historical Museum (696 Monterey Street), and the 1874 Ah Louis store (800 Palm Street). The store still sells herbs and general merchandise; in times past, it also served as bank and post office for numerous Chinese railroad workers.

In contrast to the old Dallidet Adobe and gardens, on Pacific and Santa Rosa streets is the still-modern building (now a medical clinic) designed by Frank Lloyd Wright. Keep an eye out for other discoveries along the route.

Mission San Luis Obispo. The city grew around this church—the first mission built with a tile roof. Located at Chorro and Monterey streets, the restored building is today both a parish church and a historical museum. Cal Poly students designed the attractively landscaped plaza between the mission and the creek. Footbridges cross the creek to shops and restaurants.

Following State 1 north

The attractive seaside resort-fishing town of Morro Bay spreads along the eastern shore of the estuary that gives it its name. Some travelers think of Morro Bay only as a stopover point, but this recreation area, 12 miles west of San Luis Obispo on State 1, is well worth the consideration of vacation planners or weekend sightseers. Motels and seafood restaurants ring the waterfront; a steam-wheeler paddles around the harbor for 1½-hour cruises.

The one prominent landmark that attracts your attention as Morro Bay comes into sight is high, rounded Morro Rock, looming 576 feet above the ocean just offshore from town. Unfortunately, distracting smoke stacks share the scene just inshore from the great rock. The crown-shaped rock was named by the explorer Juan Cabrillo in 1542. You can drive over a causeway from the beach area north of town to the rock.

Fishing and clamming are good. Shore fishing from piers, the causeway, and the rock coast brings in perch and flounder. (You don't need a license for bay fishing from piers, breakwaters, or jetties.)

Sportfishing boats are numerous, taking parties out to deeper waters where prospects are better.

Clamming is very popular; the shore north of Morro Rock and south to Oceano promises good catches of Pismo clams (the limit is 10; you'll need a license).

One all-year feature of Morro Bay is the Clam Taxi, which operates between the Morro Bay Marina at Fourth Street and the peninsula section of Morro Bay State Park. The water taxi takes clammers, fishermen, and assorted beachcombers across the bay to a landing area on the peninsula. From the landing area, it's about a quarter-mile hike across the dunes to the ocean beach, where you'll find the best clamming, surf fishing, and shell, rock, and driftwood collecting.

Morro Bay State Park, a mile south of town, spreads over some 1,500 acres that slope down to the bay. Spacious and verdant, it is an inviting place for camping and picnicking. You can play golf on an 18-hole course or rent a boat at the boat harbor.

Stop at the attractive Natural History Museum for a wonderful panoramic view of the bay and Morro Rock. The museum has fascinating displays and movies featuring wildlife and area history.

Montana de Oro State Park is largely undeveloped. This 5,600-acre hiker's park faces the ocean south of Morro Bay. Made up largely of rugged cliffs and headlands, it also contains little coves with relatively secluded sandy beaches. Hikers can explore Valencia Peak and other 1,500-foot-high hills that overlook nearly 100 miles of coastline from Point Sal in the south to Piedras Blancas in the north. Spring wildflowers abound; the predominantly yellow color inspired the park's name—Montana de Oro means "mountain of gold."

About 50 campsites are located near the old Rancho Montana de Oro headquarters beside Islay Creek.

Harmony, population 18, is 6 miles south of Cambria off State 1. The former dairy town has gone from grazing to glazing—now it houses a pottery shop, design studio, music box shop, antique store in a false-front building, wine cellar, restaurant, and wedding chapel.

San Simeon: a kingdom by the sea

For William Randolph Hearst to have called his San Simeon estate "the ranch" is an understatement if ever there was one. Here you'll find a strangely eclectic but glamorous collection of mansions, terraced gardens, pools, fine art objects, exotic trees, bunkhouses, garages, and shacks crowning a spur of the Santa Lucia Mountains about 45 miles northwest of San Luis Obispo. The large central structure, *La Casa Grande*, looks more like a Spanish cathedral than a castle, but its imposing ridgetop position on "Enchanted Hill" has given it the aspect of a castle when viewed from afar.

Hearst Castle today is a State Historic Monument. Only the central cluster of impressive buildings and the immediately surrounding grounds have been deeded to California. The rest of the vast ranch—the cattle range (of which the castle served as a kind of baronial headquarters), the houses and barns, the airport, and most of the village of San Simeon—remains a single private holding. Hearst properties in the area once totaled 275,000 acres.

Tours of the estate reveal many delights: a classic Neptune pool, a walk-in fireplace, Cardinal Richelieu's bed. Unlike most parks and museums, the castle is not open for families to wander through at will. Visitors take only the conducted tours, which often require reservations.

You can choose from four different tours of the castle and grounds. Tour 1 takes in the gardens, a guest house, and the main floor of the mansion. Tour 2 covers the mansion's upper level, including bedrooms and personal libraries. On Tour 3, you'll see bedrooms, sitting rooms, bathrooms, and works of art. Tour 4, offered from April through mid-October, shows you the wine cellar, hidden terrace, underground vaults, and bowling alley. Each tour lasts about 2 hours and requires considerble walking and climbing. You'll need 2 consecutive days to take all four tours.

It's wise to make reservations in advance at Ticketron offices in large cities. At the castle, tickets are sold on a first-come, first-served basis. Tour prices are moderate, and there's a separate charge for each tour. Ticketron charges a reservation fee. For monument information, phone (805) 927-4621.

Southern Sierra

In and around the southern tip of the Sierra Nevada lie some of nature's most varied attractions: giant sequoias in Sequoia and Kings Canyon National Parks; the state's highest peak; ancient bristlecone pines and Southern California's winter playground in Owens Valley; the rumpled hills and dry salt flats of awesome Death Valley; mining towns of yesterday in vast Mojave Desert; blanketing fields of wildflowers in Antelope Valley; and one of the largest towns in San Joaquin Valley, the nation's agricultural center.

Sequoia and Kings Canyon National Parks dominate the southern part of the Sierra Nevada. These large parks contain several thousand acres of the most massive trees on earth, the giant sequoias (*Sequoiadendron giganteum*). Mount Whitney's 14,495-foot peak rises from magnificent granite mountains on the eastern edge of Sequoia National Park. The rugged back country of both parks offers unsurpassed mountain scenery and a hiker's domain of spectacular peaks and canyons, threaded with an intricate trail system that includes the southern end of the famed John Muir Trail.

Owens Valley, to the east of the Sierra, offers some of the best access into the mountains. Here visitors find ghostly remains of mining communities, a 4,000-year-old forest, and an opulent display of wildflowers.

To the east also lies legendary Death Valley, distinguished from other desert valleys by its great size, low altitude, diverse topography, and colorful history.

In contrast, the Central Valley, lying to the west of the towering mountain range, is a broad agricultural belt and the setting for several of John Steinbeck's novels.

South and east of the Sierra lies the vast Mojave Desert. For many, this desert holds a special magnetism, drawing them back again and again. It lures them on to explore rugged hills and rocky canyons, thrills them with its sunsets and wildflowers, and shares the secrets of its shy creatures and hidden oases. The best time to explore the Mojave is between February and May, after the winter rains but before the intense heat of summer. In spring, the desert blushes with thousands of square miles of wildflowers. No seed was ever planted here by man; this is nature's garden, haphazard in arrangement, tended only by sun, rain, and wind. The wildflower capital of the Mojave is Antelope Valley.

Sequoia & Kings Canyon National Parks

Giant trees, awesome canyons, cascading streams, and sparkling lakes greet visitors to these spectacular mountain parks. Much of their natural beauty can be explored by road or trail. Self-guided nature trails and naturalist-conducted walks allow everyone to sample some of California's most unspoiled mountain country.

These all-year parks offer a variety of activities. Summer is the time for hikers and backpackers. You can hire saddle horses at several corrals and join guided parties for exploring the back country. Fishing is good for brook, brown, rainbow, and golden trout—you'll need a California license, available in both parks. Winter activities include Nordic and downhill skiing and sledding; snow enthusiasts head for Wolverton Ski Bowl, Lodgepole, Grant Grove, and Giant Forest.

How to get there? Sequoia and Kings Canyon, joined end to end along the Sierra ridge and administered by the same park headquarters at Ash Mountain, can be reached from the west by two main highways: State Highway 180 from Fresno, which leads through the Grant Grove section of Kings Canyon National Park,

SNOW ADDS FROSTING to
awesome giants of Sequoia
National Park. Visitors view
General Sherman Tree, world's
largest.

penetrating the canyon of the South Fork of Kings River for a short distance; and State Highway 198 from Visalia, which enters Sequoia National Park at Ash Mountain.

Through advance reservations, a park concessioner bus will meet planes, trains, and buses at Fresno. From mid-May to mid-September, call Giant Forest Reservations at (209) 565-3373.

You can take a 1 or 2-night sightseeing tour by motorcoach from Fresno. Prices include meals and lodging. For details and reservations, write Sequoia & Kings Canyon Hospitality Service, Sequoia National Park, CA 93262.

Where to stay? At Sequoia and Kings Canyon, rustic cabins in perfect harmony with towering sequoias coexist with more modern accommodations. Campgrounds are numerous, well equipped, and located in strategic and beautiful spots throughout both parks. Some allow trailers (there are no hookups). Lodgepole and a few lower-elevation sites are open all year.

Giant Forest Lodge in Sequoia has one or two-room cabins scattered among the Big Trees, and an excellent dining room. Daily rates are about $25 for two for deluxe accommodations. Some units are open the year around; others are available from mid-May to mid-October. You can rent housekeeping and sleeping cabins reasonably during the summer.

Grant Grove Lodge in Kings Canyon offers rates comparable to those of Giant Forest Lodge. Bearpaw Meadow Camp offers tent-camping with dining facilities and hot showers from the end of June until Labor Day. Farther north, Cedar Grove Camp has a limited number of canvas-top cabins.

You should make advance reservations (a deposit is required) for lodges and cabins. Write to Reservations Manager, Sequoia & Kings Canyon Hospitality Service, Sequoia National Park, CA 93262. During the summer season (May 1 to September 15), check with the 800 information operator for the current toll-free number for information and reservations.

For additional information on the parks, including a detailed map of the back country, hiking trails, and campgrounds, write to Sequoia and Kings Canyon National Parks, Three Rivers, CA 93271.

Sequoia spectacles

The first national park in California and the second in the entire national park system, Sequoia National Park was established to protect its groves of giant sequoias, found here in greater abundance than anywhere else in California—their only native habitat.

A visit to the park on the Generals Highway (State 198) is a journey not easily forgotten. This beautiful road connecting the two parks was completed in 1934. A hint of the care taken to preserve the natural scene around it is Tunnel Rock, a great boulder left in place to span the road. As you twist among the sequoias, look for other interesting spots along the 16 miles from Ash Mountain to Giant Forest.

At Hospital Rock, 6 miles inside the park, Indians lived in the shelter of another huge boulder. Legend has it that the sick were brought here for healing. Later, pioneers took refuge under it. Intriguing reminders of the Indian camp are rock paintings and mortar holes in the flat rocks. Exhibits in a nearby shelter tell the story.

The best fishing reached by road in Sequoia is along the Kaweah River's Middle Fork. You'll find turnouts for scenic vistas along this route above the river. An easy footpath takes you down from Hospital Rock.

Lodgepole is the site of Sequoia Park's visitor center and campground. Once in Giant Forest, these facilities were recently relocated to reduce damage to tree roots. Giant Forest still offers lodging and stores—but these, too, will eventually be moved to Lodgepole, leaving Giant Forest old-fashioned and unhurried.

The General Sherman Tree, the world's largest tree (though not the tallest), is 102 feet in base circumference and 36½ feet thick, with a height of 275 feet; 140 feet above ground level extends a limb 6.8 feet in diameter.

Near the General Sherman Tree is the beginning of Congress Trail, a 2-mile loop that will take you to some of the more famous and spectacular of the trees: the

BIG, BAD BODIE

"Goodbye, God, I'm going to Bodie," was the conclusion to one little girl's prayer when her family moved to what was then one of the wildest mining camps in the West. Her dismay was not unfounded—there was allegedly at least one murder a day in "big, bad Bodie." Sixty-five saloons once operated there, and the girls along Maiden Lane and Virgin Alley were sometimes rewarded with gold nuggets from the big mines.

Now a State Historic Park maintained in a condition of "arrested decay," Bodie is a true ghost town. Weeds grow freely around the dozens of old weathered buildings, and no attempt has been made to restore the buildings to their original grandeur. A few rangers and their families are the town's only residents.

Its edges curled by time, the old wooden boardwalk rises and falls along Main Street past the venerable Miners' Union Hall, the Odd Fellows Hall, and the brick post office. Other points of interest are the tiny Methodist church, the Cain home, the jail, and several "boot hills."

To reach Bodie, take U.S. 395 to a junction 7 miles south of Bridgeport (north of Mono Lake); turn east on a dirt road that winds through barren hills for 13 miles. Bring your own lunch; there are no stores or overnight facilities.

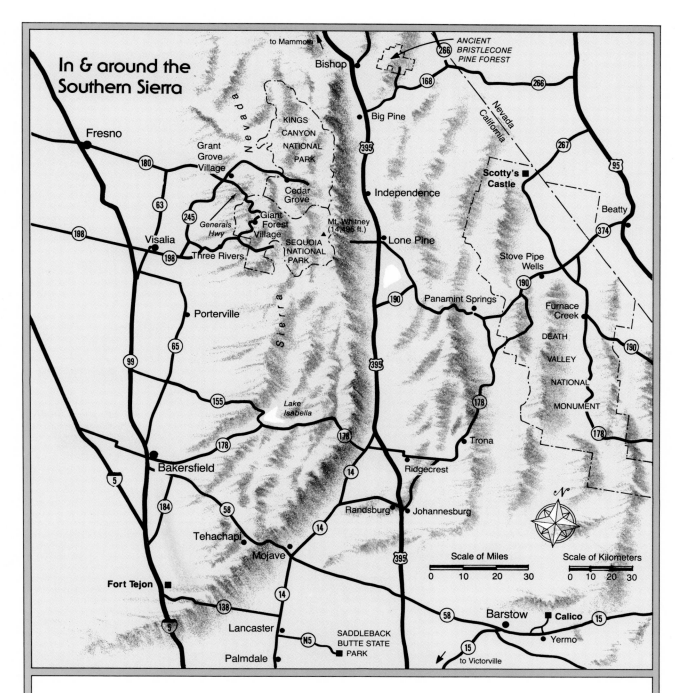

In & around the Southern Sierra

ANCIENT BRISTLECONE PINE FOREST

to Mammoth

Bishop

266

168

266

Big Pine

KINGS CANYON NATIONAL PARK

Fresno

180

Grant Grove Village

63

Scotty's Castle

267

95

198

Cedar Grove

Independence

Beatty

245

Generals Hwy

Giant Forest Village

Visalia

Mt. Whitney (14,495 ft.)

SEQUOIA NATIONAL PARK

198

Three Rivers

Lone Pine

374

Stove Pipe Wells

190

Panamint Springs

Porterville

Furnace Creek

DEATH VALLEY NATIONAL MONUMENT

65

395

190

99

155

Lake Isabella

178

178

Trona

178

178

Bakersfield

14

Ridgecrest

5

184

N

58

Randsburg

Johannesburg

Tehachapi

14

395

Scale of Miles

Scale of Kilometers

Mojave

0 10 20 30

0 10 20 30

Fort Tejon

14

58

Barstow

Calico

138

15

Lancaster

N5

SADDLEBACK BUTTE STATE PARK

Yermo

5

15

Palmdale

to Victorville

Points of Interest

Sequoia-Kings Canyon National Parks — home of giant sequoias, mighty Mt. Whitney

Pioneer Village (Bakersfield) — 12-acre collection of furnished historic buildings

Fort Tejon (Lebec) — military post once housed First Dragoons and Camel Corps; restored as park

Mammoth Country (east of Sierra Nevada)—Southland winter sports area; summer fishing at June Lake; seismic

wonders in Owens Valley. View Devil's Postpile, Mono Lake moonscape

Bristlecone Pines (White Mountains) — ancient forest of world's oldest living trees

Death Valley — dramatic desert landscape, old mining relics, Borax Museum, Scotty's Castle tour, Rhyolite house of bottles

Antelope Valley — spring wildflower wonderland around Lancaster. Tour Tropico gold camp

Calico (near Barstow) — silver mining town now regional park; mine tours, train rides, "boot hill"

DEATH VALLEY'S BADLANDS (above) are deeply etched by wind and occasional cloudbursts. Century-old charcoal kilns (right), remnants of Death Valley mining days, line up in Wildrose Canyon.

Senate, House, and Founder's groves, as well as the President, McKinley, and Chief Sequoyah trees. Posted at the beginning of the trail are guide booklets explaining the numbered stakes along the way.

The high country, for nine months of the year, is quiet, inhabited only by wildlife; this road-free domain is a playground for hikers and backpackers. The main traffic arterial is the John Muir Trail, which begins in Yosemite Valley and runs south for 225 miles to Whitney Portal.

To control the number of people in the wilderness area of the parks, backpackers are put on a permit system. Though some permits are issued on a first-come, first-served basis, it is wise to write in advance, giving the dates of your trip, your route, the number of people in your party, and whether you plan to hike or use horses. Send your request to Ranger, Sequoia and Kings Canyon National Parks, Three Rivers, CA 93271, or call (209) 565-3341.

Bearpaw Meadow provides a good sampling of the Sequoia back country in a short period; no camping permit is required here. The trip to this camp is 11 miles one way by trail from Crescent Meadow. Perching on the edge of a tremendous overlook at the base of the Great Western Divide, the camp offers comforts and good food, in addition to a spectacular view. Side trails through bold mountains lead to good stream and lake fishing. The camp, with tent accommodations and ranger station, is generally open from June through September. For information on fees and reservations, call the Giant Forest Lodge, (209) 565-3373, well in advance of your trip.

Kings Canyon attractions

Kings Canyon has the distinction of being one of the oldest and newest national parks. When established in 1940, it absorbed tiny General Grant National Park—now known as the General Grant Grove—a sanctuary set up after Sequoia was created in 1890.

The park is actually two entirely separate areas with the west side containing the only two developed sections—the General Grant Grove and Kings Canyon regions. Densely forested, it is usually comfortably cool (the elevation varies from 4,600 to 6,600 feet). A rugged mass of spectacular peaks and canyons comprises the largest area of the park.

General Grant Grove is the destination of most visitors to the area since, along with all the park facilities, it contains the famed General Grant Tree. The second largest tree in the world, the Grant Tree has a base circumference of 108 feet (actually 6 feet larger than the General Sherman Tree) but it has a smaller total volume. Both of these trees were standing in the Bronze Age more than 3,000 years ago. Because General Grant is the nation's official Christmas tree, each Yule season an impressive ceremony is held here.

Informative campfire programs are given every summer night in the amphitheater. In the village you'll find posted schedules of daily ranger-conducted trips, full of facts and park lore.

Kings Canyon and Cedar Grove are reached from a 30-mile highway that drops 2,000 feet before attaining its destination. From parking overlooks on wide sweeping curves, you can gaze into the canyons of the Middle and South forks of the Kings River and beyond to the bewildering maze of jagged peaks that constitute the greater portion of Kings Canyon National Park. These breathtaking views are the best hints you will get of the country beyond. About 10 miles before Cedar Grove is Boyden Cave, 450 to 600 feet underground, which you can tour in an hour.

Cedar Grove has a store, coffee shop, ranger station, and a few cabins. A variety of conducted trips led by ranger naturalists are offered here, as are nightly illustrated campfire programs.

East of the Sierra

The full impact of the Sierra Nevada is rarely appreciated until you see its abrupt east side—the face it turns toward the desert. This eastern side of the Sierra, to the west and north of Death Valley and east of Sequoia and Kings Canyon, offers myriad attractions for vacationers: high desert country, spectacular mountains, uncrowded trails, good fishing, ghost mining towns, wildflowers, mineral deposits—most accessible by good roads. In winter, these mountains offer excellent skiing.

One important route, U.S. Highway 395, leads north and south through the whole section, linking a chain of little towns. From this arterial highway you can go east into Death Valley or west a short distance into the towering mountains.

People may wonder why Inyo and Mono counties are considered part of Southern California when even the largest towns are 300 to 400 miles from Los Angeles. Mainly, it is because they are tied more closely with Los Angeles than with San Francisco, both economically and recreationally. Residents, too, are most oriented to the Southland.

Owens Valley

The bending and cracking of the earth's surface that created the Sierra Nevada and the parallel ranges of the White, Panamint, and Inyo mountains also sank a long, deep trough between them—Owens Valley, a place of hot springs, craters, lava flows, and earthquake faults.

Owens Valley's first inhabitants were the ancestors of the Paiute Indians; then came ranchers and farmers. Today the tourists who pass through the valley have become its most important industry.

Lone Pine is one of the points on U.S. 395 where you can turn off to the famed hiking trails of Sequoia and Kings Canyon. Going west on Whitney Portal Road, you pass through the picturesque Alabama Hills, named by Confederate sympathizers. Ringed by these knobby hills is Movie Flat, a favorite location for TV and movie westerns. One road to Movie Flat turns south from Whitney Portal Road (the same road also takes you to Tuttle Creek Campground).

Independence, the turnoff for the Kearsarge Pass entrance to the Sierra high country, is also the home of the excellent Eastern California Museum. Located at Center and Grant streets, the museum houses natural and local history displays and Indian artifacts. The museum is open daily all year; hours differ depending on the season.

One block north of Center Street on U.S. 395 is the Commander's House, the only extant structure of Camp Independence, established in 1862 to protect early Owens Valley residents from Indian attacks. It is open Wednesday through Saturday from 10 A.M. to 5 P.M.

About a mile west of the highway north of town is the interesting Mount Whitney Fish Hatchery, built of native stone in 1917.

Ancient bristlecone pines (some more than 4,000 years old) have been stunted and twisted by the harsh forces of nature so that they resemble upright pieces of driftwood decorated with green needles. The trees grow in a 28,000-acre area of Inyo National Forest; to reach them, turn east on State Highway 168 to Westgard Pass, just north of Big Pine. A winding but well-marked road takes you north to the Schulman Memorial Grove.

At the grove (open June through October), you'll find a ranger station, information center, picnic area, and starting points to Pine Alpha and Methusela groves. Travel with warm clothing, water, and a full gas tank—there are no services after Big Pine.

Bishop, with a population of over 3,000, is the bustling metropolis of the Owens Valley. Known as the world's mule capital, the city stages a colorful Mule Days celebration on Memorial Day weekend. Its Chamber of Commerce, at 125 E. Line Street, has useful travel literature for points of interest in this area. The 50-mile Petroglyph Loop Trip described in one of the chamber's folders is especially worthwhile.

At Laws, the rhythm of puffing steam engines, clanging bells, and freight platform bustle has long been stilled, but more people come to see this old Owens Valley railroad station now than ever came during its prime. The Laws Railroad Museum and Historical Exhibit has interesting daily tours of period houses and buildings (weather permitting). Located 5 miles out of Bishop and ½ mile off U.S. 6, it offers a good break from a long drive. From March through November, displays are open from 10 A.M. to 4 P.M. every day (weekends only the rest of the year).

Mammoth Country

Though Mammoth Mountain is only 30 air miles from Yosemite National Park and east of San Francisco, it serves as a Southern California playground. There's a geographical reason for this. Part of the isolated eastern crest of the Sierra Nevada, Mammoth is easily reached from the south over U.S. 395 (though the drive takes about 7 hours), but it is cut off from the west except in late summer when the mountain passes are open.

This diverse area offers excellent winter-skiing above 10,000 feet and all-year trout fishing and great inner-tubing in the 28-mile stretch of the Owens River from Pleasant Valley Reservoir to Tinemaha Reservoir.

In the intermediate elevations from Mammoth Mountain to Owens Valley are abandoned mills and mines to explore, volcanic remains to discover, and picnic spots.

Visitors to Mammoth will find a variety of lakes and creeks. Most are fishermen's retreats; others are good for swimming, boating, and viewing. Turn east off U.S. 395 on the road to the fish hatchery to reach Hot Creek. The hot springs, a 25-foot-wide natural pool, are about 4 feet deep and have practically no current. High in mineral content, the water is unusually buoyant; it can also be *very* hot. If you get too warm, paddle away from the springs into the cool eddies of the creek.

Mammoth Lakes, an area dotted with more than 30 lakes in a 9,000-foot basin, can be reached by a paved side road that cuts off U.S. 395 at Casa Diablo Hot Springs and meanders to the shore of Lake Mary, heart of the region. Five of the lakes, popular with anglers for many years, may be reached by good roads. Mountain lodges offer woodsy comfort, log fires, and hearty meals. U.S. Forest Service campgrounds are usually crowded in midsummer but are virtually deserted after the end of September. Summer aerial tram gondola rides on Mammoth Mountain are spectacular. Boats may be rented at Lake Mary and Twin Lakes, and packers offer pack and saddle animals and guides.

Mammoth Mountain skiing rivals the best in the state and certainly is the best in spring, when at 10,000 feet there is still powder snow.

The lodge at Mammoth Mountain is 4 miles from the town of Mammoth Lakes. The ski lifts serve slopes to challenge any skier; for the sightseer there's a panoramic chair ride. Snow touring is popular—on skis, snowshoes, or dog sleds. Accommodations range from dormitories to chalets. For information on housing or package ski trips, write Mammoth Lakes Chamber of Commerce, P.O. Box 123, Mammoth Lakes, CA 93546, or June Mountain and June Lake Reservation and Information Service, P.O. Box 216, June Lake, CA 93529.

Death Valley

Legendary Death Valley is distinguished from other desert valleys by its great size, low altitude, diverse desert, and colorful history.

Now a national monument, it is unique among deserts for its great extremes, one of these being its summer heat. Its record high of 134°F. was set in 1913. Up the enclosing slopes, it may not be hot at all, but down on the flats it can stay about 100° all night long.

Another of the valley's extremes is its low elevation. An area of about 14 square miles is more than 280 feet below sea level. In the salt beds west and northwest of Badwater, two places 3 miles apart and 282 feet below sea level are the lowest points in the Western Hemisphere. Nearby Telescope Peak is 11,049 feet *above* sea level, another example of the dramatic extremes to be found in this valley.

Throughout the valley you'll see evidence of human occupation, as well as geologic history. Indian petroglyphs appear in more than 200 sites. Many places carry names of pioneers and prospectors of the gold rush days. The valley, probably first referred to as Death Valley in January 1850, did not really deserve its name. Though the pioneer parties crossing the area suffered extreme hardships, only one '49er died in Death Valley (but not from heat or thirst), and a party of nine others also may have perished there. Death Valley's record of human lives lost, measured against that of the rest of the Western desert, is reassuringly low.

Natural features

All of the great divisions and nearly all of the subdivisions of geologic time are represented in the land formations of Death Valley. Fossils of prehistoric mammals discovered here show that the arid salt flats, gravel desert, and harsh peaks were once a fertile plain. As the climate became drier, ancient lakes evaporated into salt flat deposits and mud playas. Wind reduced granite to sand and blew it into dunes. Since the wind blows from all directions, the dunes remain intact.

Plants and animals

The popular belief that nothing lives or grows in Death Valley is discounted by the common animal and plant life that has tenaciously adapted to the burning heat and dryness. Almost all of the perennial plants have deep or far-spreading roots and special adaptations of leaves and stems to help tap and conserve vital water. Over 600 species of plants and trees flourish at all elevations in the monument, and 22 species—including the Panamint daisy, Death Valley sage, and rattleweed—exist only here. Bristlecone pines, thousands of years old, grow at 10,000-foot elevations on Telescope Peak.

On a favorable spring day, when the unexpected brilliance of myriad wildflowers mantle the dark, alluvial slopes and narrow canyon washes, the name Death Valley seems inappropriate.

Visitors to Death Valley see few animals, for most emerge only at night in search of food. A great variety of natural life exists in a 2-mile area between Telescope Peak and Badwater, where the desert animals can find plants to feed on. Only the plantless central salt flats are barren of animal life. Even fish live in this desert. Descended from Ice Age ancestors, the rare pupfish or "desert sardine" thrives in Salt Creek, Saratoga Springs, and Devil's Hole and is an astonishing example of super-rapid evolutionary adaptation to changing environmental conditions.

Planning a visit

Though visitors in summer may remember the blazing sun and intense heat, in other seasons they will find a mild climate. Tourist facilities are in full operation from November to mid-April. In summer, a list of Hot Weather Hints, distributed in the monument, will help make your visit safe and pleasant.

State Highway 136 from Lone Pine to Towne's Pass is the most spectacular and most improved route from the west into the valley. State Highway 178 from the south to Wildrose picnic area is another popular approach.

State Highway 127 from the southeast joins State 190 at Amargosa (Death Valley Junction). En route to the junction, the highway passes Tecopa Hot Springs, a unique watering hole where visitors partake of the baths free of charge. The curative springs once belonged to Indians whose ancestors brought their lame and sick to bathe. When they gave up the hot springs to the white settlers, it was with the stipulation that the good water be left free to all comers. And so it has remained.

Clusters of trailers around the bathhouses make the little settlement visible for miles. For information on desert camping, write to the Park Superintendent, P.O. Box 158, Tecopa, CA 92389.

Amargosa Opera House, at Death Valley Junction, has weekend performances from September through May. Reservations are necessary. In the opera house you'll be joined by an "audience" in a realistic, wall-size mural depicting 260 members of a Spanish court, ranging from bawdy commoners to sedate nobles. The painter of the mural is also the dancer in the one-woman ballet, Marta Becket. In the 1½-hour performance, you'll see both classical ballet and dance characterizations such as a dancing doll and a peasant girl.

For performance reservations, write Manager, Amargosa Opera House, Death Valley Junction, CA 92328; or call the operator and ask for Death Valley Junction toll station #8.

Tours of Death Valley are popular; check with a travel agent for specific information. Las Vegas, Nevada, is the closest air terminal. For light planes, paved landing strips are located at Furnace Creek and Stove Pipe Wells.

Where to stay in Death Valley

Lodging is not really a problem except during Easter and Thanksgiving weekends and the weekend of the Death Valley '49ers Annual Encampment in early November.

Furnace Creek Inn is a luxurious resort hotel with resort prices that include meals. The inn has a swimming pool, tennis courts, stables, and an 18-hole golf course. Furnace Creek Ranch, a mile down the road, also has resort facilities on a more modest scale. Lodging is a choice between simple cabins or newer, motel-style accommodations. The inn is open from November 1 to April 31; the ranch stays open throughout the year. For information and reservations, write directly to the Furnace Creek Inn and Ranch Resort, Death Valley, CA 92328. Write well in advance if you're thinking of going during a holiday season.

Stove Pipe Wells Hotel, actually about 6 miles from the site of old Stovepipe Wells, is a motel-style resort, open November through April. The postal address is Death Valley, CA 92328.

Campgrounds provide scenic backdrops, ranging from whispering sand dunes to sweeping mountain views. Of nine monument campgrounds, the three most improved are in the valley: near the visitor center are Texas Spring and Furnace Creek (open all year but very hot in summer); Mesquite Spring is south of Scotty's Castle.

Other campgrounds include Thorndike and Mahogany Flats; both provide fireplaces and tables, but bring your own water. The campgrounds at higher elevations are open in summer; at year-round Emigrant Junction you'll enjoy good mountain and valley views. All campgrounds require that you furnish your own firewood; at some, the water must be boiled.

In the frequented parts of the valley, camping is strictly confined to established campgrounds. But back-country campers are permitted to use outlying locations as long as they don't disturb or litter the ground, or burn the plants.

Located at 3,500 feet on the west side of the Panamint Range outside of Death Valley proper is the Wildrose picnic area, providing a nice change of pace from the campgrounds. A day-use facility only, Wildrose has tables and fireplaces. The area is open the year around.

There's life in Death Valley

At first glance, Death Valley seems little different from the desert you have driven through to reach it. But as closeup follows closeup and you make your way to both labeled phenomena and some secret finds of your own, you perceive new dimensions. The mountain face—apparently unbreached when seen from afar—is really slotted with fascinating labyrinths that lead you on and on. The featureless salt flat is a vast maze of miniature crystalline alps. The sand ridges in the distance are mountains in their own right—but mountains that yield underfoot and restore themselves to an unmarked pristine state with every fresh breeze. The unnatural splotch on the far hillside is a waste pile marking an abandoned mine, with tunnels, shafts, headframes, and railroad beds still more or less intact.

Death Valley can be explored on more than 500 miles of improved roadways. Additional miles of primitive roads wind through the back country.

Furnace Creek, because of an excellent and dependable water supply from nearby springs, has always been a center of activity. To plan your stay, stop by the all-year visitor center or call (619) 786-2331. You can buy maps and useful publications and tour a museum of local geology, plants, and wildlife.

The Borax Museum nearby exhibits an outdoor assembly of implements once used in the extraction and refining of borax and other minerals. It's a parking lot of the past: exhibited are stagecoach and buggy, buckboard and wagon, railroad handcar and locomotive. A homemade mining machine and hand-operated stamp mill are also on the grounds. You'll find smaller displays inside the oldest building left in the valley, an 1883 mining office-bunkhouse from nearby Twenty Mule Team Canyon. The great 20-mule-team wagons, nearly as sound as when they were maintaining their remarkable schedules 80 years ago, are 2 miles farther north, marking the site of the Harmony Borax Works, a restored processing plant.

Zabriskie Point, southeast of Furnace Creek on State 190, is an area of 5 to 10-million-year-old lake beds that are especially dramatic at sunrise.

Artist's Drive, off the main road south of Furnace Creek, takes you through a rainbow canyon colored by oxidation. The even more intense color of Artist's Palette is splashed on a hillside halfway through the canyon.

Badwater, a few miles farther south, is known as the lowest point in the Western Hemisphere (282 feet below sea level). Often crusted over, the salt pools at close range reveal weird formations of rugged rock salt.

Dante's View, on the crest of the Black Mountains, is one of the most spectacular scenic overlooks in the United States, rising 5,775 feet directly above Badwater.

Charcoal kilns, resembling giant stone beehives, blend into the hillside of the Panamint Mountains. They appear as good as new after nearly a century of existence. These kilns reduced pines and junipers to charcoal for the Modoc Mine smelter, 25 miles west. To reach the kilns from the Wildrose Ranger Station, follow the road to upper Wildrose Canyon.

Skidoo was the one boom town near Death Valley that really did pan out. At the end of its 2-year existence, it was ahead by $3 million.

Rhyolite, Nevada, a ghost town, is just outside the monument on State Highway 58. Here a $130,000 railroad station without a railroad houses a museum and store. The Rhyolite Bottle House, with walls built of 51,000 beer bottles set in adobe, is still occupied by a Rhyolite citizen who sells desert glass and curios. Once a spirited boom town around the turn of the century, Rhyolite thrived for only 5 years.

Titus Canyon is reached by a one-way dirt road that must be entered from State 58 on the east. This 25-mile trip through the wineglass-shaped canyon with changing colors and soaring walls is a memorable experience.

Scotty's Castle is the incredible desert mansion built by Death Valley Scotty (Walter Scott) and his millionaire friend Albert M. Johnson. Located in the extreme northern part of the monument, the Spanish-Moorish mansion, lavishly furnished, cost $2 million and took about 10 years to build. Scotty's flamboyant escapades are a part of the Death Valley folklore; the castle remains as a testimony to his natural showmanship and eccentric personality. Hourly tours are conducted daily from 9 A.M. to 5 P.M.; there is an admission charge. You can visit the grounds and picnic area without charge from 7 A.M. to 7 P.M. daily.

Colorful Ubehebe Crater, a half-mile wide and 800 feet deep, was created 3,000 years ago by a volcanic explosion. It's not far from Scotty's Castle.

The Racetrack, 27 miles south of the crater, is a mud playa, occasionally subject to high velocity winds that are responsible for the "mystery of the moving rocks." When wet, the Racetrack is so slippery that the wind can move great boulders across it.

The Mojave Desert

Parts of the Mojave have never been fully explored. Much of it is rugged terrain, fit only for the seasoned desert traveler and a well-equipped car. Though any car can handle most of the trips mentioned here, some are best made in a four-wheel-drive vehicle.

Some parts of the desert are being closed to recreational vehicles under a Bureau of Land Management plan. (The BLM manages the East Mojave National

BRILLIANT COLOR enlivens desert when spring wildflowers bloom in Antelope Valley.

Scenic Area, almost 1½ million acres of desert.) Within the off-limits areas are fragile Indian pictographs and the habitats of endangered species. Before camping off main roads, be sure you're not in such a restricted area.

Desert driving precautions

The rules for safe automobile exploration of the desert are few, but they are mandatory:

Don't turn off main roads without inquiring locally about conditions of side roads. Above all, don't hesitate to turn back if travel becomes difficult; back roads are likely to become worse, not better.

Remember that you often gain necessary traction in sand by deflating your rear tires to about half normal pressure (take along an air pump so you can reinflate tires when you're back on hard surface). Be sure in advance that your engine's cooling system is in good working order. Always carry adequate supplies of water, gasoline, and oil. Don't count on desert springs as water sources—they are often dry. If stranded in the desert during the summer, don't leave the shade of your car.

Maps

Up-to-date, detailed maps are necessary to any back-road exploring. You can usually get good ones from counties, the U.S. Forest Service, state monuments and parks, and the U.S. Geological Survey. The Bureau of Land Management, the agency in charge of much of California's desert country, has section maps that indicate private or government-owned lands within the desert. For a free map, write to the BLM, 1695 Spruce Street, Riverside, CA 92507.

In the northern Mojave

The vast northwestern Mojave Desert is a land of great contrasts. To the west rise the high, imposing peaks of the Sierra Nevada; yet throughout this desert can be seen the low, crystalline sinks of primeval lakes. Human history is recorded in ancient Indian drawings on the rocks and in old mines and mining towns left by 19th century prospectors. Today, man is making his mark here with secluded military establishments and missile sites. At Brown, off U.S. 395 on State 58 north of Edwards Air Force Base, is the world's largest open-pit borax mine. Still active, the great pit yields snow-white hills of processed borax.

Randsburg, a gold town but not a ghost town, is hidden from U.S. 395, which passes through its neighbor, Johannesburg. From a distance Randsburg still resembles old photographs of early mining communities. Houses, some built with wood from dynamite boxes, stand weather-beaten and full of memories. The town has lived through three booms: gold (it had one of the richest mines in Southern California), tungsten, and silver. The Desert Mining Museum has miners' and Indian artifacts and objects from the famed Yellow Aster Mine. Nearby Koehn Dry Lake, resembling a snowstorm on the desert, is the site of still another kind of mining—salt mining.

At China Lake, in the Coso Mountains, you can see the most extraordinary concentration of prehistoric rock pictures in North America. The site in Renegade Canyon, within the China Lake Naval Weapons Center firing range, is now a National Historic Landmark. The Navy and the Maturango Museum, a geological treasure trove located on the center, team up to conduct day-long caravans to the pictographs. There is no definite schedule for the tours; if you would like to join one, write to the museum at Box 5514, China Lake, CA 93556.

To reach the museum, leave U.S. 395 or State Highway 14 at the Ridgecrest-China Lake exit and drive to the end of the road, where you'll come upon the Naval center's main gate. The museum is open only on weekends from 2 to 5 P.M.; admission to the museum is free. You will need a pass from the main gate.

Little Lake, just off U.S. 395 about 20 miles north of the road to China Lake, is worth a stop for a look at some notable Indian pictographs. You can see some of the rock drawings from the lakeshore, but others are best sighted from a rowboat (for rent at the boathouse at the north end of the lake). The greatest concentration of drawings is found on the basalt cliffs on the west shore and at the southeast end of the lake.

The fee for overnight camping includes bank-fishing privileges. All campsites have tables, fireplaces, and water.

To reach Fossil Falls, turn east from U.S. 395 onto Cinder Road, almost 3 miles north of Little Lake. Turn southwest at the first intersection, left at the next intersection, and drive to the end of the road. It's a short hike to the falls on a marked trail. The falls were formed by ancient lava flows from the Coso Mountains.

Trona Pinnacles make a logical side trip from the popular Wildrose Canyon route into Death Valley; you can see them at a distance.

Rising from the desert floor south of the crystalline Searles Lake, the spires are believed to have been built up by algae from an ancient sea.

The northern approach to the Pinnacles is very primitive but gets you there in the least amount of time. If there have been very recent rains, a safer approach is on the rough but all-weather road from the south that runs more or less parallel to the Trona railroad tracks.

A leisurely lunch stop among the formations will give you time for a brief exploration. You could easily spend a day investigating the area. You can camp overnight on the east side of the Pinnacles in the shadow of some of the tallest spires.

In and around Barstow

An old mining center, Barstow lies at the junction of two main Interstate Highways: Interstate 15, a heavily traveled freeway between Los Angeles and Las Vegas, and Interstate 40, which heads southeast for the Colorado River and the California-Arizona border. Along both routes you'll discover some spots to explore, but to do so you may have to get off the fast interstate, and drive once-famous U.S. Highway 66.

Barstow is a good base for exploring the surrounding countryside. You can venture into canyons, climb mountains, hunt gemstones, or follow trails leading to historic landmarks and old waterholes.

The Mojave Valley Museum (open daily) has a variety

of desert artifacts, mining exhibits, and a small Indian collection. For information on wildflowers, make this your first stop in Barstow; conducted tours are held during spring. The museum is located in Dana Park.

Southeast of Barstow, an area has been set aside for driving the ubiquitous dune buggies and motorcycles—so they won't overrun the entire desert.

Calico, founded in 1881 as the result of one of the West's richest silver strikes, is experiencing a new boom: an influx of tourists instead of prospectors. The town was named for the multicolored mountains that lie behind it. The original residents were proud of the local saloon (Lil's), hotel, mercantile store, bank, railroad station, and schoolhouse—but especially of the high-producing Maggie Mine. Today you can explore its tunnels, ride the Calico-Odessa Railway, take a cable tram ride, and visit the buildings that are probably a bit more orderly and better scrubbed than before, but still colorful. There's a slight admission charge for cars, as well as charges for specific attractions.

Calico was restored and opened to the public by Walter Knott of Knott's Berry Farm, whose uncle grub staked the original Calico Hills prospectors. Later, the area was deeded to San Bernardino County, which now manages it as a regional park with emphasis on its mining history. Visitors enjoy Calico's Ghost Town spring festival in May and "Calico Days" in October. For dates and other information, call (714) 254-2122.

A campground in the area allows you to spend the night in the "Old West." In addition, there are motels in nearby Yermo and Barstow. Calico is 9 miles east of Barstow (3½ miles west of Yermo) off I-15.

Apple Valley

Situated east of the Mojave River and north of the San Bernardino foothills, Apple Valley has the clean dry air, beauty, warmth, and solitude of the desert. Once a sanctuary for early Indians, Apple Valley is now a resort community with golf courses, guest ranches, swimming pools, and fishing lakes. The resort also offers an airport favored by sailplane pilots, riding stables, and a thoroughbred breeding farm where you can observe horses in training. Ranch clothes are in order here. Barbecues are reached by hay wagons, and Western entertainment centers around a crackling campfire.

The Apple Valley Inn—center of most visitor activity in town—offers accommodations in detached cottages. Inside the inn, you'll find game trophies, antique rugs, and old portraits. The Roy Rogers Museum, formerly on the grounds, was moved to Victorville some time ago to form the nucleus of a new entertainment center—Western World, a 300-acre complex reached by taking the Palmdale offramp from I-15.

Apple Valley is located southeast of Victorville on State Highway 18, which continues east through Lucerne Valley (also offering enjoyable guest ranches) on its way to Big Bear Lake. An unusual rock formation in Lucerne Valley is Hercules Fingers, a granite boulder 60 feet high. Drive out Camp Rock Road to the second power company road; turn east for approximately 3 miles; small bamboo sticks mark the road.

Mojave Narrows Park is near here. This great oasis, halfway between San Bernardino and Barstow, is one of Southern California's least-known parks.

Along a 2-mile stretch where the underground Mojave River rises to the surface, the park is an inviting expanse of green meadows, cottonwoods, willow thickets, and year-round water in river channels, creeks, bogs, ponds, and two small lakes. Birds and small animals visit from the desert, and beavers build dams here.

The park is open daily; there is a modest car entry fee. To get there, take the Bear Valley cutoff from I-15 east to Ridge Crest Road and then go north to the entrance.

BASQUE FESTIVAL marks late summer in Bakersfield. Drinking from a bota (above) and whirling through native dance (right) are watchable arts.

Antelope Valley

This corner of the Mojave Desert slopes gradually upward to the west as it narrows between the rolling foothills of the converging Tehachapi and San Gabriel mountains. The pastoral aspect of much of Antelope Valley sets it somewhat apart from the rest of the Mojave. Without its Joshua trees, it would not look like desert. Yet it is a part of the Great Basin, 2,000 to 3,000 feet above sea level, where cold winters, hot summers, and harsh winds discourage human settlement. Plants from the desert, from the Central Valley, and from coastal hills grow in Antelope Valley, making it a beautiful and popular destination in the spring. Even in other seasons there is much to observe. Antelope Valley's largest town, Lancaster, has fine motels and restaurants and is a convenient base for exploring open

country a few miles to the west and east. Accommodations are also available in Palmdale, Mojave, Tehachapi, Lebec, and Gorman.

You get more than just a scenic view of the valley if you pull off State 14 (heading north) at the lookout point a few miles south of Palmdale. You can also see the valley's geologic features that have been formed by California's dominant rift zone, the San Andreas Fault. A plaque at the lookout shows the location of the fault line, extending west of Palmdale across the valley to its highest elevation at Big Pines Summit (6,862 feet).

Wildflower viewing is often at its best in Antelope Valley. Sometimes the show is shimmering and brilliant, but it is always unpredictable.

The Jane S. Pinheiro Interpretative Center (located in the Antelope Valley California Poppy Reserve) features exhibits of local wildlife and plants, most notably California's state flower, the poppy. The center is open all year, but perhaps the best time to visit is during the spring floral fireworks display. The Lancaster County Chamber of Commerce, (805) 948-4518, can tell you when and where wildflowers are blooming. To reach the center, take State 14 northeast to Avenue I in Lancaster; then go west on Avenue I for 13½ miles. The center is on your right.

One suggested loop trip centers around State 14. Drive north from Lancaster to Rosamond and west to visit Burton's Tropico Gold Mine and Museum. Continue 3 miles west to almost-deserted Willow Springs (just off the highway), a former stage and freight station and, in the early 1900s, a health resort. Head north to Backus Road; turn right past the headframe of the Cactus Mine.

Saddleback Butte State Park is 17 miles east of Lancaster on Avenue J. At the park's northwest corner, a small headquarters building, a parking lot, and some picnic tables are all the civilized embellishments you will find. Beyond is a splendid, sunny, 2-mile sweep of yucca-studded desert, culminating in alluring Saddleback Butte. Ask the ranger where to find the large waxy wildflowers known as desert candles.

Burton's Tropico Gold Mine and Museum lies 4 miles west of Rosamond, not far from Mojave, at the edge of a big forest of Joshua trees.

The mine yielded one of the most successful strikes in the Southland. In its shadowy interior, you'll see gold ore and miners' gear; proceed through a stope (the sloping cavity left after a vein is mined) to view the 900-foot-deep shaft, in operation until 1956. A tour guide explains common mining methods and procedures as you follow the vein out to the "glory hole," an open pit created by steam-shovel mining.

In the buildings, you'll see displays of mining equipment, a collection of rocks and gems, and relics such as period clothing and old newspapers. A safe guards the collection of gold nuggets.

To reach the mine, drive 11 miles north of Lancaster on State 14 to Rosamond Boulevard, then go west about 5 miles to Tropico Mojave Road and follow the signs uphill. The mine and museum displays are open for touring all year long, from 10 A.M. to 4 P.M. Thursday through Sunday. Expect a modest admission charge. For further information about the mine and museum, call (805) 256-2644.

San Joaquin Valley

A flat basin dotted with small towns, the San Joaquin Valley is the southern half of California's Central Valley—the only extensive expanse of flat land in the state (the northern half is the Sacramento Valley). It is a major agricultural producer of cotton, grapes, and other products that thrive in summer heat.

Hot, dry summer weather limits recreational opportunities in the valley itself, and with few exceptions, residents look to the nearby mountains or to the cool coast for their vacation and weekend activity. Still, significant vacation areas have developed around Fresno and Bakersfield, the area's two largest cities. Artificial reservoirs, a part of large-scale irrigation systems, are sources for boating, fishing, and swimming.

Valley cities are also "gateways" to national parks and the high country of the Sierra Nevada. For this reason, they're centers of hurried summer activity.

Years ago, to enter the southern half of California's Central Valley from Los Angeles you followed the "Grapevine," a twisting road with all the thrills of an amusement park ride on the Ridge Route over the Tehachapis and down into the outer limits of Bakersfield. No longer an obstacle course, today's road is a smooth freeway (Interstate Highway 5) that gives no indication of the troubles experienced in building a wagon route over this same pass.

Just south of Bakersfield, I-5 and U.S. Highway 99 divide. Interstate 5 heads through an almost isolated section of the San Joaquin Valley, marked only by turnoffs, a few gasoline stations, and restaurants at posted intervals.

Bakersfield

Situated on the south bank of the Kern River in the southern end of the San Joaquin Valley is Bakersfield—county seat for Kern County and a junction of major highways through Southern California. Primarily a market city, Bakersfield is in the midst of an area rich in oil, minerals, and agriculture. Along the foothills to the east of the city lie the large oil fields; between the fields and city lie ranches, pastures, vineyards, and orchards. This area was depicted in John Steinbeck's *The Grapes of Wrath* as the promised land for Oklahomans who drove west to escape the dust bowl of the Great Depression.

Country music fans call Bakersfield "Nashville West," thanks to Merle Haggard, Buck Owens, and others. You can hear the country sound around town.

Kern County Museum's Pioneer Village, a 12-acre indoor-outdoor museum, makes frontier history come alive. Outdoors, about 40 historic structures (originals and restorations) are laid out as a model town of the 1870–1910 period.

Indoors, the main museum houses fossils from the nearby McKittrick oil field area, a diorama of birds and mammals, Indian relics, and the most unusual curiosity—a dog-powered butter churn. The museum at 3801 Chester Avenue and the village are open weekdays from 8 A.M. to 5 P.M., weekends and holidays from 10 A.M. to 5 P.M. Admission to the museum is free; there's a slight charge for the outdoor displays.

Fort Tejon, an old military post established by the U.S. Army in 1854, is handily situated for today's travelers, just off the freeway near Lebec (30 miles south of Bakersfield). Fort Tejon once quartered the Army's most unusual unit—the First Dragoons and Camel Corps.

Abandoned in 1864, the post was restored as a State Historic Park. It's open daily the year around. You can picnic on the grounds in the shade of some lovely old trees. On the third Sunday of each month from May through October, a "Civil War" skirmish takes place at 10 A.M., 11 A.M., and 2 P.M.

Index